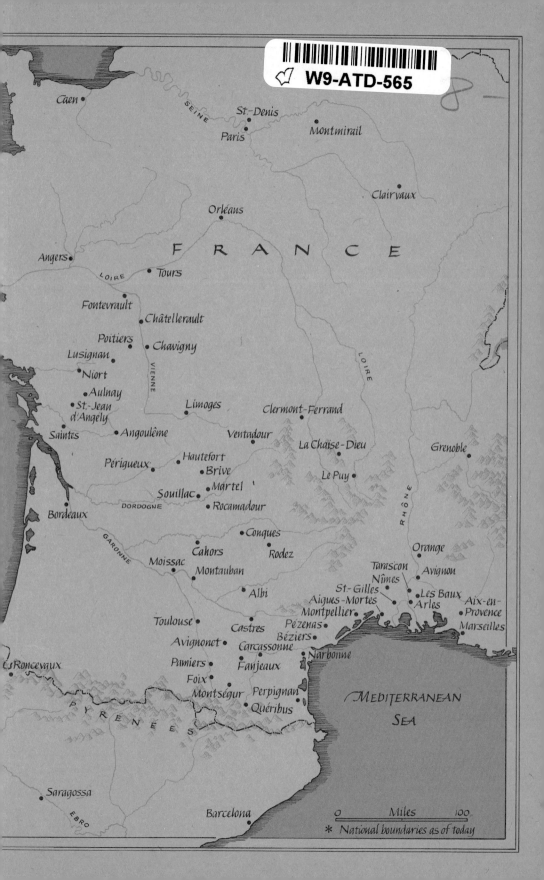

Caen

SEINE

St.-Denis

Paris

Montmirail

Clairvaux

Orléans

F R A N C E

Angers

LOIRE

Tours

Fontevrault

Châtellerault

Poitiers

Chavigny

Lusignan

VIENNE

Niort

Aulnay

St.-Jean
d'Angely

Limoges

Clermont-Ferrand

LOIRE

Saintes

Angoulême

Ventadour

La Chaise-Dieu

Grenoble

Périgueux

Hautefort

Brive

Le Puy

RHÔNE

Souillac

Martel

Bordeaux

DORDOGNE

Rocamadour

Conques

GARONNE

Cahors

Rodez

Orange

Moissac

Montauban

Tarascon

Avignon

Nîmes

Les Baux

Albi

St.-Gilles

Arles

Aigues-Mortes

Aix-en-
Provence

Montpellier

Toulouse

Castres

Pézenas

Marseilles

Avignonet

Carcassonne

Béziers

Pamiers

Fanjeaux

Narbonne

Roncevaux

Foix

MEDITERRANEAN

Montségur

Perpignan

SEA

P Y R E N E E S

Quéribus

Saragossa

EBRO

Barcelona

0   Miles   100

* National boundaries as of today

Pilgrims, Heretics, and Lovers

Frontispiece—Page from the Chansonnier Provençal *in the Pierpont Morgan Library. MS 819, fol. 100. The troubadour Guiraut de Borneilh is represented in the right-hand margin. (The Pierpont Morgan Library, New York)*

PILGRIMS, HERETICS, AND LOVERS

A Medieval Journey

CLAUDE MARKS

MACMILLAN PUBLISHING CO., INC.

NEW YORK

Library of Congress Cataloging in Publication Data

Marks, Claude.
    Pilgrims, heretics, and lovers.

    Bibliography: p.
    Includes index.
    1. France—History—To 987.   2. France—History—Capetians, 987-1328.   3. France—Civilization.
I. Title.
DC61.M37   914.4'03'1   74-31037
ISBN 0-02-579770-0

Macmillan Publishing Co., Inc.
866 Third Avenue, New York, N.Y. 10022
Collier-Macmillan Canada Ltd.

FIRST PRINTING 1975

Printed in the United States of America

To

SUE

who has shared

the journey

Can la frej 'aura venta
Deves vostre pais,
Vey aire m'es qu'eu senta
Un ven de paradis.

> When the cool breeze blows hither
> From the land where you dwell,
> Methinks I do feel
> A wind from Paradise.

BERNART DE VENTADOUR

Ah, l'alentir vas me l'aire
Qu'en sen venir de Proensa.

> I breathe the gladsome air
> That blows from fair Provence.

PEIRE VIDAL

For love is no sin, but a virtue that makes
The bad good, and the good better.

Now Joy and Courtesy offend the great
So wicked have they grown.

GUILHEM MONTANHAGOL

Contents

Foreword

IMPORTANT ASPECTS OF our modern Western civilization had their origins in Central and Southern France at a particular time in history which is unfamiliar to many people but fascinating in itself.

We no longer view the Middle Ages as a monolithic society obsessed by religious dogma. An age of faith it certainly was, and the salvation of the soul was of great concern even to those who dared defy the authority of the Church. The medieval period was neither as static, as hostile to the pursuit of knowledge, nor as blind to the beauties of nature as was once believed.

In the varied and extensive territory where the melodious *langue d'oc* was spoken, an area extending from Bordeaux on the Atlantic coast to Grenoble at the foot of the Alps, and from the Loire to the Pyrenees, the feudal system was far less rigid than in the North, and a more gracious life style developed which culminated in the brilliant courts of Poitou, Toulouse and Provence and in the poetry and song of the troubadours.

The greater freedom and mobility of society in those regions which are now increasingly referred to in Southern France as Occitanie (from *oc*) favored diversity rather than conformity, in ideas and individuality. To the male-dominated feudal society of the North, the comparative freedom and respect enjoyed by women south of the Loire was incomprehensible. While the sublimated concept of love voiced by many of the troubadours may be hard to accept in our more realistic post-Freudian world, and while some of their conventions of language and courtship may seem remote from modern experience, the *gai sçavoir* (joyous science), as troubadour poetry was later called, marked an essential stage in the emancipation of women, and consequently of human beings generally.

The theme of travel constantly recurs in the Middle Ages. Thousands of pilgrims passed through France every year on their way to Rome, Jerusalem and especially Santiago de Compostela. The Crusades in Spain and the Orient, which were themselves regarded as pilgrimages, failed in their objective to convert the infidel, but succeeded, to quote Stendhal, in revealing to the Westerners "that there were pleasures sweeter than pillaging, raping and fighting." Contact with the Moslem world and the semi-Oriental culture of Byzantium influenced the arts, music, poetry and costume and contributed to a greater refinement in everyday living.

The relative openness and tolerance of Provençal society made it receptive to every intellectual and spiritual current, Jewish as well as Arabic. These territories were regarded by the Church authorities as breeding grounds for heretics, and the Cathars, or Albigensians, some of whose leaders were women, made thousands of converts, including many nobles. This dynamic, pluralistic culture was ruthlessly suppressed in the 13th century by the Crusades against the Albigensians and by the forces of the Inquisition; but though stifled, it did not completely die out, and its influence has been much greater than is generally realized. In that period of crisis in the 13th century the troubadours were not silent, and there were as many songs of protest as of love.

This life-affirming spirit found an early exponent in the Merovingian queen Radegonde during the Dark Ages, and five centuries later produced the colorful Count Guilhem VII of Poitou, the first troubadour, and his extraordinary granddaughter Eleanor of Aquitaine.

A host of poets and singers, men and women, some noble, some of humble birth, renewed the language of lyric poetry and created an ideal of gallantry, sincerity and joyousness which has influenced our own "pursuit of happiness," so often proclaimed and all too seldom achieved.

In translating extracts from poems written in the musical and concentrated *langue d'oc*, I have tried to preserve the rhythms and wherever possible the rhymes. However, in a poet such as Bernart de Ventadour, it would take a Yeats to create an equivalent of his subtle and emotionally charged verse, and even then it would be a paraphrase, not an actual translation. It seemed advisable in some of his poems to abandon any attempt at rhyme in order to convey his meaning as faithfully as possible. Of course, the original poems were meant to be sung, and music was an integral part of their structure. If the sentiments sometimes seem commonplace today, it should be remembered that they were fresh and original when first expressed by the troubadours.

Traveling through the "troubadour country" is a wonderful experience, as the land is as varied and fascinating as its history. It includes the gentle landscape of Poitou and the Charente, the wild gorges of the Dordogne and Hérault, the densely wooded foothills of the Pyrenees and the lonely stretches of the Camargue—Romanesque churches along the pilgrimage routes and ruined Cathar castles on precipitous heights—remote and mysterious Auvergne, and Provence, which the poet Frédéric Mistral called "the empire of the Sun." Each city, despite the passage of time, preserves its individual color, texture and *saveur*. The weathered gray stone of Poitiers, where this rich civilization had its birth, is very different from the dramatic rose-red brick of Toulouse, or the soft ambers and golds of Aix and Avignon with their distant echoes of Italy. The people of every region take pride in their past, and a whole new Occitan movement, with its singers, poets and scholars, is struggling to preserve the identity of the Midi while keeping pace with the modern world.

I should like to express my thanks to the following museums, organizations and individual photographers for their cooperation in furnishing illustrative material:

The Metropolitan Museum of Art and the Pierpont Morgan Library, New York; the British Museum and The Victoria and Albert Museum, London; the Archives Photographiques (Caisse Nationale des Monuments Historiques) and the Bibliothèque Nationale, Paris; the Bibliothèque Municipale and the Centre d' Etudes Supérieures de Civilisation Médiévale, Poitiers; Reportage Photographique YAN (Jean Dieuzaide), Toulouse; Bernard Biraben, Bordeaux; A. Necer and Hélène Plessis, Poitiers; N. Bourgouin, Studio Baluteau, Matha (Charente-Maritime); Photo Cap Roger-Viollet and R. Henrard,

Etablissements J. Richard, Paris; Pierre Pons, Lavelanet (Ariège); The University Library, Heidelberg; Bildarchiv Foto Marburg (Lahn); Bildarchiv der Oesterreichischen Nationalbibliothek, Vienna; and Sue Marks, New York.

My thanks are due to Mr. John Ciardi for permission to quote a passage from his translation of Dante's "Inferno," and to New Directions for the quotation from Ezra Pound's "Sestina: Altaforte."

I would also like to thank the following people for their assistance and advice: Professor Pierre Bec and M. Henri Renou of the Centre d' Etudes Supérieures de Civilisation Médiévale, Poitiers; Monsieur J. Guérin, curator of the Bibliothèque Municipale, Poitiers; Mme. Jean Dieuzaide of the Atelier YAN, Toulouse, for her invaluable help; M. René Nelli, one of France's greatest authorities on the troubadours and Cathars; M. Ousset, whose delightful bookshop in Toulouse, La Bible d'Or, has been a great source of inspiration; M. Calestroupat, director of the Musée du Vieux Toulouse; Professor Charles Camproux of the Paul Valéry University, Montpellier; M. Claparède, director of the Société Archéologique, Montpellier; M. Robert Joudoux, director of excavations in the castle of Ventadour (Corrèze); Mlle. Lamache of the Centre Culturel, Fanjeaux (Aude); M. Robert Cazilhac of Narbonne and M. Daniel Aubert of Arles for their information about the young Occitan movement in the Midi; Mme. Denise Breyne of Arles, who showed me parts of Provence I would otherwise not have seen; my friends in Paris, Gérald and Marie-Claude Brown-Sarda for their constant help and encouragement; Elizabeth Brown of Brooklyn College for her perceptive comments on Eleanor of Aquitaine; the Public Relations Department of Shell Oil Company, Houston, Texas, for information on pilgrims' scallop-shells; M. A. Sirventon of the Syndicat d'Initiative, Pézenas (Hérault); and my wife Sue, for her patient and understanding assistance in the preparation of this book.

Pilgrims, Heretics, and Lovers

CHAPTER I

A Light in the Darkness—
Radegonde in Poitiers

LIKE OTHER MEROVINGIAN RULERS, Clotaire, King of the Franks, son of the great Clovis, maintained a harem at his court in Soissons, a bevy of concubines docile to their lord and master but all intriguing for the privilege of being legally wedded to him "by the ring." Among the very few women who refused to submit to this arbitrary form of male dominance was the outstanding Thuringian princess Radegunda, better known by her Gallicized name, Radegonde.

After routing the Visigoths near Poitiers in 507, Clovis and thousands of his Frankish warriors had been baptized by St. Rémi, Bishop of Rheims, but beneath a veneer of Christianity there was still a hard core of barbarism. This was evident in the years of chaos and misrule that followed Clovis' death in 511. The cruelest and most ambitious of Clovis' four sons was Clotaire, who instigated the murder of his brother Clodomer's children and seized the cities of Tours and Poitiers.

In 529 he and his brother Theodoric invaded the kingdom of Thuringia in central Germany, laid waste the country and massacred its inhabitants. Among the victims were Radegonde's uncle, King Berthaire, and his queen. Berthaire had raised his niece as his own child after killing her father, Hermanfried. Radegonde was only ten

[*1*]

years old at the time of the Frankish invasion, but had already, in the words of *Macbeth*, "supp'd full of horrors." Years later she described to her biographer and friend Fortunatus how "my father's sister, with her milk-white complexion, her red hair brighter and more shining than gold, lay mortally wounded on the ground," how the countryside was strewn with unburied corpses, and how women, "their hands tied and their hair in disarray . . . were led off into slavery."

Radegonde and her young brother were among the survivors. Lots were drawn, and the two children were given to Clotaire as part of the "spoils of war." We are told that the beautiful ten-year-old girl aroused "a violent desire in the heart of the conqueror," who resolved to make her his wife as soon as she had reached marriageable age.

Impressed by her beauty, grace and intelligence, Clotaire sent Radegonde to the royal villa of Athies in Vermandois in upper Picardy, where, without realizing the fateful consequences of such a step, he had her taught reading and writing. This, and the fine education she received from tutors, were most exceptional for the period. Clotaire, an unlikely Pygmalion, believed that he owned in Radegonde a "pearl of great price" who would add luster to his crown. Radegonde acquired such an appetite for learning that she soon became familiar with the writings of many religious and secular authors.

When Radegonde was nineteen, royal messengers arrived at the villa with orders to escort her to Vitry near Châlons to be married to Clotaire. Despite the relatively sheltered life she had enjoyed at Athies, Radegonde had learned enough about the riotous Merovingian court at Soissons to realize what she would have to face as Clotaire's queen. She knew that Clotaire already had four "wives," Ingunda and her sister Aragunda, Gondieuque and Chunsina—not counting the many concubines. And she could never forget that Clotaire had brought death and destruction to her family and her people. She made the momentous decision to flee, accompanied by a few faithful attendants.

When he heard the news, Clotaire set out immediately in pursuit. The fugitive was caught, brought back to the palace and compelled to marry him. Radegonde's unprecedented display of independence must have made her seem even more extraordinary and precious to her tyrannical but enamored husband. He showered her with gifts, but her proud, sensitive spirit could never be at ease at a court that seemed to her gross, licentious and brutal. The hours she spent at prayer caused some of the courtiers to say that Clotaire had married not a queen but a nun. The breaking point was reached when Clotaire, determined to destroy the last male descendant of the Thuringian kings, cruelly murdered Radegonde's brother.

Life at the palace could no longer be endured, and she fled a second time, taking with her the costly gifts she had received from her royal husband. According to a popular legend, at one point during her flight Radegonde and her two female companions took refuge in a cornfield to escape their pursuers. The corn sprang up miraculously, so that a few minutes before the arrival of the grim Clotaire and his men-at-arms, the three women were completely hidden from view by the tall stalks.

After a period of wandering, Radegonde arrived at Noyon, where St. Médard, bishop of the city, consecrated her a nun, in spite of the danger to himself. She deposited her royal jewels on the altar as a token of humility.

Clotaire relented in his pursuit, but Radegonde took no chances. Acting without delay, for her self-willed husband could always change his mind, she went to the Loire Valley and founded a monastery at Tours, after praying at the tomb of St. Martin, the city's patron saint, whose shrine was an important pilgrimage center.

Later she traveled south into Poitou, which was part of Clotaire's domain, and settled in its ancient capital, Poitiers. To everyone's amazement, Clotaire agreed to a formal separation, and even contributed to the building of a monastery founded by Radegonde within the Gallo-Roman walls near the southernmost city gate. The monastery was later named Sainte-Croix and was the earliest of all religious houses for women in Gaul, except for the one in Arles, established around 507 by St. Césaire. In 555 Radegonde entered the newly founded monastery. She humbly declined the office of abbess, selecting instead one of her companions, Agnes. She wrote, "*sororem meam Agnetem . . . Abbatissam institui*"—"I have installed my sister Agnes as abbess."

Even then Clotaire had not abandoned all thoughts of "reclaiming his queen," but was dissuaded from taking any action by St. Germain, Bishop of Paris, who in 560 consecrated Agnes as Abbess of Sainte-Croix. Clotaire's death the following year removed a major source of anxiety, and a new chapter in Radegonde's life began.

Fig. 1. Detail from a page from the Life of St. Radegonde by Fortunatus, late 11th century MS 250 (136), fol. 24. (Bibliothèque Municipale, Poitiers, Photograph by A. Necer)

On a page in an 11th century illuminated manuscript of the life of St. Radegonde, as she later became, by Fortunatus in the Poitiers Municipal Library, three episodes from her earlier life are depicted with the naïve intensity of the Romanesque style (Fig. 1). She is seated at a banqueting table next to a still well-disposed Clotaire, possibly trying to persuade him to change his ways. In an adjoining scene she is praying in her private chapel. Below, Clotaire is stretched out on his deathbed, and Radegonde, still wearing her crown, prostrates herself. She could be praying for his soul, or giving thanks for her own deliverance.

Apart from Radegonde's cell and oratory, heavily restored in 1912, hardly a trace remains of the original monastery buildings which housed two hundred nuns, all of noble and some of royal birth. The convent was named Sainte-Croix when the Byzantine emperor Justin II sent a fragment of the True Cross to the Queen's monastery in 568. The nuns enshrined it in a silver reliquary which, along with other mementos of St. Radegonde, was transferred in 1965 from Poitiers to the Benedictine convent of La Cossonnière near the charming little village of Saint-Benoît, just outside Poitiers. Her small wooden desk is adorned with Merovingian Latin crosses and the earliest-known representations in Gaul of the symbols of the four evangelists—the winged man of St. Matthew, the lion of St. Mark, the bull of St. Luke and the eagle of St. John (Fig. 2).

Sainte-Croix with its gardens and fountains resembled a fortified Gallo-Roman villa, and was a peaceful oasis in the turbulent Merovingian world. Radegonde's second biographer—a woman, Baudovinia—wrote in the early 7th century that the former queen was by no means isolated from events on the outside. During the recurring fratricidal strife between the Merovingian kings of Neustria and Austrasia (there was not yet a unified Frankish kingdom), Radegonde would write to the two rulers imploring them "not to let the country perish," but in that age of chronic warfare her entreaties went unheeded.

Daily life in Sainte-Croix and other early convents followed a fixed routine. With the exception of the abbess and the provost, all of the sisters had to take turns in cooking, washing and other domestic tasks. More important in that age of almost total illiteracy, all had to learn to read and write; some even transcribed manuscripts. Two hours a day were devoted to intellectual pursuits. During the night, at certain regular times, the nuns would awaken and rise up from their beds to sing psalms.

Radegonde's own life in the Sainte-Croix monastery was a strange mixture of asceticism, learning and sociability. She spent much of the day in her cell practicing the most rigorous religious exercises. She wore a hair shirt, and during the Lenten season used an iron chain as a belt, so tightly fastened that it cut into her flesh. At times she would apply red-hot metal to her body. To the modern mind this cruel self-mutilation with its contempt for the flesh is among the most odious aspects of medieval Christianity; to a believer of the time it was a way of re-enacting the sufferings of Christ and the tribulations of the martyrs. For Radegonde it was also an extreme reaction against the wild license of the Merovingian court with its noisy rabble of soldiers and concubines. She distributed alms to the poor at the gates of Sainte-Croix, and tended the blind and even lepers. She also found time for the pleasures of the mind, and the cultural life of the monastery was greatly enhanced by the arrival in Poitiers in 567 of the Italian poet and scholar Venantius Fortunatus, then visiting the sanctuaries of Gaul.

Venantius Honorius Clementianus Fortunatus was born near Treviso in northeastern Italy in 530. He studied at Milan and Ravenna, and was fired with the ambition to excel as rhetorician and poet. Fortunatus composed an "epithalamium," or wedding hymn, in Latin, celebrating the marriage of Sigebert, the Frankish king, with the Visigothic princess Brunhilde, whose ruthlessness and cruelty were at that time still unsuspected by the many admirers of her beauty.

After remaining for two years at Sigebert's court, Fortunatus traveled in various parts of France, walking all the way, and composing short Latin poems whenever the spirit moved him. He heard reports of the celebrated Queen of the Franks who had taken the veil but who still had an aura of regal majesty. He settled in Poitiers in 567 and was ordained a priest. This gave Fortunatus an entry into the monastery of Sainte-Croix. His intellectual and literary gifts, combined with his agreeable personality, won him the friendship of Radegonde and Abbess Agnes. Fortunatus became superintendent and later almoner of Sainte-Croix. His religious poems, with their easy, flowing rhythms, were much admired and imitated in the Middle Ages. He is regarded as the last important writer of Latin poetry in Merovingian Gaul, and his hymn "Vexilla Regis prodeunt"—"the banners of the King go forth"—composed in 568 to celebrate the arrival in Poitiers of the fragment of the True Cross, has been incorporated into the Catholic liturgy and is still sung on Good Friday.

Between Radegonde and Fortunatus there was a "marriage of true minds," and despite the monastic setting, there is something remarkably modern in this need of an educated woman of the 6th century for a "friendship of the heart." She addressed elegies to Fortunatus in Latin, for which he thanked her in these flowery words: "You who give honey to the thirsting cells have sent me big verses on little tablets, and also little verses full of charm, whose every word captivates my heart."

Fortunatus addressed his poems to Radegonde not only as a woman but as the very incarnation of purity. In a transference of ideas more easily comprehensible to the medieval than to the modern mind,

Fortunatus celebrated the immaculate Virgin *through* Radegonde and her spiritual daughter, Agnes. His exalted language makes Fortunatus a distant forerunner of the tradition of *l'amour courtois*, in its more sublimated aspects, as sung over five hundred years later by the troubadours. However, even the most idealized images of women in troubadour poetry were never intended to symbolize the Virgin Mary: this only occurred in the period of decline in the late 13th and 14th centuries.

The friendship between Fortunatus, Radegonde and Agnes was not always conducted on a rarefied and mystical level. Meals at Sainte-Croix were generally frugal, but Fortunatus enjoyed special favors and was served the best fare that the monastery kitchen could provide, "meats of all kind, seasoned in a thousand ways, and vegetables flavored with gravy or honey, served on silver, jasper and crystal dishes." Small wonder that the pampered and aptly named Fortunatus composed gastronomic poems to entertain the nuns!

With naïve delight he declared in verse: "Greedy and gluttonous as I am, I did justice to everything. I devoured everything." He described his belly "stretched tight like that of a woman about to give birth." He sang the praises of wine, admitting that he "is not exempt from the accidents that befall most drinkers."

Whenever Fortunatus was invited to dine with Radegonde and Agnes, the dining hall was decked with garlands of fragrant flowers and the tablecloth was covered with rose petals. The three friends would call each other by pet names, "my life, my light, delight of my soul," which might seem to an outsider somewhat at variance with the sublimated ideal of "intellectual love." It was all very skittish and chaste, but it indicated that even in that constricted environment natural human instincts needed an outlet and could not be completely suppressed.

The tradition of lively correspondence by letters between clerics and nuns inaugurated by Fortunatus persisted, and was obviously not without its hazards. An ordinance issued by Charlemagne in 789 forbade the exchange of *epistolae amatoriae* between nuns and members of the clergy.

Radegonde died on August 13, 587, at sixty-nine, a venerable age for that period. The famous theologian and historian of the Franks, Gregory of Tours, came to Poitiers to officiate at her funeral. He was shown her cell, her books and her spindle. According to tradition, Radegonde, shortly before her death, had a vision in which the

Saviour appeared in her cell and announced that she would soon die, but that glory awaited her in Heaven, where she would be one of the "pearls of His crown." As He vanished He left the imprint of His right foot on a flagstone of the cell. After Radegonde's death, a small chapel was built next to her cell to house the stone bearing the *"pas de Dieu."* The chapel was demolished in 1798 in the wake of the Revolution, and in 1893 the stone was removed to the Church of Sainte-Radegonde, where it can still be seen, in a chapel hollowed out of the right-hand wall of the nave. The stone is usually strewn with paper money and coins as votive offerings.

Gregory of Tours described how, as the funeral procession passed by the ramparts, the nuns were gathered on the walls, sobbing, clapping their hands in despair (one of the usual gestures of mourning in antiquity) and tossing flowers on the bier. Radegonde was buried in the church she had founded on the site of a pagan temple. It was near the monastery but outside the walls, and was known as Sainte-Marie-Hors-les-Murs. After her burial there it became the Church of Sainte-Radegonde. During the Norman invasions the saint's body in its stone sarcophagus was hidden away, but was brought back to Poitiers in 868.

The 6th century building has disappeared, but the crypt of the present church, built in the late 11th century on the identical site, contains Radegonde's tomb, the tomb of St. Agnes, and that of another of their companions, St. Disciola. In 1422 the Bishop of Poitiers, Simon de Cramaud, had the tomb opened in the presence of the Duc de Berry, who was then governor of Poitou. The story goes that the Duke, an ardent collector of gems and other *objets d'art*, took Radegonde's wedding ring without any difficulty, but when he tried to take her nun's ring, the finger of the skeleton closed tightly to prevent this sacrilege!

For centuries pilgrims would make the journey to Radegonde's tomb on her saint's day, August 13, and in the 19th century she became the object of a fervent cult by mothers of sick children. The traditional rite required that the child crawl under the sarcophagus and go several times back and forth on its hands and knees between the stone blocks supporting the tomb. It is not recorded how many cures were effected by this unusual treatment.

In front of the dark sarcophagus a startling white marble statue in a classical Baroque style is supposed to represent St. Radegonde. It has the full-blown features of the queen-mother Anne of Austria, widow of Louis XIII, who commissioned it in 1658 from the sculptor Nicolas Legendre to give thanks for the cure of her young son Louis XIV, for whom she was acting as regent. Every year on August 13, or on the following Sunday, this statue is carried in procession through the city. In 1887 it was given a crown, a privilege reserved in the Church only for the most illustrious madonnas.

Many miraculous cures are attributed to Radegonde by the flocks of pilgrims who have visited her tomb over the years. The walls of the crypt, nave and ambulatory bear innumerable ex-voto tablets, some of recent date. Thanks are given for the healing of an arm or leg, the return from a dangerous journey, the passing of an exam and even the winning of a local election.

Among the recently restored stained-glass windows on the north wall of the nave, four show various episodes in the life of St. Radegonde, not presented in any chronological order; all stress her gentleness and charity. In one she is interceding with a tax collector for the release of some unfortunates who had been imprisoned for nonpayment. Some of the panels date from the 14th century. Radegonde wears her royal robes, and her mantle is anachronistically decorated with golden fleurs-de-lis (Fig. 3).

The genial Fortunatus became Bishop of Poitiers in 599. His addiction to the pleasures of the table was evidently not judged too harshly, for after his death around 609 he was canonized by the Church. The abbess who succeeded St. Agnes in Sainte-Croix had worldlier inclinations and admitted to playing dice and entertaining laymen at meals.

In secular Merovingian society, women were either helpless chattels or, in exceptional cases, ruthless, power-hungry queen-consorts who took on the ferocity of the masculine jungle around them.

Fig. 2. The reading desk of St. Radegonde, before 587 A.D., from the Abbey of Sainte-Croix, Poitiers.

Shakespeare's Goneril and Regan in *King Lear* had their prototypes
in such terrifying figures as Queen Fredegunda and her rival Brunhilde, ferocious and bloodthirsty Merovingian queens.

Radegonde chose a different course, and proved that a woman
of beauty, intelligence and courage could create her own milieu,
although admittedly it took royal prestige to bring this about. Monks
in their monasteries had long been active in transcribing ancient manuscripts and pursuing learned studies, but with Radegonde this world
became accessible to women—although a limited number. It is also
significant that one of the first literary works in France produced by
a woman should have been the life of Radegonde, written by
Baudovinia, presumably during the saint's lifetime (unfortunately,
much of her text has disappeared).

Whatever ordeals Radegonde imposed on her own body at the
dictates of piety, she never inflicted suffering on others. The cause
of women would have to wait many centuries; a Church council
assembled at Mâcon in 585 was debating "whether woman has a
soul." In broad human terms, Radegonde's extraordinary life in a
barbaric age was a shining illustration of the moral of La Fontaine's
delightful fable "Phoebus and Boreas": the sun and the north wind
vie with each other to see who can make the traveler shed his cloak,
and the sun's warm rays prevail. La Fontaine ends his fable with the
words *"Douceur fait plus que violence"*—"Gentleness wins where
violence fails."

*Fig. 3. St. Radegonde,
from a 14th century
stained-glass window in
the church of Sainte-
Radegonde, Poitiers.*

CHAPTER II

The Dawn of Gallantry:
The First Lords of Poitou and Aquitaine

THE CHURCH PROVIDED THE ONLY ELEMENT of continuity in Poitiers during the troubled decades that followed the death of Fortunatus. A count, appointed by the Merovingian kings, was designated ruler, but the bishops held the real power. Ansoald, Bishop of Poitiers from 677 to 697, founded the first hospital in the city, a room with beds for twelve sick people, in memory of the twelve apostles. This symbolism of numbers was typical of medieval thinking, but bore of course little relationship to the problems of illness. The hospital had an oratory dedicated to St. Luke, the patron saint of physicians and also of painters, for according to tradition he had painted the Virgin's portrait. The Merovingian kings were too busy maintaining order in their northern domains to concern themselves with the region south of the Loire.

After crossing the Pyrenees in 732, the Arabs, or the Saracens as they were called throughout the Middle Ages in the West, charged northward on their small, swift thoroughbred horses, burning and ransacking churches and monasteries on their way. They bypassed Toulouse, and apparently intended to cross the Loire and reach Tours. Even the sight of Poitiers' massive Gallo-Roman fortifications, still intact after four centuries, did not deter them, although they contented themselves with pillaging the sanctuaries outside the walls, Saint-Hilaire and Sainte-Radegonde.

Not far from the city, the Saracens were suddenly faced with the combined armies of Eudes, lord of Aquitaine, and the powerful Frankish prince Charles Martel, called "the Hammer" for his prowess in battle, who had already subjugated many of the German tribes across the Rhine. There is no certainty where the battle took place, except that the battleground was somewhere between Poitiers and Tours. The Saracen horsemen, loosely organized and counting on a quick victory, were routed by the disciplined and heavily armed Franks and their Poitevin allies.

The Franks did not pursue the Saracens as they fled southward. Some groups formed pockets of resistance. In the little town of Saint-Sauveur-de-Givre-en-Mai (Frost-in-May), in the present arrondissement of Bressuire, west of Poitiers, the Saracens attempted to entrench themselves. The citizens fought back, until the Arabs promised that they would surrender if there was a frost, an unlikely event in the month of May. The next morning the trees, bushes and meadows were white with frost. The Saracens surrendered and peacefully settled in the region.

During the initial invasion, some of the Arabs from Spain moved eastward and attacked Provence. They took Arles, raided the tomb of St. Césaire, and marched on to capture Avignon. The Saracens became for a brief period the masters of Provence.

In 739, Charles Martel launched a third attack on the Saracens in Provence. His final victory expelled them from the area and brought Provence under Frankish rule.

From the point of view of today's Occitan movement in Southern France, which seeks greater regional autonomy for the Midi and takes pride in the rich and diverse cultural and ethnic background of Provence, this Frankish domination was yet another example of Northern subjugation of the South—first Clovis' battle-ax and then Charles Martel's hammer! The skeptical Anatole France went even further in the late 19th century and shocked orthodox French opinion by describing the defeat of the Saracens by Charles Martel's armies near Poitiers, not as a glorious turning point in European history, but as a "retreat of civilization before barbarism." A high degree of culture had certainly been achieved in Spain under Moslem rule. Although the Arabs were fierce in battle, they were generous in victory, and showed far more tolerance toward other races and religions than did their Christian adversaries.

Compared to the refinement of many aspects of Islamic civilization, the West of the 8th century did indeed appear uncouth and primitive, especially when the authority of a violently autocratic rule was bolstered by harsh religious dogma. But just as the most vital creations in art often spring from the resolution of opposites, many of the crowning achievements of the Middle Ages in Europe resulted from a combination of the subtle, sensuous, mystical and, at that time, intellectually inquiring spirit of the East, and Western clarity, energy and organizing skills—a fusion that transcended religious and military antagonisms.

Although supported by the Pope and the Church, Charles Martel, who had invaded and occupied Aquitaine in 735, never assumed the title of King, but he acted like a monarch in dividing his Frankish territories between his sons Pepin the Short and Carloman. In 747 Carloman retired to religious life, and four years later Pepin the Short deposed the last Merovingian puppet—King Childeric III, whom he forced to enter a monastery. Pepin had himself proclaimed King of the Franks, and was the founder of the Carolingian dynasty, named after his father, Charles Martel.

Life had never been more expendable, and the right of might was the only law. A pious monk absorbed in his devotions could be transformed in an instant into a bloodthirsty warrior burning and looting, convinced that he was doing the right and noble thing. All that the common people could hope for was the bliss of Paradise. The accession of Charles Martel's grandson, Charlemagne, gave promise of a more orderly and civilized world.

Charlemagne succeeded his father, Pepin, as King of the Franks in 768. His coronation as Emperor of the West in St. Peter's Basilica in Rome on Christmas Day 800 opened up visions of universal order. It was hoped that the new Holy Roman Empire would revive the glories and stability of the original Empire of the Caesars, but strengthened by the Christian faith. Even though the reality fell short of this lofty ideal, Charlemagne's rule as Holy Roman Emperor embraced many different peoples and did in fact usher in a new era of civilization, as the shadows of the Dark Ages began to recede.

Charlemagne was described by his biographer, Einhard, as heavily built and "seven times the length of his own foot," which would suggest that he was over six feet tall, a towering height for that period. Although he learned to read only late in life and could never master spelling or writing, he labored consistently for the rebirth of learning and the arts. Charlemagne rebuilt the towers and ramparts of Poitiers. In 781, in a prudent attempt to reconcile the independent spirit of the region with the interests of his own dynasty, he raised the duchy of Aquitaine to the status of a kingdom for his son Louis the Pious, later Emperor Louis I.

With his great ability and prestige, Charlemagne was able to establish some kind of order in Aquitaine, but the situation under the military chiefs he appointed was always precarious. In spite of the pious stories that later formed part of the "Charlemagne legend," there was little improvement in the condition of the people. The so-called "Carolingian Renaissance" hardly touched Poitiers, and there was no real equivalent in Poitou of the famous monastic schools and palace workshops founded by Charlemagne in Tours, Metz, Saint-Denis and Rheims—nothing to compare with the splendid manuscript illuminations and book covers, ivory carvings and goldsmith's work produced in those remarkable centers of royal and ecclesiastical patronage. However, men of learning were becoming increasingly familiar with the heritage of classical antiquity.

A court was appointed by Charlemagne to govern Toulouse, which was then the capital of the Carolingian kingdom of Aquitaine, Languedoc and Provence. When Louis the Pious succeeded Charlemagne as Emperor of the West in 814, these southern provinces became incorporated into the Holy Roman Empire. Throughout the Middle Ages certain regions in the Midi continued to owe allegiance to the Emperor.

The Charlemagne of legend meant more to the Midi and to France generally throughout the Middle Ages than the actual historical ruler ever did. The Charlemagne of history, with his gigantic figure, round face and drooping blond mustache (Fig. 4), became transformed in the popular imagination into the majestic patriarchal figure, "the emperor with the flowery beard" described in the medieval *chansons de geste*. These epics, originating in Northern France after the year 1000, were spread by wandering clerks and minstrels throughout the land. Although the historic Charlemagne was a staunch ally of the Church, he kept four concubines. His daughters had several illegitimate childen, two by an abbot: Charlemagne's court was as loose-living as that of his Merovingian predecessors, though less brutal.

In legend he became the ideal Christian ruler, a paragon of chivalry and defender of womanhood. The real Charlemagne was not a great warrior, and his invasion of Spain in 778, in an attempt to wrest the country from its Arab rulers, ended in disaster. The annihilation of the rear guard of his army by Basque mountaineers at Roncevaux as the Franks were retreating through the passes of the Pyrenees was so magnified in the medieval imagination that it became the very crown of the whole Charlemagne legend—especially in the *Chanson de Roland*. In this epic cycle, the historical Hruodland, Margrave of the Breton March, who was among the slain at Roncevaux, became the valiant, impetuous medieval hero Roland, one of Charlemagne's twelve peers and his beloved nephew. The Basques were transposed into fierce Saracens, and the puppet shows of Sicily still perform the exploits of Orlando, or Roland, with much clanking of armor and the spilling of bucketfuls of blood! Other legends made Charlemagne the first Crusader of the West, who went with his army to help beleaguered Christians in the Orient, put the infidels to flight and delivered the holy city. As a reward he had, so the story goes, received relics from the Patriarch of Jerusalem, and from the Byzantine Emperor, whom he had visited in Constantinople.

One of Charlemagne's paladins, Guilhem, the hero of the medieval epic *Chanson de Guillaume*, did exist. Born in 752, he was, on his mother's side, a grandson of Charles Martel, and was brought up with the children of Pepin the Short, including the future Charlemagne, with whom he formed a lifelong friendship. Although his father was governor of Narbonne, Guilhem was a younger son without land. After Charlemagne became King of the Franks, Guilhem was one

Fig. 4. Denier (silver coin) of Charlemagne, in the Bibliothèque Nationale, Paris.

of his most loyal companions-in-arms. He was made Duke of
Aquitaine and defended the right of Charlemagne's son Louis to the
throne against barons seeking to displace him.

A Saracen invasion of the Midi led to fierce battles in which
Guilhem won victories at Nîmes, Orange and Narbonne. The facts
are heavily overlaid with legend. According to one account, Guilhem,
on a pilgrimage to Rome, defeated the Saracen giant Cursolt in single
combat. But the Saracen cut off the end of his nose, and from then on
he was nicknamed Guilhem Courtnez.

In the 12th century chanson, Guilhem, at the head of an army of
"needy and brave knights," took Nîmes by a stratagem, and entered
the beautiful city of Orange, with its palaces and gardens, while its
Moorish king was away. The lovely Moorish queen Oreble was
there and was held captive. When the Saracen king returned, the
Frankish knights murdered him, and Guilhem immediately married
Oreble, had her baptized and renamed Giboure. These pious Christians saw nothing wrong in killing a pagan king, seizing his lands
and marrying his widow. Color and race, however, were no obstacles
to marriage. The chanson's description of Orange as an earthly
paradise suggests that the greater refinement and luxury of Saracen
civilization was already exerting a spell on the West.

As a reward for his victory, Charlemagne gave Guilhem the principality of Orange. This would make him the ancestor of the House
of Orange from which the royal house of the Netherlands is
descended.

Guilhem won his last battle with the Saracens at Barcelona. He
was forty-eight when he returned to France and learned that his
beloved wife Giboure had died. He yearned for solitude, and leaving
the principality of Orange to his son, he went to Paris to tell the
Emperor of his desire to retire from the world. Unwilling to lose his
boyhood friend, Charlemagne kept him at court as counselor. Guilhem accompanied the Emperor to Rome, where Charlemagne
received from Pope Leo III a three-inch-long piece of the True
Cross, supposedly deposited by St. Helena, the mother of Constantine the Great, in the church at Jerusalem.

On his return to Southern France, Guilhem visited his estates in
the wild and beautiful Hérault region northeast of present-day
Montpellier. In a lonely ravine of the Hérault Gorge, he built a
Benedictine monastery in 804, and Guilhem settled there with
a few monks.

Fig. 5. Saint-Guilhem-le-Désert (Hérault).

After a last tearful reunion in Paris with Charlemagne, who gave him the holy piece of the True Cross, Guilhem returned to his monastery in the little village of Gellone, and deposited the relic in the church of the abbey. After Guilhem's death and canonization, pilgrims on their way to Santiago de Compostela would stop at Gellone, later called Saint-Guilhem-le-Désert, to worship the True Cross. No trace of the Carolingian buildings remains, but today the famous relic is preserved in the crypt of the beautiful little abbey church built in the 11th and early 12th centuries, one of the purest gems of the Romanesque to be seen anywhere (Fig. 5). The apse of the church, with its crown-like frieze of arches, rises among the village's ancient gray and amber houses covered with mellowed red-tiled roofs. The façade of the church on the peaceful little square is almost hidden by an enormous plane tree. The interior, with plain barrel vault and transverse arches, is in its absolute simplicity a splendid example of intelligent and sensitive restoration. Even the late 18th century organ does not detract from the overall harmony.

A shock comes on opening the door from the south wall that leads into the cloister; only two of the original arches remain in the bare space where the cloister used to be. The rest was sold in 1906 to the American sculptor George Grey Barnard and became part of the fabulous collection of medieval sculpture and architectural material assembled by him in New York and presented in 1925 to the Metropolitan Museum of Art; it is now part of the "The Cloisters," that unique museum of medieval art. The splendid 12th century capitals, carved in the elegant transitional style between Romanesque and Gothic, are inspired by the local fauna and flora (Fig. 6) of Hérault.

Guilhem is credited with one last exploit after his retreat to the monastery. The region was plagued by the outrageous acts of a terrifying Saracen giant called Don Juan, who had come from the Spanish marches and lived in a castle on top of a precipitous rock overlooking the village. Guilhem in his monk's habit sought out the giant and challenged him to single combat. In the presence of the inhabitants of Gellone kneeling in prayer, Guilhem slew the infidel Goliath with one thrust of his sword. The ruined castle high up above the village is still pointed out as *le château de Don Juan*.

After this heroic deed, recalling his earlier days as a warrior, Guilhem returned to his cell and spent the rest of his life in prayer. Guilhem, the famous Duke of Aquitaine, Count of Toulouse and Prince of Orange, died in 812 and was solemnly buried in the abbey church. A century later, the village of Gellone took the name of Saint-Guilhem-le-Désert.

One of the very few representations in art of St. Guilhem is an anonymous early 16th century painting of the School of Montpellier in that city's fascinating Société Archéologique, which also contains five sculptural fragments from the Church of Saint-Guilhem-le-Désert. In the painting, the saint holds his crozier and Bible; the other saint on the panel is a woman, St. Apollonia, an early Christian martyr who holds in her right hand a pair of pincers with an extracted tooth! But she did not become the patron saint of dentistry.

The most curious medieval custom to survive in Saint-Guilhem-le-Désert is the Procession of Snails. Every year on May 3 at dusk, by the light of oil lamps made out of snail shells, small loaves of bread shaped like crosses are blessed at a special Mass and preserved as talismans against thunder and lightning. At the season of transhumance—that is, when the cattle and other animals are moved to more favorable pastures—one of these little crosses of bread is fixed between the horns of the ram who leads the flock. After the Mass, there is a procession through the village with the snail-shell lamps. In the Middle Ages the pilgrims on their way to Compostela would take part in this parade, after worshipping the fragment of the True Cross. Saint-Guilhem-le-Désert was also the center of a pilgrimage in the 13th century enforced on Cathars who had renounced their heresy.

Fig. 6. Capitals and abacus from the cloister of the Abbey of Saint-Guilhem-de-Désert (Hérault), late 12th or early 13th century. (The Metropolitan Museum of Art, The Cloisters Collection, Purchase 1925)

Several even more illustrious pilgrimages either originated or grew in importance during the Carolingian era. Charlemagne was the first of many high dignitaries to make a pilgrimage to the sanctuary of Le Puy on the heights of Mont Cenis in the rugged and grandiose Velay region in Auvergne. The cult object was a huge Druidic stone slab, known as the *pierre des fièvres*, or fever stone. Originally it was part of a prehistoric dolmen, but after the arrival of the first Christian missionaries it was credited with miraculous healing powers, due to the intervention of the Virgin. Paralytics and other afflicted people would lie down on the stone and go to sleep. After the Virgin appeared to them in a dream they would wake up cured—provided, of course, that they had the necessary faith.

The earliest sanctuary housing this stone was built in the late 5th century. It was made more holy by being used as an altar, surmounted by a statue of the Virgin. This was not the famous Black Virgin of Le Puy, which from the 13th century became a venerated object of worship for countless pilgrims. Le Puy had long been the center of the cult of the Virgin Mary that so profoundly influenced medieval Europe. When the present basilica of Notre-Dame-du-Puy, one of the strangest and most interesting churches in all France, was completed in the 12th century on the steep hill overlooking the town, the miracle-working stone was placed at the head of the flight of steps leading through the cavernous portico into the nave of the church.

Hospices on the Alpine passes for pilgrims on their way to Rome or Jerusalem had already been built in the Carolingian period, but there is no evidence for the belief, widespread in the Middle Ages, that the most popular of all medieval pilgrimage-resorts in Europe, Santiago de Compostela in the Spanish province of Galicia, owed its origin to Charlemagne. An illumination in a 15th century manuscript, preserved in the archives of the Toulouse Municipal Library, shows Charlemagne asleep in bed, wearing his crown, and being visited in a dream by the apostle St. James (Fig. 7). Charlemagne had been dreaming of the Milky Way. St. James, who, according to legend, had preached in Spain, ordered Charlemagne to follow the Milky Way into Galicia in northeastern Spain to rescue his tomb at Compostela, which had fallen into the hands of the infidels, and to build a shrine there. In reality, the earliest account of the transference of the saint's relics from Palestine to Spain dates from the 10th century, and the first accounts of bands of pilgrims from Germany

Fig. 7. St. James appearing to Charlemagne in a dream. From the Grandes Chroniques de France, *15th century MS in the Archives Municipales, Toulouse.*

and France were written a hundred years later. There is no mention of Compostela in the *chansons de geste*.

Not all the theologians who surrounded Charlemagne were in favor of pilgrimages, as they considered many of the pilgrims activated by extremely dubious motives; also the many temptations and distractions in the cities they passed on their long journeys too often proved irresistible. Many pilgrims, it was felt, returned less devout than when they started out! These theologians were particularly opposed to women going on pilgrimages.

When the abbess Ethelburga of Fladbury in Worcestershire, England, found that the pilgrimage to Rome that she had planned was impracticable, Alcuin, the eminent English churchman and educator at Charlemagne's court, and the moving spirit of the Carolingian Renaissance, wrote to her saying that it was "no great loss" and that God had better designs for her: "Expend the sum thou has gathered for the journey on the support of the poor, and if thou hast given as thou canst, thou shalt reap as thou wilt."

In his last years Charlemagne had been concerned about the danger from the Vikings, and had ordered the building of a fleet, knowing that the Norsemen, or Normans, as the blond, bearded pirates were later called, could only be challenged successfully in their own element, the sea. In the period of anarchy that followed Charlemagne's death in 814, these orders were never carried out, and conditions were ripe for a Norman invasion by land.

As King of Aquitaine, Charlemagne's son Louis the Pious—also nicknamed le Débonnaire, the easygoing or compliant (Fig. 8)—had resided in the palace of Chasseneuil, near his birthplace of Poitiers. He maintained a "scriptorium" for the copying of ancient manuscripts, and entertained traveling scholars at his court. After he became Emperor of the West in 814, Louis received many gifts from the Byzantine court, and from Al-Mamoun, the Caliph of Baghdad—

Fig. 8. Louis the Pious, also called "le Débonnaire," from a 9th century MS in the Biblioteca Apostolica Vaticana, Rome.

rich fabrics and precious objects which gave the Carolingian nobles a tantalizing glimpse of the splendor and refinement of the East.

Louis the Pious' Frankish astronomer expressed horror at the free-and-easy ways of Aquitaine. This was the first among many scandalized reactions on the part of devout and serious northerners to the more relaxed, worldly atmosphere south of the Loire.

In 817, to revive an old custom, Louis divided his empire among his sons, Lothair I, Louis and Pepin I. Each of the sons was dissatisfied with his portion, and they at once began quarreling among themselves.

Aquitaine was caught up in the general disorder. Pepin I founded the Abbey of Saint-Cyprien in Poitiers in 828. In the following year, he joined his brother Lothair in temporarily deposing their father, Louis the Pious. For two years King Louis and his proud and beautiful queen, Judith of Bavaria, a stronger character than her husband, were kept prisoners in the monastery of Sainte-Croix. In 831 Louis was restored to power, and Pepin I had to contend with a new adversary, his father's youngest son by a second marriage, Charles the Bald, who claimed the kingdom of Aquitaine. Pepin I died in 838 and was buried in Sainte-Radegonde, but the struggle for Aquitaine continued between his son Pepin II and Charles the Bald, who on his father's death in 840 became King of the West Franks. In the course of a sterile and seemingly endless war, Aquitaine, Poitou and the city of Poitiers were constantly changing hands between Pepin II and his uncle Charles the Bald. These fratricidal struggles between the Frankish rulers made their lands especially vulnerable to a Norman invasion.

After 843 the Normans, numbering no more than five thousand, engaged in a series of raids along the banks of the Seine and the Loire and in lower Poitou. The sight of the Viking "long ships" with their striped, square sails and high prows elaborately carved with grimacing, vividly painted animal figures, struck fear into the inhabitants of Poitou, and since the ships' draft was small they were able to sail into relatively shallow rivers, lagoons and marshes. Although the Normans were fierce and predatory in battle, and as pagans were unawed by crucifixes and holy relics, they were intelligent and resolute, by no means the savage, ruthless barbarians described by monkish chroniclers. It was largely the barrenness of their Scandinavian homeland that had prompted their seagoing expeditions, which were carefully prepared. The aim was not merely to amass booty but also to settle in more propitious territory, free from the ordeals of hunger and cold. Their adaptability and organizing skills became evident when in the 10th century they conquered Normandy, accepted Christianity, and abandoned piracy and raiding without losing their spirit of adventure. Their conquest of England in the 11th century and their successful rule of Southern Italy and Sicily brought out the true qualities of this extraordinary people, and in the 12th century a great king of Norman descent, Henry II of England, would rule in Aquitaine.

But all this lay in the future. The population of Poitou, exhausted by decades of war, felt nothing but panic when in November 855 the Normans, contrary to their usual practice, arrived on foot before the walls of Poitiers. As experienced seamen, they realized that the swift, raging waters of the Clain, then in flood, were impossible to navigate. Like the Arabs over a century earlier, they were stopped short by the powerful city walls, and retreated after setting fire to the Abbey of Saint-Cyprien and other buildings on the outskirts.

When the Normans reappeared before Poitiers two years later, the city was spared by the payment of a ransom. They made a third attempt in 860. Pepin II, who still claimed the kingdom of Aquitaine, had temporarily wrested control of the city from Charles the Bald, and in order to thwart his uncle's plans he opened the gates to the Normans. Pillage was widespread, and the pagan invaders were eager to loot the wealthy abbeys and sanctuaries. They sacked and destroyed the church and monastery of Saint-Hilaire, but were unable to find its treasures. The monks had secretly hidden them and fled to Le Puy in Auvergne, taking with them the precious relics of their patron saint. They returned with them to Poitiers after the danger had passed.

Charles the Bald soon retook Poitiers and drove out his nephew, Pepin II.

The Normans made a further assault on Poitiers in 868, accompanied by their willing collaborator, Pepin II. They met with unexpected resistance, led by the Count of Poitiers, Ramnulf II. The inhabitants of Poitiers were outraged by the Carolingian prince Pepin II's treachery and rallied around Ramnulf. The Normans were routed, and Pepin was taken prisoner. Ramnulf handed Pepin over to Charles the Bald, who imprisoned his nephew at Senlis, where he remained in captivity until his death in 870.

Ramnulf II's loyalty to his Carolingian overlords was not adequately rewarded until many years later. In 889 Charles the Bald's grandson Charles III, the Simple, shared the throne of France with Eudes, Count of Paris. By a strange coincidence, both these warriors were founders of a ruling family. King Eudes, ancestor of the royal Capetian dynasty of France, confirmed Ramnulf as Count of Poitou as well as of Poitiers and Duke of Aquitaine—there were to be no more Kings of Aquitaine!

This was the beginning of the long line of count-dukes who for three centuries, until the time of Eleanor of Aquitaine, made Poitiers the capital of a vast region stretching from the Loire to the Pyrenees and Languedoc, a sovereign state more extensive, richer and more fertile than the territories held by the King of France. As Counts of Poitiers and Dukes of Aquitaine, these powerful lords paid a purely nominal and symbolic allegiance to the French king. They considered themselves his superior, and maintained their proud independence, with far-reaching consequences. With their quick intelligence, energy, worldliness, diplomatic skills and their awareness that the ambitions of the Church were not confined to religious matters, they were far more advanced, more "modern" in outlook than the other feudal lords of their day.

Love for the arts and letters and the relative freedom that prevailed at their court and in their domains gave rise to a civilization that embodied the most dynamic and mercurial qualities of the Midi. In the long run these qualities have enriched and enlivened *l'esprit français* in general, even though in the Middle Ages the Occitans—those who inhabited the regions where the *langue d'oc* was spoken—did not regard themselves as Frenchmen. The count-dukes dreamed of establishing an autonomous realm in the South completely independent of Northern France. Their ultimate failure to achieve this was due to internal weaknesses in the feudal system itself and to overwhelming pressures from the outside, not to any lack of talent or vision.

The name Guilhem had been one to conjure with in the Midi ever since the days of Charlemagne, when the Emperor's valiant companion-in-arms, the first Duke of Aquitaine, renounced his worldly estate and founded the monastery and church in the wilds of Hérault that became Saint-Guilhem-le-Désert. Guilhem was the name of a long line of outstanding rulers of Poitou and Aquitaine. The first

Guilhem, nicknamed Tête d'Etoupe, or Towhead, because he wore a flaxen wig, was Count Guilhem I of Poitou, but Duke Guilhem III of Aquitaine, and from that time on the numbering of the Guilhems varies according to whether they are being referred to as Counts of Poitou or Dukes of Aquitaine. Their titles as Counts will be given to avoid confusion.

The Kings of France watched the rise of the vigorous new dynasty south of the Loire with growing alarm. The weakened Carolingian monarchs depended on their powerful vassals, the Counts of Paris, to assert royal authority, and Hugh the Great, Count of Paris and Duke of the Franks, wielded more actual power than his overlord, the French king Louis IV, nicknamed d'Outremer ("from overseas," because he had spent his boyhood in England). Hugh resented Guilhem's title as Duke of Aquitaine, and unsuccessfully laid siege to Poitiers in 955. He set fire to the fortified *bourg* of Sainte-Radegonde. The people of Poitiers remained loyal to tow-headed Guilhem, whose prestige was enhanced by his fearless stand.

After Guilhem's death in 963, his son Guilhem II, called Fier-à-Bras, or Proud Arm, because of his exceptional courage, obtained in 970 from Hugh the Great's son and successor, Hugh Capet, an unqualified recognition of his ducal title, and proudly proclaimed himself "*Dux totius monarchiae Aquitanensium.*" The agreement was given added weight by the marriage of Hugh Capet to Guilhem's sister Adelaide of Poitiers.

A new era began in 987, when, after the last Carolingian king, Louis V, died without children, Hugh Capet was elected King of France by the prelates and nobles. Hugh was the founder of the Capetian dynasty, which was to rule France continuously for many generations. Hugh's surname, Capet, may have been derived from the Latin *capa* or *cappa* (cape) that he wore as lay abbot of Saint-Martin at Tours. It was not, as was sometimes claimed, an allusion to a playful and youthful habit of snatching caps from his entourage.

While Hugh Capet owed his throne largely to the Church, it was a woman who helped to establish the new dynasty on a firm basis. After Hugh's coronation in 987, the legitimacy of the new dynasty was challenged by the Empress-regent of Germany, Theophano. Hugh Capet countered this move by sending his wife Adelaide for a personal confrontation with Empress Theophano. Adelaide was successful and returned in triumph with a treaty of alliance, and Capetian rule was assured for centuries.

Resistance came unexpectedly from Hugh's brother-in-law Guilhem II of Poitou, who at first refused to recognize Hugh's election, considering him a usurper. There was another war, and another unsuccessful French attempt to capture Poitiers. Guilhem retained his titles, and the duchy of Aquitaine enjoyed virtual autonomy until, weary of his political struggles, Guilhem the "proud of arm" retired to the monastery of Saint-Maixent in the Sarthe region, where he died in 994. Ending one's days in a pious retreat was known in the Middle Ages as "making a good death" or "dying well."

The emergence of Poitiers as a brilliant center of culture dates from the reign of Guilhem III, the Great, who succeeded his father in 994. Guilhem III was a clever, energetic and fearless ruler of whom a chronicler wrote, "no man dared raise a hand against him." In many of his actions he showed a magnanimity and courtesy in marked contrast to the barbarism that had prevailed in Western Europe in the 10th century.

Unlike the early Capetian kings, who owed most of their power to the Church and enjoyed participating in religious ceremonies, the Counts of Poitiers, though lavish in their gifts to monasteries, were suspicious of the clergy's ambitions, and insisted on what would centuries later be called the separation of Church and State. They were "believers," but more from individual choice than compulsion. Guilhem III spoke contemptuously of the "insignificance" (*vilitas*) of his mild, weak-willed cousin Robert the Pious, who had been crowned as co-ruler of France during the lifetime of his father, Hugh Capet, and who became sole king on Hugh's death in 996.

In spite of his piety, Robert had his troubles with the Church. In order to marry his cousin Bertha, with whom he was madly in love, Robert repudiated his first wife, Rosala, who was much older than he. The Church could not accept this marriage with a kinswoman, and in 996 Robert was excommunicated by Pope Gregory V, a terrible burden for so devout a monarch to bear. Surprisingly, Robert, fortified by his love, braved the anathema for five years, but around 1002 reluctantly yielded and gave up Bertha. Instead of recalling his first wife, Rosala, he married Constance, daughter of William I, Count of Arles. The Church raised no objection since there was no blood relationship. Constance, a scheming and ambitious woman, made life miserable for her compliant husband. With her fiery southern temperament she despised the people of the North, whom she regarded, with some justification, as barbarians. As was to be

expected, the rough courtiers and solemn priests in Robert's entourage were scandalized by the extravagant costumes and easy morals of
Constance's compatriots, whom she had summoned from Provence
and Aquitaine. She had a cruel streak and was capable of having
negligent guards and other offenders blinded or tortured as a warning to others. In addition to many vexations, Constance gave Robert
the Pious four sons, so that the future of the Capetians was assured.

At this time in Poitiers, Count Guilhem III was becoming an outstanding ruler. He owed his nickname, the Great, not to any military
conquests, but to his personal qualities, his skill as administrator and
diplomat, and his princely way of life. Guilhem resided in the palace,
which in Merovingian times had been the seat of justice. The palace
had most probably been erected on the site of the Roman Capitol,
since it was the custom to build new structures upon old, favorable
places. Today, after many additions and modifications, it still serves
as the Palace of Justice, and is one of many buildings in Poitiers that
provide an extraordinary sense of continuity and of the direct heritage
of past ages. Guilhem III remodeled the palace and began construction of the Great Hall. He also rebuilt the cathedral, which had
been destroyed by fire.

The princes of Europe dealt with Guilhem III as an equal, but his
chief claim to fame derives from the warm welcome and encouragement he gave scholars and men of learning. His father, Guilhem II,
Fier-à-Bras, had never learned to read or write. Driven by a keen
intellectual curiosity rare among rulers in those early feudal days,
Guilhem III installed a library in the palace and would often read
and study far into the night. He took great pride in showing visitors a
manuscript illuminated with golden letters, presented to him by King
Canute of England.

Guilhem III donated the Abbey of Saint-Maixent, where his father
and grandfather had died, to the monk Rainaud, a man of such
outstanding intellect that he was nicknamed Plato. Guilhem III was
also the friend and patron of the learned prelate Fulbert of Chartres,
who established several schools in Poitiers and was made custodian of
the priceless treasury of Saint-Hilaire.

The wide-ranging interests of Guilhem III extended to religious
questions then stirring many people throughout Christendom. The
doctrine of Manichaeism, with its belief in the conflicting dualism
between the realm of God and the realm of Satan, was of serious

concern to the Church, and reappeared two centuries later in the Cathar heresy. Poitou-Aquitaine was always a fertile ground for this and other unorthodox beliefs, and the Occitan rulers in general were more inclined to tolerate than to persecute those who sought their own path to salvation.

Guilhem III died in 1030 in Maillezais, near Niort, on an island in the Poitevin marshes, where his father, Guilhem Fier-à-Bras, had founded a Benedictine abbey. Its ruins are still standing, but the most interesting monument in Maillezais is the impressive, if overrestored, parish church, built later in the 11th century in the robust Poitou-Romanesque style. One of the jambs of the entrance door is decorated with a relief carving of men standing on each other's shoulders (Fig. 9). They could have been inspired by the acrobatics of traveling mountebanks. We can find a parallel to this motif in the rise of the Count-Dukes of Poitou and Aquitaine, each of whom built or tried to build on the achievements of his predecessor—though nothing could have been further from the unknown sculptor's intention.

A turbulent interlude followed Guilhem III's death in 1030. Agnes of Burgundy, his ambitious widow, hastily married Geoffroy Martel, Count of Anjou, the head of a rival dynasty, in order to thwart her stepson, Guilhem IV, the Fat. War broke out, and Guilhem IV was captured by Geoffroy Martel and imprisoned; on the payment of an enormous ransom raised by his wife Eustache, who mortgaged

Fig. 9. Detail of the portal of the parish church of Maillezais (Vendée).

the treasures of the abbeys of Poitou, Guilhem IV was released, but he died soon after leaving prison.

The history of Poitou-Aquitaine is complicated by the succession of Guilhems. Agnes of Burgundy had borne to Guilhem III a son who was also named Guilhem, and after the death of Guilhem IV, he became Guilhem V, and was nicknamed Aigret, from the Latin *acer*, meaning lively, impetuous. There always was another son named Guilhem to step into his father's place. Guilhem V died in Poitiers in 1058, and his son and successor, Guilhem VI, was destined to reassert the authority and prestige of the ruling dynasty of Poitou.

Guilhem VI was also known as Guy-Geoffroy. He proved to be a redoubtable warrior and a skillful, if at times devious, negotiator— quick to make promises, but not always scrupulous in keeping them. He extended Poitou and Aquitaine to include the fertile region of Saintonge, which he won from the Counts of Anjou. Guy-Geoffroy (Guilhem VI) also imposed his rule on Gascony. But his greatest exploit was his campaign against the Saracens in Spain in response to an appeal from the Count of Barcelona in 1065.

Guy-Geoffroy had another Spanish ally, King Sancho-Ramiro of Aragon, who was striving to push his domain southward at the expense of the Emirate of Saragossa. The term "crusade" did not yet exist; this campaign against the Moslems was an early phase of the "reconquest of Spain" by the Christian princes. Guy-Geoffroy did not succeed in driving the Moors from Tarragona, but he scored a decisive victory by capturing the rich Moorish citadel of Barbastro near Saragossa.

Fig. 10. A Concert, from The Loves of Bayad and Riyad, *a 14th century Hispano-Moresque MS in the Vatican Library, Rome.*

Part of the booty of this Spanish campaign was the gift to Guy-Geoffroy's commander, Guillaume de Montriel, of no less than fifteen hundred young Moorish girls, many of them accomplished musicians, dancers and singers. Some of these girls were sent to the Byzantine Emperor in Constantinople, but many were brought by Guy-Geoffroy to Poitiers, and they had an influence on the development of the music of the region. We do not know if they resembled the round-faced, black-haired, dark-eyed harem beauties in early Islamic wall paintings and Hispano-Moresque miniatures (Fig. 10), but we can be sure they had some impact on the warm-blooded young nobles of Poitou. Guy-Geoffroy's young son, also named Guilhem, would have seen and heard these young Moorish performers at his father's court in Poitiers, where the exotic rhythms could be appreciated even without a knowledge of the Arabic language.

Guy-Geoffroy's campaigns, fought in alliance with the Spanish nobles, and even the most fanatical crusades of the next generation provided continuous contact with the refinements of Arab culture and began to work subtle changes in the rougher patterns of the early feudal society of Christendom.

Buoyed by his triumph at Barbastro, which had great repercussions throughout the Midi, Guy-Geoffroy felt strong enough not only to deal with the weak and unpopular King of France as an equal, but also to challenge the authority of the formidable Pope Gregory VII and defend his second marriage to his kinswoman, Adélarde of Burgundy. This scandal was eventually resolved in his favor when he promised to dissolve the marriage and to build a monastery in Poitiers for the Cluniac order; this organization of Benedictine monks, with its center at Cluny in Burgundy, was vital to Gregory's program of Church reform. Poor Countess Adélarde was discarded and removed like a pawn from the political chessboard, but she was allowed to continue to live quietly at the court. The buildings of the Cluniac monastery, Saint-Jean-de-Montierneuf, were completed after Guy-Geoffroy's death in 1086 by his son Guilhem VII.

Little remains of the 11th century church apart from the apse, similar in style to that of Saint-Hilaire, and the ambulatory, which is far more spacious than in most Romanesque churches. A stone tablet on the wall of the north aisle near the pulpit commemorates the consecration of the altar in 1096 by Pope Urban II, who had come to France to rouse enthusiasm for the First Crusade. The church also

Fig. 11. Elephants, from a capital from the Abbey Church of Saint-Jean-de-Montierneuf, Poitiers, ca. 1077–1088: now in the Musée des Beaux-Arts, Poitiers. (Photograph by Sue Marks)

contains the much-restored tomb of the founder of Montierneuf, Count Guilhem VI, Guy-Geoffroy. But the importance and sense of prosperity that surrounded Montierneuf in medieval times is gone. During the Revolution in the late 18th century the church was used as an army barracks and stable. The only reason the Romanesque capitals in the ambulatory were spared is that they were concealed by the piles of hay used as fodder for the horses. The capitals include some delightful paired elephants (Fig. 11) by a sculptor who probably had never seen one; he may have found a similar motif in Byzantine or oriental fabrics.

Poitiers had grown and prospered under Guilhem VI's energetic guidance. The ravages of the Normans were a distant memory, and the only disaster to strike the city was an "act of God," an earthquake on October 18, 1083, followed by a terrible fire. The destruction was quickly repaired, and a new wave of building began.

Guilhem VI died suddenly in the castle of Chize, near Poitiers, during a hunting expedition in September 1086, one year before the death of his great contemporary, William the Conqueror, the powerful Duke of Normandy, whose conquest of England began a new era in that country's history. Since the nave of the still unfinished Church of Saint-Jean-de-Montierneuf was not ready to receive the remains of its founder, he was buried in the chapter hall of the abbey. A year or so later the thick stone sarcophagus was taken to the nave opposite the main altar and buried two feet below the ground. A splendid mausoleum with marble columns was erected above the tomb with a recumbent effigy of Guy-Geoffroy, his feet resting on a dog, the symbol of fidelity.

In 1822 the tomb was dug up and opened; the count's body was described as being a little under five feet six inches tall, dressed in a black woolen garment that fell to his ankles: over it was another garment that came to his knees, with a hood covering what seemed to be a very large head. The mausoleum was replaced by a monument designed in a hybrid style that reflects the enthusiasm of the early Romantic period for the Middle Ages. An inscription gives credit to King Louis XVIII for the preservation of the tomb and the erection of the new monument. The sculptor dressed the recumbent figure in a costume full of anachronisms, including the full breeches and court shoes of the Louis XIII period. A coronet indicates his rank, but his small clean-shaven features and bobbed hair suggest a *"preux chevalier"* or "gentil, parfyt knight" of the age of St. Louis rather than an 11th century noble.

Few medieval portraits exist but it can be assumed that Guilhem VI, like most of the count-dukes, had a handsome presence and a quality of "charisma." In spite of his considerable achievements, he remains a shadowy figure, eclipsed in the eyes of posterity by his brilliant, mercurial son, Guilhem VII, the first of the troubadours.

CHAPTER III

Guilhem VII: The First Troubadour

T HE YEAR 1000 HAD COME AND GONE without the dreaded apocalypse destroying the world. A more ordered society was evolv-
ing, although life was certainly harsh and perilous. Nobles, while
often highhanded and unscrupulous, were no longer the rough, illiterate semibarbaric warlords of the Dark Ages. In Central and Southern
France rulers and their entourages showed greater respect for learning and peaceful pursuits, and relied more on diplomacy than violence
to achieve their ends.

As slowly but inevitably the patterns of daily life changed, women
found new activities and new ways to express themselves. The
cheerless existence of a feudal lord's wife in the 10th century,
largely confined to the women's quarters in the upper story of a
hastily built wooden tower, was very different from that of a noble
lady of the 11th and 12th centuries in her stone castle, where, during
her husband's absences, she often exercised the powers of the liege
lord. Even if there was little physical comfort by modern standards, her existence had a more dignified and less restrictive setting
than in the rough and primitive 10th century. Needless to say, these
improved conditions were true only of the more privileged women,
who were "noble," according to a Provençal saying, because they

went "neither to the baking oven nor to the washhouse nor to the mill."

Feudalism was less rigid in the Occitan territories than elsewhere, and there was greater tolerance of diverse opinions. Typical of the more flexible character of southern feudalism was the *alleude* (from the Latin *allodium*), a system whereby hereditary property was exempt from all indebtedness to an overlord. The fief, on the other hand, one of the bases of feudalism in both North and South, was granted in return for certain services. North of the Loire the prevailing maxim was "No land without a lord," and the peasants were serfs, bound for life to their master's estate. In Guyenne and further south, the saying was reversed—"No lord without a lawful claim"—and serfdom was by no means universal. Many peasants were freemen, owning their own property. The northern barons tended to hoard their wealth, often acquired by warring with their neighbors; one of the most admired virtues of the great and lesser nobles of the Midi was *largueza*—generous, even extravagant, spending to increase their prestige and benefit larger numbers of people.

Generalizations are dangerous, and it would be wrong to paint too idyllic a picture of life in the Midi, but there is no doubt that Occitan feudalism had a more peaceful character than its northern counterpart, and that there was greater respect for human beings. For one thing, a woman in the Midi could inherit a fief; in the more rigorous system of the North only males could inherit property, and since feudal society was based on force, it was assumed that a woman could not be capable of defending her landed estates as a warrior, weapons in hand. The castles in which the Counts of Poitiers and Toulouse resided dominated their respective cities, but were regarded by the inhabitants as symbols of protection rather than oppression. In the 11th century the new ideals of chivalry began to emerge, aristocratic and militantly Christian, yet with a broad human base. This was reflected in the evolution of the *chansons de geste*. Origins of these epic poems in the French vernacular have been much disputed, but the first chansons were probably composed around the year 1000 by the combined efforts of itinerant clerks and minstrels, later known as jongleurs. Their aim was to attract pilgrims to the shrines where the heroes of the epics were supposedly buried, or to honor the pious founders and patrons of the abbeys stationed along the main pilgrimage routes. The subject of each of these epics was a series of historical facts or *gesta*; the sources were the monastic chronicles containing records of the saints and heroes whose relics were preserved in the churches and monasteries. Inevitably the recorded exploits of the distant past were heavily embroidered with legend, but so vivid and naïve was the popular imagination that the chansons were accepted as real history by those who heard the minstrels' songs.

Wandering jongleurs, or "cantators," would sing to the accompaniment of a primitive viol. The most illustrious of the central figures around whom these cycles were grouped was Charlemagne, and the oldest and finest extant *chanson de geste* is the *Chanson de Roland*. Legends surrounding Charlemagne's favorite paladin probably began in the monasteries on the route to Roncevaux in the Pyrenees, where Roland met his death in 778. Only one version of the *Chanson de Roland* has survived; the date of its composition has been placed somewhere between 1066 and 1095. The unknown author lived at or near the sanctuary of Mont-Saint-Michel in Normandy.

The 12th century Franco-Norman poet Wace, from the island of Jersey, records that the bard Taillefer sang of Roland's deeds against the Saracens in Spain to inflame the Normans before their victory over King Harold's Saxons at Hastings in 1066. It is uncertain whether Taillefer used the version we know or an earlier one. Sometimes the minstrels accompanied the warriors into battle, like the Scottish bagpipers of a much later era. Wace describes Taillefer

Fig. 12. Jongleur accompanying Crusaders into battle, as they ride against the Saracens in the Holy Land. The cross on the spire indicates that the city has been occupied by the Christians. From a mural in the Chapel of the Templars, Cressac (Charente), ca. 1170–1180.

Fig. 13. Battling Warriors. Detail of a capital in the Romanesque pilgrimage church of Conques-en-Rouergue (Aveyron), 12th century. (Photo Reportage Zodiaque YAN)

flinging his sword into the air as he sang rousing stanzas from the *Chanson de Roland* before the Norman army.

A late 12th century mural in the chapel of the Knights Templars in Cressac, in Charente, shows a bareheaded young minstrel with his viol riding alongside some stern-looking Crusaders in the Holy Land (Fig. 12). The treatment is lively, but the pictorial space is so ambiguous that the position of the bard, who is much smaller in scale than his heavily armed companions, is far from clear. He must be riding an unseen horse, but looks as if he were tucked into the central knight's shield.

The best of the early *chansons de geste* were written in ten-syllable verse, divided into stanzas of different lengths. Their general character has been described by Edmund Gosse as "hard, coarse, inflexible, like the march of rough men stiffened by coats of mail." The battling warriors on a carved capital in the pilgrimage-church of Sainte-Foy in Conques (Fig. 13) reflect the martial spirit of the *chansons de geste*. Scenes of this kind, also found in other Romanesque churches, may sometimes refer to the Crusades in Spain, but in general they are

thought to represent earthly combat, the struggle here below, as con-
trasted with the bliss of Paradise. Not all the poems had the grandeur
of the *Chanson de Roland*. Their celebration of warlike qualities was
a legacy of the Teutonic vigor of the Franks, but these epics sprang
entirely from the soil of France, mostly from the North and Northwest. Their fierce martial energy was tempered by the altruistic
values of Christianity, and the chansons did much to foster what
became known as the spirit of chivalry.

Even the *Chanson de Roland* praised the "valiance" and "chivalry"
of the Saracen enemy. These were not empty words, for an Arab
knighthood developed simultaneously with, or possibly even earlier
than, Christian knighthood, and with similar ideals—the cult of
honor, contempt for cowardice, faith in the nobility and perfectibility
of man, protection of the weak and devotion to the spirit of disinter-
estedness and magnanimity. The vizier El Fadl ben Yahya declared,
"Chivalry is the forgiveness of wrongs," and "If you triumph, be
merciful."

In the Christian world, knighthood became distinct in many ways
from feudalism, with its strict hierarchy, and had its own ethical
standards, which were not always identical with those of the Church.
The knights were members of a military aristocracy recruited in a
more or less democratic fashion, and were accepted on the basis of
courage, intelligence and other personal qualities rather than for considerations of social class. In the Midi the chivalric virtue of *prets*
(merit or valor) later became one of the basic elements of courtly
love as sung by the troubadours. Once a man was a knight he enjoyed
the protection of the entire order and great freedom of movement.
He could go from castle to castle and be received as an equal by the
noble castellans. A knight in chain mail, attended by his bearded
squire, stands before a richly attired lord (Fig. 14) in a carved
relief in the cloister of the Cathedral of Sainte-Eulalie in Elne in the
Pyrénées-Orientales. The exact meaning of the scene is not clear; it
may represent part of a ceremony of allegiance. After his ritual
initiation he was pledged to keep certain secrets, like the Freemasons
of a later time. This may account for the esoteric symbolism, the
hidden meanings, often present in the poetry of 12th century troubadours, many of whom were themselves knights.

Although the 11th century *chansons de geste* helped to create the
values of chivalry, the notion of *l'amour courtois* had not emerged.
Women in the chansons were to be rescued from danger and pro-

tected but had little personal identity and minimal freedom of choice and action. A girl whose father had died, or a young widow, had to rely on the king or an overlord to provide her as soon as possible with a husband.

In one chanson, Hélisseut, daughter of Yon of Gascony, travels to Paris and is received by Charlemagne. After bowing respectfully she goes straight to the point: "My father has been dead for two months. I ask you for a husband." In the chanson of *Girard de Vienne*, the

Fig. *14. A knight and his squire in the presence of a lord. Relief in the cloister of the Cathedral of Sainte-Eulalie, Elne (Pyrénées-Orientales), 12th century. (Reportage Photographique YAN)*

Duchess of Burgundy addressed the king in most practical terms. "My husband has just died, but what use is mourning? Find me a powerful husband, for I need him to defend my land." The king first considered giving her to his loyal vassal Girard, but decided that she was so attractive that he would keep her for himself.

But marriage was no guarantee of security, for it could be annulled on any number of pretexts, and wives were often "repudiated" on grounds of consanguinity or for other reasons, to suit the political or acquisitive desires of the husbands. The troubadours of the next generations often celebrated the joys of extramarital love. This did not necessarily mean a glorification of adultery *per se*, but was an honest reflection of prevailing attitudes and social conditions. Marriage was an entirely practical arrangement in which emotion or personal choice played little or no part.

The earlier troubadour Count Guilhem VII grew up in a society molded to a large extent by the values of the *chansons de geste*, but tempered by the amiability and relative freedom of the court of Poitiers. With his lusty temperament and roving eye, Guilhem combined the chivalrous posture of "champion of women" with a pagan appetite for enjoyment—only occasionally are there hints of the courtly love of the troubadours.

The *chansons de geste* stressed the so-called "aristocratic" virtues, but in spite of this, the itinerant jongleurs who sang or recited them found a wide audience, not only of knights, pilgrims and burghers but also of artisans and peasants. Who were these minstrels who provided this vital cultural link between so many regions of France and such diverse classes of society?

The medieval minstrel has been described as a cross between the court bard and singer of the Dark Ages and the agile mime of classical antiquity. Even after the theater, as it had existed in pagan Rome, had been banned by the Church and classical culture had all but disappeared, the descendants of the old mimes continued to travel about Europe entertaining the masses with their rough, unliterary and unsophisticated art. There are references to them in Gallo-Roman times, and they were especially numerous in the Germanic countries. Until the 9th century they had little or no contact with the court singers or bards. The 6th century Roman author Cassiodorus mentions that Theodoric the Great, King of the Ostrogoths, sent a singer and harpist to the Frankish king Clovis. Even though these court singers of heroic lays do not seem to have enjoyed much prestige, and few of their names have come down to us, they held themselves aloof from the popular entertainers who were considered no better than "rogues and vagabonds." Singers and minstrels of every kind were attacked by the Church. Charlemagne's court theologian, Alcuin, declared, "He who brings actors, mimes and dancers into his house is forgetting the host of devils that he lets in along with them."

As a result of the Carolingian Renaissance, the courtiers began to prefer classical and learned poems to heroic epics. With the loss of their audiences and the growing hostility of the clergy, the court singers found themselves in the same déclassé circles as the lowly mimes. In order to compete with them they were forced to widen their repertory and become mimes themselves. They were no longer merely poets, singers and musicians, but also dancers, jugglers, clowns, acrobats and even animal trainers and bear-leaders. The liveliness and wealth of picturesque detail in the *Chanson de Roland*, in contrast to the mournful solemnity of many of the heroic sagas of the Dark Ages, owed much to the animation and inventiveness of these versatile performers, who usually recited or sang to the accompaniment of a primitive viol. In their versions the epic chansons combined nobility of content with the vigor of folk art.

Itinerant minstrels were increasingly referred to in France in the 11th century as *jongleurs*—in Provençal *juglar*, a term which spread to Spain early in the 12th century. Lexicographers have disagreed about the origin of the word. One possible derivation is from the Latin *joculator*, jester, or comic entertainer, from which "juggler" also stems. In addition to songs, recitations and dancing, the roving minstrel was often a nimble mountebank, adept at juggling, sleight of hand and various types of acrobatics. Some of the earliest references to those performers can be found in a very important Latin manuscript of the early 11th century in the Bibliothèque Nationale, known as the *Tropaire-prosier*, a collection of prose passages to be sung during Mass. St. Martial, first Bishop of Limoges, who preached the Gospel in Aquitaine in the 3rd century, is mentioned in the text. The manuscript probably came from the famous Abbey of Saint-Martial in Limoges, erected on the site of the tomb of the "Apostle of Aquitaine." From the late 10th century on, Limoges was one of the most important centers for musical studies in the West, and greatly influenced the development of Church music and the liturgical drama.

Above: Fig. 15. Flute player and juggler, from the Tropaire-prosier of the Abbey of Saint-Martial, Limoges Bibl. Nat. MS Lat. 1118, fol. 112 V. (Bibliothèque Nationale, Paris)

Right: Fig. 16. Female dancer with cymbals, from the Tropaire-prosier of the Abbey of Saint-Martial, Limoges. Bibl. Nat. MS Lat. 1118, fol. 114 R. (Bibliothèque Nationale, Paris)

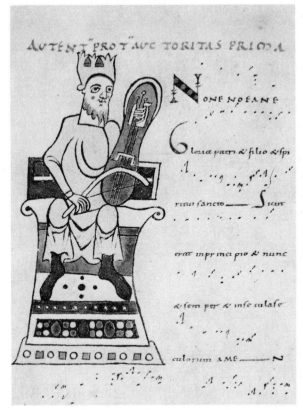

Fig. 17. King playing the "crouth" from the Tropaire-prosier *of the Abbey of Saint-Martial, Limoges, late 10th or early 11th century. (Bibliothèque Nationale, Paris)*

One delightful illustration in the *Tropaire-prosier* (Fig. 15) shows two male jongleurs. The taller one plays a *chalumeau*, a double flute. His companion is smaller and looks younger, but given the arbitrary proportions of early Romanesque art, it is not certain that he is meant to be a young boy. Another illumination (Fig. 16) represents a woman dancing, and playing what appear to be small cymbals or castanets. She wears a blue mantle, a yellow dress, a blue overdress and green shoes. It is tempting to think of these colorful jongleurs as members of those traveling families of entertainers so frequent in medieval France and England, the forerunners of the *commedia dell'arte* troupes and strolling players of a later era.

Jongleurs were considered outcasts by many churchmen, and one clerical writer declared that they "have no use or virtue" and "are beyond hope of salvation." But the very fact that the *Tropaire-prosier*, produced by monks, represents these sinful, disreputable outcasts so vividly is an indication that the jongleurs had captured the popular imagination. Also, where music was concerned, it was not easy to separate the sacred from the profane. Another page shows a king seated and playing the *crouth*, an early form of viol, possibly King David composing the Psalms (Fig. 17). The Bible also states that David danced before the Altar of the Lord. The text accompanying the *Tropaire-prosier* picture of David begins, "Glory to the Father and to the Son and to the Holy Ghost." The female dancer adorns a text beginning, "Alleluia!" The Church accepted music if it was "for the Glory of God" and if the words were in Latin. Songs performed by the jongleurs were in French or in the *langue d'oc* of Provence, and the themes, whether epic or lyric, were largely secular.

The visual arts were almost entirely in the service of religion, and the more acrobatic antics of the jongleurs provided a varied repertory of gestures and bodily positions to sculptors and miniaturists and artists in other media at a time when there was only the most rudimentary knowledge of human anatomy. In two early 13th century medallions in the Copenhagen Museum in champlevé enamel from Limoges, a city famous for its enamel industry, jongleurs are important elements of the design. In one (Fig. 18), a jongleur achieves a seemingly impossible acrobatic dance in front of a seated harpist; in the other (Fig. 19), a smiling viol player performs for a dancing-girl who holds narrow rectangular castanets. The imagery suggests that these medallions may have had a secular use.

Left: Fig. 18. Harpist and acrobat, from a medallion in champlevé enamel. Limoges 1200–1220, in the Copenhagen National Museum.

Right: Fig. 19. Viol player and dancer with castanets, from a medallion in champlevé enamel. Limoges 1200–1220, in the Copenhagen National Museum.

A meeting of jongleurs is recorded as having taken place at Fécamp in Normandy in the year 1000, during Lent, a slack season for the minstrels, since the Church disapproved of the jongleur's profession and forbade all performances in those weeks of fasting, repentance and self-denial. This meeting would have provided an opportunity to exchange ideas and learn new songs and styles of performing. The songs were not usually original creations, but were memorized and adapted over the years, and the names of the authors were unknown.

Jongleurs also performed at weddings and other festive occasions. The anonymous poet of the romance of "Flamenca," writing in the late 13th century, describes a type of gathering that had existed for many decades. In the hall of the vast palace of Bourbon d' Archambaut in Provence, many jongleurs took part in the wedding celebrations and vied with one another in singing or reciting ballads and narrative poems with such titles as "The Lay of the Honeysuckle" and "The Lay of the Faithful Lovers," all with musical accompaniment. Mention of a "Lay of Tintagel" points to the abiding popularity of the Arthurian legend (Tintagel Castle in Cornwall was King Arthur's reputed birthplace). Ballads were so called because the songs were accompanied by a dance or *balla*.

None of these anonymous pieces has survived, but it is clear that by the end of the 11th century, shortly before Guilhem the Troubadour began to write poems, there was already a popular oral tradition of song and verse in the vernacular, spread by the wandering minstrels to an increasingly varied and receptive public. While the epics preserved their appeal, intimations of a warmer, more lyrical spirit were already, as the French say, *dans le vent*, in the wind—especially in the lands where the melodious *langue d'oc* was spoken.

In Northern France the dialects were variations of the *langue d'oïl*, as distinct from the *langue d'oc* prevalent in most territories south of the Loire. *Oïl* and *oc* were the respective words for "yes." Among the *langue d'oïl* dialects, that of the Paris region gradually supplanted all the others as the standard idiom and developed into modern French, *oïl* being the ancestor of *oui*. The area where *langue d'oc* was spoken was much more extensive than present-day Provence; it reached north as far as the Loire and included Poitou, Saintonge, Aquitaine, Périgord, the Limousin, Burgundy, Auvergne, Gascony, the Narbonnais and Provence itself. These were the native lands of the Provençal troubadours, who were usually of a higher social class than the jongleurs. However, the term "Provençal" often used to describe the literature of those regions did not become current until the 13th century. This was probably due to the Italians, since Provence was the part of France with which they had the closest ties. It should be noted that in Poitou and Limousin, both central provinces, the dialects of *oc* and *oïl* existed side by side.

In addition to the Provençal songmakers, some of whom crossed the Pyrenees into Spain, there were in Languedoc and elsewhere in the Midi both male and female singers of Moorish love songs. But neither the minstrels, whatever their origins, nor their appreciative but uncultivated popular audiences had any thought of giving these anonymous songs literary form. Priests and clerks, following the example of Fortunatus five centuries earlier, composed poems and songs in Latin for an educated but limited audience. They looked with scorn on the crude entertainments for the unlettered public, and their own works had no direct influence on popular poetry.

Guilhem VII, Count of Poitiers and Duke of Aquitaine, a powerful prince, was the first important figure to lend the prestige of his name and the richness of his creative gifts to this widely diffused but undefined type of poetry. By spreading the taste for songs and ballads in the vernacular among the nobles of Limousin and Provence, Guilhem gave a new dimension to lyrical poetry in the Western world.

Guilhem VII was not quite fifteen at the time of his father's death in 1086. Young nobles matured rapidly in those days, and at fifteen Guilhem was declared to have attained his majority. He was given a nickname, the Young, which, like Louis VII in the following century, who had also succeeded his father at a tender age, he continued to bear until the end of his rule.

Adélarde, Guilhem's mother, resumed her title of Countess. She had continued to reside in the palace after she had been repudiated by Guilhem VI to avert the threat of excommunication, because of their blood relationship. She had neither the desire nor the ability to act as regent for her son.

The barons who had been in awe of the imperious Guilhem VI thought they would be able to handle a mere boy without difficulty. They soon discovered that the new count-duke, handsome, intelligent and self-willed, had every intention of being his own master. A contemporary chronicler, Gottfried of Vendôme, described the young ruler as "moving like a God among men." Even the Church, with whom Guilhem was later to have violent clashes, regarded him at first with great favor, impressed by the generous gifts he made to religious institutions in Poitiers and Bordeaux (his second capital). Guilhem made successful visits to his domains in Saintonge and Gascony, and skillfully countered the machinations of some of the more ambitious local barons.

He was less fortunate than Guy-Geoffroy in his choice of counselors and in his delegation of authority. His intimate friend Hugh the Devil, Count of Lusignan, and Guillaume Taillefer, Count of Angoulême, tended to encourage the young ruler in his thirst for adventure. When they governed during his absence, the people of Poitou and Aquitaine enjoyed less security than they had during the reign of his father.

There is no authentic portrait of this most gifted and colorful of the Counts of Poitou, whose chief claim to immortality was as the virtual creator of troubadour poetry. If he and other outstanding personalities of the Middle Ages stand out less vividly in our minds than those of later periods, it is not because they lacked vitality and complexity, but because of the very nature of medieval imagery, rarely concerned with realistic portraiture. We do not know what they *looked like*, so we have no visual image to remember.

The only contemporary representation of Guilhem the Troubadour is on a much-damaged seal preserved in the Municipal Archives of Poitiers, and originally attached to a deed of donation made in 1107 to the monks of Saint-Jean-de-Montierneuf. The count, then aged thirty-six, is shown on a galloping horse with a round shield attached to his left arm, brandishing a sword with his right. His left hand holds the horse's bridle. He is bareheaded and bearded, with long hair, and although the features are obliterated, his head is not concealed by a helmet. Even in its original state, the seal can have been no great work of art, yet it has a "verve" and sense of movement which suggest the mercurial, impulsive character of Guilhem VII, who, according to his biographer, Orderic Vital, "knew well how to sing and make verses, and for a long time he roamed the land to deceive the ladies." His portrait in the troubadour manuscript in the Bibliothèque Nationale (Fig. 20) is pleasing but purely imaginary.

Neither Guilhem's poetic gifts nor his philandering propensities were apparent when in 1088 he married Ermengarde, daughter of his neighbor to the north, Foulques, Count of Anjou. Foulques' nickname was le Réchin, an archaic French word best translated as "the Sullen" or "the Contrary." Ermengarde, three or four years Guil-

Fig. 20. Guilhem VII, Count of Poitou, an imaginative portrait in an early 14th century manuscript of troubadour poetry. MS fr. 12473, fol. 128. (Bibliothèque Nationale, Paris)

hem's senior, appears to have inherited some of her father's contrariness. Though beautiful, well educated and gracious in manner, she was subject to frequent and sudden changes of mood. Periods of solitary retreat in a cloister alternated with spectacular appearances at court when she would dazzle everyone with her charm and animation. Her changeable nature and a certain domineering tendency soon alienated her young husband, and the marriage was of short duration. It was dissolved in 1091, but it is not known what pretext was used to break the union. In any event, the Church raised no objection, and, as was usual at the time, Ermengarde remarried the following year, becoming the wife of the Duke of Brittany.

Guilhem's second marriage was brought about by momentous events that took place south of the Pyrenees. The Christian princes of Spain had renewed the campaign against the Almoravides, the Berber Moslem dynasty then governing much of the peninsula. One of the leaders of the attempted Christian reconquest was Sancho-Ramiro, King of Aragon. In 1086 he had married Philippia, daughter of Guilhem IV, Count of Toulouse—not to be confused with the Guilhems of Poitou. According to southern custom, she was the rightful heir of the county of Toulouse. The situation was complicated by the fact that her father, Count Guilhem IV of Toulouse, had lost two sons from two successive marriages and, weary of power, decided, in 1088, to abandon all his ties and responsibilities and leave for the Holy Land.

Guilhem of Toulouse died in Palestine around 1093. His brother Raymond, Count of Saint-Gilles, had administered the county in his absence. After Guilhem's death, his daughter Philippia's inheritance was still intact. King Sancho-Ramiro of Aragon could have advanced his claim to the county of Toulouse through his wife, but he was too busy with his campaign against the Moors. In 1094 Sancho-Ramiro was mortally wounded at the siege of Huesca at the foot of the Pyrenees, and his young widow, Philippia, then just over twenty, found herself in a precarious position. She did not wish to remain in war-torn Spain at the court of her stepsons, Peter I, King of Aragon, and his brothers, who were older than she was. Neither could she return to Toulouse, where her uncle, Raymond of Saint-Gilles, had assumed the title of Count and would not have tolerated her presence since she had a stronger claim to the county. Her alternatives were either to enter a convent or to remarry.

Among the suitors who came to the Aragonese court to seek Philippia's hand, the young, vigorous and charming Count of Poitou, Guilhem VII, was the obvious favorite. Guilhem spent the summer and autumn of 1094 wooing and winning Philippia and preparing the wedding festivities. Apart from his personal qualities, Guilhem could offer Philippia a position as brilliant as the one she had enjoyed at Aragon. They were married only a few months after she became a widow.

Guilhem was so carried away by the delights of the Aragonese court that he ignored various small disturbances that had broken out in Poitou during his absence.

Although the Aragonese were at this time fighting the Moors, Aragon was the most "Arabized" of the Christian kingdoms in Spain and had a strong Moorish population. Christians and Moslems lived side by side, and the aim of the Spanish rulers in Aragon and the other Christian kingdoms was not to expel the Moors from the peninsula, but extend their power over the two religions. There was none of the fanaticism that developed in the later stages of the reconquest. The Spanish rulers of Aragon, León and Castile were of partly Visigothic descent and had inherited their ancestors' tolerance of different races and creeds.

In the parts of Spain ruled by the Moors, the Christians were, on the whole, well treated, and there was frequent intermarriage. Whatever the political and military conflicts, there was much cultural

Fig. 21. Hispano-Moresque ivory casket, A.D. *968, bearing the name of Al-Moughira. Musée du Louvre, Paris. (Archives Photographiques)*

interchange between the two civilizations, and this was reflected in art and architecture as well as in music, dance and poetry. The art known as Hispano-Moresque has a certain "classical" quality partly derived from the West—the Mosque of Cordova is an outstanding example in architecture—and Christian Spain, while sharing many of the characteristics of the early Romanesque style in Europe, shows many traces of Oriental influence.

The Moors achieved a high level of refinement and beauty in the decorative and sumptuary arts, especially in ivory carving, fabrics and embroideries, and the Christian courts of Spain often displayed an almost Oriental luxury and splendor. Even the Church valued precious objects produced by Moslems or made under Moslem influence. Reliquaries in Spanish cathedrals sometimes contain richly embroidered linings of Moorish design.

At the time of Guilhem VII's eventful stay in 1094 the Aragonese court would certainly have possessed many fine objects of Moorish workmanship, including exquisitely carved ivory caskets. One lovely example in the Louvre from Cordova (Fig. 21) dating from 968 bears the name Al-Moughira, and contains the earliest-known representation of a lute player. A standing male musician is flanked by two seated attendants, and the group is enclosed in an ornate medallion.

The profuse decoration of the casket also includes animals, birds and fabulous beasts symmetrically paired in the Oriental and Byzantine manner. The Moslem ban on figurative art was rarely applied to secular works of this kind. Similar motifs executed with equal exuberance but greater breadth would later appear in the Romanesque stone carvings of the West.

Each of the musicians on the ivory caskets in the Louvre plays a lute (Fig. 22). Except for the harp and the zither, which originated in the Orient at an earlier period, all of the musical instruments used in the Middle Ages were of Moorish origin, developed in Andalusia and adopted by Christian Europe. The *rabab*, ancestor of the violin, was imported from Persia, but the Arabs invented the bow, and in the 10th century introduced the lute into Europe (from the Arabic *al 'ud*) with its pear-shaped body and fretted neck. The lute and the viol became the troubadours' favorite instruments.

A school of music had been founded in Cordova early in the 9th century by Bagdadi Ziryal, and was still flourishing two centuries later. Some of this tradition has been preserved in modern Morocco by descendants of the Moors who were expelled from Spain in the late 15th century, but the passage of time has brought changes.

Fig. 22. Lute player, from a 10th century Hispano-Moresque ivory casket in the Louvre.

The strong, simple cadences of Hispano-Moresque music influenced the monodic melodies of medieval Languedoc and Provence. (In a monodic composition there is only one vocal part, with or without musical accompaniment.) Castanets, which have contributed so much to the distinctive rhythms of music and dance in Spain, were known in Andalusia long before the coming of the Arabs and were mentioned in Roman times by the Spanish-born poet Martial. The French and Provençal jongleurs often used wooden castanets to accompany their dances.

If our knowledge of Arab music in medieval Spain is fragmentary, enough of Hispano-Arabic poetry has been preserved to convey the spirit of this highly developed culture. Moorish love poetry, sung to the accompaniment of instrumental music, anticipated Provençal lyrics by over two hundred years. Rhythm was as important in the poetry of the Moors as in their music, and it was the Moors who introduced rhyme into Europe. (Latin verse was scanned but not rhymed.) A typical metric form was the Andalusian *zajal*, which was popular among all classes of the mixed population.

The *zajal* was a lyric poem usually sung in a mixture of Arabic and Romance, and was an adaptation in the vernacular of the *muwassaha* written in the classical Arabic favored by more learned and cultivated circles. The basic form of the *zajal* is three rhyming verses with a refrain (AAAB). The fourth verse of each stanza rhymes with the refrain.

In his book *Literary History of the Arabs*, R. A. Nicholson translates a *zajal* by the poet Hariri, who died in 1122 and was Guilhem VII's contemporary:

> I ride and I ride
> Through the waste far and wide,
> And I fling away pride
> To be gay as a swallow;
>
> Stem the torrent's fierce speed,
> Tame the mettlesome steed,
> That wherever I lead
> Youth and pleasure may follow.

Although Guilhem may not have known this poem, most of his surviving songs have rhythms similar to the *zajal*, and there are affinities in metrical structure with the more popular types of troubadour lyrics such as the *aube* (dawn song) and the *ballade*.

The hybrid character of the *zajal* was paralleled by the diversity of the singers, who might be dark-skinned Moors or Spaniards trained in the Moorish musical tradition. Many of the singer-musicians were women; they were in great demand at the Christian as well as the Moorish courts of Spain and were popular in towns and villages. This cultural coexistence still prevailed in Spain in the 13th century, for a Castilian miniature from a manuscript in the Escorial of the *Cantigas de Santa María*, compiled by King Alfonso X of Castile, shows two male jongleurs, one a Moor and the other dressed in the Provençal fashion, singing a duet (Fig. 23). According to records of the year 1293, the Castilian court employed twenty-six *juglares*, of whom thirteen were Moors, twelve were Christians, and one was a Jew. Two of the Moors were women who sang "profane" songs and danced. In the 12th century, Moorish jongleurs and "jongleresses" traveled in many parts of Christian Europe, where their art was much admired. Even assuming that they sang and played melodies of European origin, they probably improvised in the Oriental fashion. The dances that accompanied their songs were known as far away as England, where "Moorish dances" became "Morris dances."

Since his early childhood Guilhem VII had been familiar with the sound of Arabo-Andalusian music and song, for there were hundreds of slave girls, many of them singers and dancers, at his father's court. He might have known some Arabic, a few words here and there. His visit to the Aragonese court further increased his knowledge and appreciation of the insistent rhythms of Arabic verse and music. The

Fig. 23. Duet performed by a Moorish minstrel and a Christian jongleur, from a 13th century MS of the Cantigas de Santa María *in the Biblioteca del Escorial.*

influence of the actual themes of Arab love poetry is far more problematic, especially as Guilhem's own poetic compositions were not written until his return from the Orient in 1102.

All that can be said with certainty is that as early as the 10th century Hispano-Moresque poetry had a strongly romantic quality, combining sensuousness and spirituality in a manner which anticipated the cult of courtly love in troubadour poetry—not so much in the works of Guilhem VII, with his lusty paganism, as in the later Provençal poets.

Ancient Arab poetry, written in the hieratic language of the Koran, glorified battles, horses and the valor of the tribe. They were the Moslem equivalent of the epic sagas and *chansons de geste* sung by European minstrels, except that the Arab poems were recited, not sung. In the 10th century, over a hundred years before the first troubadour songs, a new type of poetry had arisen in Moslem Spain which broke with the old conventions. It was lyrical and erotic in content and, to the horror of Moslem purists, was sung in the Andalusian vernacular (a mixture of Arabic and Romance) to a musical accompaniment. The new poetry flourished at the Moorish courts of Cordova and Seville and was also popular in Aragon, which until the 11th century was under Moorish control.

Far from being only sensual, as is so often believed, Arab lyric poetry has a spiritual content which owes something to the mystic Moslem movement of Sufism. This movement was strongest in Persia and included some of the greatest Persian poets, but it also had many adherents in Moslem Spain. The Sufis regarded love as a symbol of the soul's union with God, love being the primary cause of creation. Love could mean love of all creation, but also the love of man and woman which was sublimated into an expression of personal union with the Divine. This idealization of love had a pre-Islamic origin, for the Sufism which emerged in the late 10th century borrowed ideas from neo-Platonism, Buddhism and Christianity. There was nothing anemic about the Sufis' exalted vision of women, for they believed that divine love could not be understood by anyone who had not experienced the transports of profane love—a concept not far removed from the *gai sçavoir* of the troubadours.

These ideas are eloquently expressed in a verse treatise on love with the poetic title of *Tauk al-Hamama* (*The Dove's Neck Ring*), by Ali ibn-Hazm of Cordova, who died in 1064 or 1065, about the time of the capture of Barbastro by Guilhem VI. The work is divided into thirty chapters, with titles—"Of Love-Messages," "Of Fidelity," "Of Hints from the Eyes," and "Of the Submissiveness the Lover Owes His Lady"—and other themes close to the *fin 'amor* of the troubadours. The Platonic idea appeared when Ibn-Hazm declared that "the union of the spirit is more beautiful than the union of the body."

In the chapter "Of Love by Description" there are stories of love for a "distant lady" known only by hearsay. The origin of love is always through the senses, especially through the impression of sight, "for love enters most often through the eyes, which are the gateways of the mind, and thence spreads throughout the whole soul."

The sublimated sensuality of Hispano-Moresque love poetry appeared in some verse by the 10th century poet Ibn-Darrach, who wrote of his beloved, after describing her charms with great enjoyment:

> She is like an orchard of which I taste
> Only the beauty and the perfume;
> For I am not as the beasts of the field
> To whom a garden is but a pasturage.

It would be many decades before similar sentiments found their way into European poetry. Also the Arab poets show an awareness of the subtle nuances of love completely absent in the simplistic psychology of the *chansons de geste*. The poet Ibn-Hazm made the perceptive statement that "love often begins jestingly, but its end may be very serious."

The Moorish poet closest in feeling to Guilhem VII of Poitiers was Ibn-Quzman of Cordova, who died in 1159. His *Divan* (collection of poems), composed in the Arabo-Romance vernacular of Andalusia, included several varieties of *zajal*—love poems, spring songs, drinking songs, licentious verses, and satirical and moralizing pieces. While singing the praises of love which "takes its origin from sight" and the power of feminine beauty to "quicken the spirit," Ibn-Quzman mocked those poets who sublimated passion into an unattainable ideal and who "will depart from this life without ever having enjoyed it." Guilhem VII had an equally down-to-earth approach, but there is no evidence that when he began to write poetry after his return from the Orient he actually imitated Ibn-Quzman. The Moorish poet was twenty-four years younger than Guilhem, and although they were both writing verses at the same time, it would be truer to speak of an affinity of style, mood and content than of a direct influence.

The relationship of Arab and Provençal lyric poetry continues to be debated. Even assuming that Guilhem and the other troubadours knew little or no Arabic and could not have read the Moorish poets in the original, there were many Jews in the courts and cities of Spain and Southern France who were skilled translators and acted in various capacities as intermediaries between Moslems and Christians. These Jews could be scholars, officials attached to the rulers or princes, doctors or merchants, but some were professional poets and musicians. In the 13th century, a noted Jewish troubadour, Bofilh, lived in Narbonne.

Research has shown that in the early days of Islam the harems of Moslem Spain were very different from those of later times. The women living in Moorish palaces, some of them Spaniards, were not required to wear the veil and often received the same education as the men. In the 10th and 11th centuries these women were certainly more cultivated and had more independence than women in Christian countries, even in Provence. A number of women were skilled transcribers of manuscripts which were admired for their beauty. Others were gifted poets, and some of the princesses of the Moslem dynasties of Spain themselves composed verses and patronized poets. Whatever the differences between Moorish Spain and the semifeudal society of Provence, the emergence of an ideal of chivalry, followed by the awakening of lyrical passion and the cult of love, developed at about the same time in both cultures. The Crusades would bring about an even richer interchange between East and West, although that certainly was not their intention.

Only a few months after Guilhem's return to Poitiers events in the Near East took a dramatic turn. Arab rule in the Holy Land had been tolerant, and no obstacle had been placed in the way of the Christian pilgrims until in the 11th century the ruling Fatimid dynasty, claiming descent from Mohammed's daughter Fatima, destroyed the Church of the Holy Sepulcher in Jerusalem and assaulted and enslaved the pilgrims. The Seljuk Turks penetrated into the Byzantine Empire, moved southward and captured Jerusalem in 1070. The Christian world was shocked and angered, but it was not until twenty-five years later, when the revivalist zealot Peter the Hermit traveled through Italy, Germany and France in 1095 demanding a Holy War to rescue the hallowed shrines of Christendom from the infidel, that the movement gained sufficient impetus to spur the attack. Pope Urban II, moved by Peter the Hermit's fiery words, put himself at the head of those who inspired the First Crusade.

Pope Urban, who was of French origin, went to France, where he had been a Cluniac monk and where he had powerful friends. He summoned the Council of Clermont in Auvergne, which was attended by the leading churchmen of Aquitaine and other high ecclesiastical dignitaries. Guilhem VII was one of the few French lords present.

The Pope exhorted the leaders of Christendom to take up arms to rescue the Holy Sepulcher from the infidel. He promised that the journey would count as full penance for all sins and that the homes and lands of all who "took the Cross" would be protected by a truce during their absence. A Holy War was declared by acclamation and the cry went up, *"Deus Vult"*—"It is the Will of God."

The first great prince to respond to Urban II's appeal and take the Cross was Raymond IV, Count of Toulouse, who was also Count of Saint-Gilles and Marquis of Provence, and the uncle of Guilhem's wife, Philippia. Raymond became the chief planner and organizer of the Crusade, and Guilhem resolved to take advantage of his absence to advance his own claims to the county of Toulouse based on his wife's right of inheritance.

In Clermont, where he received the Pope with great ceremony, Guilhem expressed sympathy with his purposes without committing himself. He invited the Pope to visit Aquitaine, and Urban felt, in view of Guilhem's great reputation among the local clergy, that he could rely on Count Guilhem's complete support. The Pope celebrated Christmas of 1095 in Limoges, and arrived the following January in Poitiers, where Guilhem gave him a splendid reception. It was on this visit that Urban dedicated the abbey church of Montierneuf and blessed the altar, especially erected for this solemn occasion.

The aged Pope and the young count conferred in Poitiers for twenty-five days. What they talked about is unknown, but it has been suggested that Guilhem may have hinted at his designs to make what he considered his rightful claim on Toulouse. If Philippia's inheritance was indeed mentioned, the Pope might well have demurred, for Raymond of Toulouse was then preparing to leave for the Crusade, which was, after all, the main object of the Pope's journeys in France.

From Poitiers, Urban II went to Angers, Vendôme and Tours, and east to Burgundy. He consecrated the high altar at his home monastery of Cluny, and turning back to the west, stopped to bless monasteries, dedicate churches, present golden roses to nobles whom he particularly favored, all the while stirring up enthusiasm for the Crusade. Wherever he went, wrote an ecclesiastical chronicler, he "urged men to take the Cross, to march on Jerusalem and deliver the Holy City from Turks and other Gentiles. Thereupon a multitude of nobles and non-nobles, rich and poor, from all countries, with one accord began to take the road to the Holy Sepulcher, having shed all their possessions."

But Guilhem was not among them. He decided to bide his time.

In October 1096, Raymond of Toulouse, with his wife Elvira of Castile and their infant son (who died on the journey), left at the head of three thousand Crusaders for the Holy Land. Raymond hoped to establish a ruling dynasty in the Orient, and vowed never to return. His eldest son, Bertrand, was left in charge of the county of Toulouse, the county of Saint-Gilles and other seigniories in Provence, a territory almost as extensive as the county of Toulouse itself.

Guilhem saw his opportunity, and in the spring of 1098 he invaded Bertrand's domain. The city of Toulouse was taken without a blow. Guilhem limited his occupation to the lands he claimed as the patrimony of Philippia, and made no attempt to expand eastward at Bertrand's expense. However questionable the invasion might appear to others, Guilhem did not regard it as aggression or conquest, but as the assertion of a just claim.

A triumphal entry into Toulouse by Guilhem and Philippia marked their victory. They took the great basilica of Saint-Sernin under their personal protection and gave it special rights and privileges. Certain ecclesiastics, including the Bishop of Cahors and most of the Toulouse clergy, protested violently against the count's actions and tried to persuade the Pope to threaten excommunication. The Bishop of Poitiers went to Rome to intercede for Guilhem at the Papal Court and prevented ecclesiastical censure, but the count's relations with the Church grew considerably cooler.

In 1099, Philippia, who ruled as a virtual sovereign in Toulouse while her husband was visiting other parts of his realm, gave birth to a son, who became Guilhem VIII and the father of Eleanor of Aquitaine.

The news of the capture of Jerusalem by the Crusaders, led by Raymond of Toulouse, reached the Midi in July. Accounts of this exploit, greatly magnified, fired the imagination of many who had resisted Urban II's original appeal. Guilhem's thirst for adventure was aroused and he determined to head his own expedition to the Orient. A natural skeptic, Guilhem was certainly not motivated by religious zeal, but neither was he driven by the lust for plunder that animated many of the Crusaders. It was to be a glorious adventure opening up new experiences and new delights.

Since Guilhem wanted to lead this expedition in style, money was an urgent necessity. He was too well disposed toward his vassals and the population of Poitou-Aquitaine to impose oppressive levies and taxes, so he decided to mortgage his domains. Messengers were sent to England's turbulent king, William Rufus, son of the Conqueror, pledging the duchy of Aquitaine in return for money for his Crusade. Rufus eagerly accepted because, according to Guilhem's biographer, Orderic Vital, he longed to add Aquitaine "to his father's duchy and kingdom"—that is, Normandy and England. Boasting that he would hold court in Poitou by Christmas, William Rufus collected a huge sum to consummate the agreement with Guilhem and was about to cross the Channel at the head of his army when on August 2, 1100, he was killed while hunting in the New Forest. There have been theories of conspiracy—William Rufus' mocking anticlericalism caused him to be regarded by the Church as a monstrous blasphemer, and he was never a popular ruler—but the cause of his death seems to have been the arrow accidentally shot by his close friend Walter Tirel. Hunting was a dangerous sport in those days and such deaths were not uncommon, although in Rufus' case the clergy saw it definitely as an act of God.

Thwarted in his plan, Guilhem turned, surprisingly, to young Bertrand, Count of Saint-Gilles, then living in Provence, with an offer to mortgage Philippia's patrimony. Bertrand was only too glad to regain his former territories, and Guilhem relinquished his rights to the county of Toulouse in exchange for a considerable sum. Such trading, but usually on a smaller scale, was common practice among would-be pilgrims as well as Crusaders.

Guilhem "took the Cross" in Limoges in 1100, and in March of the following year about thirty thousand Crusaders from Aquitaine and Gascony gathered in Poitiers and placed themselves under his leadership. This army of soldiers and pilgrims crossed the Rhine and joined forces in Germany with Guelf, Duke of Bavaria, and Ida, Markgravin of Austria. On foot and on horseback, accompanied by heavily laden mules, wagons piled with provisions, tents, bedding as well as military supplies, this vast procession of over sixty thousand proceeded to Constantinople. Many women—some devout, some going along for the adventure, some professional "camp-followers"—joined in the march.

At the Byzantine court in Constantinople, Guilhem was not over-awed by the resplendent Emperor Alexius Comnenus (Fig. 24) but treated him as an equal. He showed the same directness and natural-ness in his dealings with people of every class in his own domains. Once when passing through Saint-Jean-d'Angély he saw a former retainer who had become a monk and embraced him publicly with great warmth. Guilhem's straightforwardness and friendly informal-ity were among his most attractive qualities.

Begun with enthusiasm and exalted hopes, this Crusade ended in disaster. In a barren mountain region in Anatolia in Asia Minor, Guilhem's forces were trapped in a ravine and pounced upon, as they stopped by a stream to quench their thirst, by the Turks, who were concealed and who had waited for this opportunity. Thousands of Crusaders were slaughtered and most of the others fled in panic. A chronicler relates: "The Count of Poitou, standing on a nearby moun-tain surrounded at its foot by infidels, watched the rout of his followers. At the sight of the slaughtered soldiers the Frankish prince wept bitterly." Guilhem escaped with four hundred horsemen. He was not captured, as Orderic Vital erroneously stated, but after a brief stay in Tarsus he finally arrived in Antioch on the southern coast of Asia Minor with a mere handful of retainers.

Fig. 24. The Byzantine Em-peror Alexius I Comnenus (reigned 1081–1118), from a Greek MS in the Vatican Library, Rome.

Antioch had been won from the Seljuk Turks by the Crusaders in 1098, and was the capital of a powerful principality with close ties to the newly founded Latin kingdom of Jerusalem. At the time of Guilhem's arrival, Bohemund I, the Prince of Antioch, was being held captive by the Moslems, but his nephew Tancred, who was acting as his regent, gave the hapless Guilhem a magnificent reception.

After several months as Tancred's guest, amid the luxuries and pleasures of Antioch, Guilhem recovered from the shock of his defeat and the annihilation of his army. The court of Antioch had something of the splendor of Byzantium—without its ritualistic formality—combined with the exotic flavor of the Orient.

Serious-minded commentators were later to lament the supposedly demoralizing effects on the pleasure-loving Guilhem of this "decadent," semi-Oriental atmosphere, but his stay in Antioch undoubtedly helped to shape his poetic vision. The Moorish songs then current in Syria were more passionate and rhythmical than the simpler anonymous songs of the jongleurs which Guilhem must have known.

In September 1102, Guilhem went with his host, Tancred, to Jerusalem. Baldwin of Flanders, a leader of the First Crusade, who had been crowned King of Jerusalem, was consolidating the Latin states of the East and planning further campaigns against the Moslems. Guilhem had no desire to participate in these thankless military enterprises; the constant attacking and defending of fortresses had no appeal for him. In October he was back in Poitiers, after an absence of eighteen incredible months.

Guilhem quickly recovered from his shattering experiences in the Orient, and his natural resilience enabled him to take up the challenge of politics and the delights of love and poetry. He felt no further need to seek adventure overseas.

Orderic Vital relates that the count, on his return from the Crusade in 1102, "sang, before the princes and the great assemblies of the Christians, of the miseries of his captivity among the Saracens, using rhymed verse jovially modulated." Vital's unreliability has already been noted, and Guilhem was never in captivity, but the chronicler conveys the count's talent for turning his experiences, whether sad or joyous, into the subject for songs. The barons and knights among his audience had some knowledge of the *Chanson de Roland* and other epics, and many were themselves able to recite verse. None of these early compositions by Guilhem have survived, but they were presumably in the general style of the *chansons de geste*. Later he composed a completely different type of poetry, reflecting not only his own impetuous, irreverent and ardent nature but also the new and vital spirit that was stirring in the land.

Philippia had governed his domains while Guilhem was on his Crusade to the Orient. The serious-minded countess ruled most effectively, and there was greater calm in Aquitaine than before the count's departure, or after his return. During her husband's absence Philippia had become passionately religious. She was strongly influenced by the ideas of the Breton hermit and reformer Robert d'Arbrissel, whose preachings were beginning to stir up the population.

Robert d'Arbrissel had been an active propagandist for the First Crusade, but in other respects he took issue with the Church authorities. His sermons were based on the perversity of the world in which falsehood, murder, adultery and simony—that is, the purchase and sale of ecclesiastical preferment—were widespread. Although he remained within the Church, some of his beliefs paralleled those of the Cathars and other medieval sects who sought individual paths to salvation.

In one respect he was unique. At a time when some churchmen were still debating "whether woman has a soul," Robert proclaimed not only the equality but also the superiority of women. As he roamed barefoot through Brittany, Anjou and Maine, he was followed by huge crowds of men and women calling themselves the "Poor of Christ." The men wore long beards and were poorly attired. They slept out-of-doors at night. Around 1099, the year of the capture of Jerusalem by the Crusaders, Robert and his followers settled at Fontevrault, an isolated spot on the borders of Anjou, Touraine and Poitou, ideal for meditation and the communal religious life. Helped by the generosity of neighboring lords, especially Count Foulques of Anjou, Robert built an abbey dedicated to the Virgin Mary, and installed a double foundation for monks and nuns under the rule of an abbess—a startling innovation. A noblewoman, Pétronille de Chenille, was the first abbess in charge.

Robert's belief that qualified women were often better administrators than men was vindicated by the success of Fontevrault. Until the Revolution of 1789 ended the abbey's six hundred years as a religious organization, monks and nuns alike were continuously subject to the authority of the abbess, who was usually a widow. Robert believed that a woman with the experience of raising a family and managing a household would have greater skill in organization than one who had led a celibate life removed from the world. Guilhem VII's first wife, Ermengarde, had been one of the first ladies of noble birth to enter Fontevrault. Over the years the abbey became famous as a retreat for highborn ladies, the most famous of whom was Eleanor of Aquitaine.

Within the high, plain monastery walls there were originally seven buildings, among them a convent of St. Mary Magdalen for repentant harlots, a leper hospital called Saint-Lazare, homes for aged monks and nuns, a guest house and the abbess's residence. The splendid Romanesque abbey church, Sainte-Marie-de-Fontevrault, was begun in 1104. Its tall pillared choir was consecrated by Pope Calixtus II fifteen years later, and the entire building, with its magnificent roof of domes in the Périgord style, was completed in 1150. Later it became the funerary church of the Plantagenets.

The most unusual building in the vast abbey complex is the Tour d'Evrault. According to a legend current among the local peasantry in the Middle Ages and later, the tower was once inhabited by a bandit called Evrault, who terrorized the region until the arrival of Robert d'Arbrissel. (The tower was built by Eleanor long after his death.) This myth maintained that Evrault would place a lantern at the summit of the tower to lure travelers, whom he would then rob and murder. Actually this tower was merely the highest chimney of the monastery kitchen (Fig. 25), an octagonal building with five fireplaces and twenty chimneys that could be used simultaneously. It was quickly darkened by smoke, and its eerie aspect, strange silhouette and somber color haunted the imagination of the peasants and prompted the circulation of the legend of Evrault the bloodthirsty bandit. The kitchen at Fontevrault is the only surviving one of the Romanesque period except the abbot's kitchen in Glastonbury, in Somerset, England.

Although there was an increasing cult of the Virgin Mary in the early 12th century, the exaltation of women as preached and practiced by Robert d'Arbrissel was altogether exceptional. He wrote to the representative of the Bishop of Poitiers: "You know that everything that I have built in this world was for the nuns . . . I and my disciples have submitted ourselves to them for the good of our soul." That this view of feminine supremacy was far from universally accepted is shown by an amusing carved capital in the cloister of

Fig. 25. The Tour Evrault, former monastery kitchen, Fontevrault, 12th century. (Archives Photographiques)

Notre-Dame-du-Puy in Auvergne, in which an abbot and an abbess are fighting over a crozier in their struggle for the rule of a monastery (Fig. 26).

Philippia, living in Poitiers, where the memory of Radegonde was still cherished, was deeply impressed by Fontevrault and its founder. Her freethinking husband Guilhem VII had given only token support to the foundation of Fontevrault, and had no mystical feelings, but he was aware of the principles and new ideas being developed there. Like his ancestor Guilhem the Great, his curiosity was stimulated by the various movements which arose periodically on the soil of Aquitaine, some more "heretical" in the eyes of the Church than others.

Count Guilhem, only thirty-one years old when he returned from the Orient, was a notorious philanderer. However, while he was not at all inclined to put women on a pedestal, Guilhem was not unsympathetic to Robert d'Arbrissel's policies, which were one step forward toward the gradual emancipation of women.

As his court became a magnet for spirited, free-living young nobles and a school for troubadours, and his relations with the Church were increasingly strained, Guilhem grew bored with Philippia's religious

Fig. 26. Monastic battle of the sexes: an abbot and an abbess contend for the rule of a monastery. Capital in the cloister of Notre-Dame-du-Puy (Velay).

preoccupations and was irritated by the hold the monks and priests had over her and some of the other women of his household. A more immediate source of discord was the scandal of his notorious affair with "La Maubergeonne."

While traveling through Poitou, Guilhem met a seductive lady with the picturesque name of Dangerosa, or Dangereuse, the wife of his vassal Aimery I, Viscount of Châtellerault. She became enamored of the young and charming count, who returned her passion. In 1115 Guilhem abducted her and installed her as his mistress in a splendid tower called the Tour Maubergeon (Fig. 27), which he had added to his palace in Poitiers. The people of the city nicknamed her "La Maubergeonne" after the tower. She was one of the first of those "official mistresses" who have played important and colorful roles in French history.

Philippia had endured Guilhem's infidelities, and had ignored the veiled references to his conquests and escapades in his songs and poems. She had borne him two sons and five daughters and had managed his realm during his absence on the Crusade with ability and success. The presence of the beautiful viscountess within the precincts of the palace was insupportable. Around 1116, about a year after Dangerosa began her residence in Poitiers, Philippia withdrew to Fontevrault. She had had enough.

In 1121, still captivated by his mistress, Guilhem arranged for the marriage of his eldest son (by Philippia) to her daughter Anor (by the Viscount of Châtellerault). This young couple were to become the parents of the great Eleanor of Aquitaine.

Guilhem's abandonment of Philippia and his liaison with La Maubergeonne increased his problems with the Church. In 1114, one year before his abduction of the viscountess, he had been threatened with excommunication by the Bishop of Poitiers for what the Church considered an infringement on its tax rights and privileges. There was a stormy confrontation in the Cathedral of Saint-Pierre. As the bishop was about to pronounce the anathema, Guilhem rushed at him, his sword in hand, seized the startled prelate by the hair and shouted, "You will die if you do not give me absolution!" The bishop resolutely completed the words of the anathema, bared his throat and said, "Strike then!" Guilhem scornfully retorted, "No, I do not love you enough to send you to Paradise!" The bishop was

Fig. 27. *The Palais de Justice (formerly the Palace of the Counts), Poitiers, with the Tour Maubergeon on the right. The landscaping has been greatly improved since this photograph was taken. On the left are the remains of the Gallo-Roman wall. (Photo Cap Roger-Viollet)*

exiled to the Castle of Chauvigny, east of Poitiers, where he died soon afterward.

Gérard, Bishop of Angoulême, who was also the papal legate in Aquitaine, renewed the sentence of excommunication on the grounds of the count's adulterous relationship with La Maubergeonne. Guilhem taunted the bishop, who was completely bald, and said, "Your hair will need a comb before I part with the viscountess!"

To the Church, the worldliness of the court of Poitiers and Guilhem's liaison with La Maubergeonne were as scandalous as the spectacle of Salomé dancing before Herod (Fig. 28), a scene frequently represented in medieval art.

Wary of any increase in the temporal power of the Church and

Fig. 28. Salomé dancing before Herod, from a 12th century capital from the Church of Saint-Etienne, Toulouse, in the Musée des Augustins, Toulouse. (Reportage Photographique YAN)

undeterred by its condemnation, Guilhem went his independent way, improvising his policies and alternating between bursts of energy and spells of indolence. As an administrator, he lacked his father's consistency of purpose, but he was serious in his artistic endeavors and contributed far more to the cultural life of his time than the warlike Guy-Geoffroy had done. Guilhem's court at Poitiers differed from those of his predecessors and most contemporary rulers in its emphasis on youthfulness and gaiety, the cultivation of poetry and song and the increasing presence of women and the importance given them in social activities.

Guilhem's poems in the *langue d'oc*, written after 1102, reflect the changes in society. His more robust and ribald songs suggest rough male companionship, but in other poems there are the first hints of *l'amour courtois* that was to be a dominant theme of the troubadours and was certainly intended for a mixed audience of men and women. The new life style among the Occitan nobility involved lavish spending, *largueza*—largesse, instead of the miserly hoarding of wealth practiced by most feudal barons elsewhere in France.

The new "courtliness" did not develop in the North until after 1150. Another factor determining the difference in manners was the comparative freedom of Occitan society from the rigid structure of feudalism; there were of course certain class distinctions and the ruling aristocracy had considerable power, but the system had greater flexibility than in the North and there was greater respect for the individual. An underlying *convivencia*, or spirit of coexistence, favored diversity and spontaneity, a most propitious atmosphere for the development of the arts.

The complex question of the origins of the troubadour lyric may never be completely resolved, but all the evidence points to Guilhem VII's key role in inaugurating a new era in European poetry. He fully deserves his title of "The First Troubadour."

Before considering some of the possible influences on his art, it may be helpful to examine the word "troubadour" itself. In Provençal the word is spelled *trobaire*, or *trovador*, and is derived from *trobar* (*trouver* in French), meaning to find, to invent. The word is most appropriate, since Guilhem and his fellow poets did indeed "find out" new and striking metrical forms to express ideas and feelings hitherto unknown in poetry. By writing their lyrics in the vernacular, the *langue d'oc*, they raised it from a dialect to a literary vehicle of great richness and subtlety. The poets and singers of Northern and Central France, who in the late 12th and throughout the 13th century followed the troubadours' example but composed in the *langue d'oïl*, were known as *trouvères*. They too used music in their performances, but much less is known about their lives, and their lyrics rarely achieved the same sophistication and complexity as those of the Occitan poets.

In theory the troubadour was of noble birth with a knightly background, as distinguished from those who made song their profession, but many of the greatest troubadours were of humble origin. By virtue of their poetic gifts they became part of a fraternity comparable to that of chivalry, but more open, and with an even larger social influence. They enjoyed exceptional privileges of speech and criticism, and were living examples of the Provençal ideal of *paratge*, a word hard to translate but implying a spiritual equality based on merit, *prets*, rather than rank, power or riches. *Paratge* also conveyed the idea of a gallant, generous and open-handed life style.

The rise of the troubadour led to a change in the status of the lowly jongleur. The troubadour, whether he stayed in one place or traveled from court to court, was often accompanied by his *joglar*, who provided a musical setting for his words and sang the poet's verses in public. The jongleur belonged to a lower caste than the troubadour, but in time the distinction was blurred. As a rule only the needier troubadours were their own jongleurs.

Some jongleurs, like Cercamon (who will be discussed later), were not content to perform the works of others but composed songs of their own. By their talent and originality they themselves acquired the status of troubadours. The stigma attached to the word "jongleur" did not altogether disappear, for one of the last troubadours, Guiraut Riquier of Narbonne, expressed his irritation at a fellow poet being referred to as a jongleur, and thus being put into the category of sword swallower, monkey trainer and mountebank!

Although some churchmen continued to fulminate against the jongleurs as "ministers of Satan," their calling was given spiritual significance early in the 13th century by St. Francis of Assisi, who urged his disciples to practice poetry, saying, "We are the jongleurs of God . . . whose vocation is to uplift the hearts of men."

Without knowing Arabic, Guilhem VII could have been aware of some of the themes of Moorish lyrics through the translations made by Spanish Jews, many of whom settled in Montpellier and other towns of the Midi and helped to spread Moorish culture. Opponents of the "Arabist" theory have claimed a Latin origin for troubadour poetry—not the classical poems of Virgil or Ovid, but the medieval Latin verse composed by the clergy. The "Latinists" have pointed out that it was in Poitiers that Fortunatus in the 6th century had written poems in praise of Radegonde, and it was in Poitiers that Guilhem VII began writing his poetry. Even if we are justified in seeing in Fortunatus a distant forerunner of *l'amour courtois*, there is a world of difference between the flowery, sublimated, mystical verses of Fortunatus, with their varying rhythms and many mythological allusions, and the thoroughly Provençal directness of Guilhem's *cansos*.

A contemporary of Guilhem, Hildebert de Lavardin, wrote

eloquent letters in Latin verse to nuns, which, though couched in spiritual terms, often seem to border on profane love. The "dialectic" or spiritual delight they express is hardly the same as the *fin 'amor* of the troubadours, which, however idealized, existed in the worldly ambiance of a court or castle. Also, Hildebert wrote in a scholarly Latin for an audience of literati.

According to one chronicler, Guilhem knew "only enough Latin to say his prayers." In troubadour songs there are no allusions whatever to Eros, Cupid or Venus, who figured so prominently in Medieval Latin verse. The *fin 'amor* of the troubadour was not a mythological deity, but a set of values, a state of mind, based on the progressive sublimation of desire and the exaltation of *la domna*— woman. The cult of the Virgin Mary may have influenced both the Latin and the Provençal poets, but the two literary trends, clerical and secular, were parallel rather than interdependent.

Although musical notations of some of the troubadour songs have survived, their exact tempo is uncertain. This is also true of medieval religious music, but we can assume that its rhythms were often slower and statelier. In secular music, much may have depended on the individual performer, and the poetic stress of the words may also have determined the musical accents. Modern transcriptions must always be largely conjectural. Some of the songs, even love songs, have a liturgical sound to our ears. *Ballades* and other songs using tambourine or tabor accompaniment have livelier beats, sometimes reminiscent of Moorish dances, of which there are still traces in the "farandole" of the Midi.

A more direct Latin contribution to the troubadour lyric may have come from the so-called "goliards," or wandering scholars, also known as *vagantes*. Some were unfrocked or runaway priests, some were students who had abandoned their studies—medieval "dropouts." Like many of the jongleurs, they led a restless existence on the fringe of society and were considered equally disreputable. They were in closer contact with nature and the people than the monks and clerks who wrote for a more scholarly audience. In lilting Latin rhymes, similar to the *pastourelles* favored by Provençal poets, the *vagantes* sang of "love in the springtime."

Women in the goliard lyrics were usually presented in a harsh and unromantic way, an expression of the sour antifeminism so frequently found in the Middle Ages, and fostered by orthodox Church teachings in which woman, the cause of man's fall from Eden, was denounced as a "Gateway to Hell." A few of the troubadours, notably Marcabru and the Monk of Montaudon, were inclined to be cynical, but the majority of them presented women with respect and attacked only "false love." Even in the lustiest, most pagan poems of Guilhem VII there is no real misogyny: women are seen as a source of delight, not as objects of scorn.

Musicologists have pointed out the similarities of the "verses," or metrical lines, composed by Guilhem and the earliest troubadours to the "tropes," or vocal exercises, based on the word "Alleluia" as sung by the monks in the Abbey of Saint-Martial in Limoges. Guilhem had strong ties with the city of Limoges and chose the Limousin dialect of the *langue d'oc* for his poems. He could well have known such works as the *Tropaire-prosier* of Limoges with its illustrations of a royal musician, jongleurs and a jongleresse. He may have been influenced by these sources even if the content of his poems was completely different. The troubadour, or jongleur, had far more latitude in vocal interpretation and tempo than the clerics who sang the Gregorian chants and canticles or followed the musical system of Limoges.

As an anticlerical skeptic, Guilhem was not inspired by mysticism or homage to the Virgin Mary. He created a courtly, secular and worldly mystique based on the cult of *la domna*.

Although troubadour poetry was cultivated in the courts and castles of the nobles, it had a wide popular appeal, due not only to its use of the *langue d'oc* but also to its incorporation of motifs deeply embedded in folklore, notably the celebration of spring. Festivals in the villages went back to pagan times and were imbued with primitive magic. In the 11th century it was still customary at the end of April for young girls, with flowers in their hair, to plant May-trees and cut green branches in the countryside. Joyous processions were organized by the clergy—as in so many instances, the Church was quick to adopt certain pagan practices and make a place for them in its own program. The month of May was a time for free courtship, which is perhaps why June has become the popular month for marriages. A Queen of May was chosen, who at that time was almost always a married woman. Married women were allowed to dance in this special season with a symbolic "lover" of their choice in spite of the jealousy of husbands.

There was always an element of danger in the frolicking at the spring festivals. Even a symbolic revolt of women against the constraints of society could be considered a threat. Nevertheless, the excitement of the idea of extramarital love, transcending conjugal ties, was carried over into troubadour poetry, with the jealous husband always playing a role. In Arab poetry a similar cast of characters can be found: the "jealous one" and flatterers, slanderers and mischief makers who try to cause trouble for the lovers.

Any great new movement in art or literature is the result of the coming together of many forces, given fresh life and meaning by the creative genius of one or more individuals. Guilhem VII and his fellow troubadours derived their inspiration from Hispano-Moresque poetry and music, the May festivals, the rhetorical Latin verse of the clerics, the cadences of Church music, the rituals of chivalry, the ribald, colloquial "dog Latin" songs of the goliards and the anonymous ditties and ballads in the repertory of itinerant jongleurs sung in the vernacular.

A charming anonymous "Ballad of the Queen of April" in the tradition of the spring festivals was current in Poitou and Limousin in Guilhem's time. The *ballade* was a poem to be danced to, and was simpler in form than the *dansa*. Young women and *bacheliers* (unmarried apprentice knights) would dance in the open air in a circle to an unaccompanied song (children's games have evolved from this kind of play dance—"A-Tisket-a-Tasket," "The Farmer in the Dell," etc.). A singer, either male or female, would sing the verses and everyone would join in the refrain. "The Ballad of the Queen of April" begins:

> *A l'entrada del tens clar—eya!*
> (At the coming of the fair season—eya!)

The refrain "eya" occurs at the end of the first three lines of each stanza. The "Queen of April" is watched over by an old and jealous king. The verse continues:

> *Per joia recomencar—eya!*
> *E per jalos irritar—eya!*
> *Vol la regina mostra—eya!*
> *Ou 'il 'est si amorosa.*

> To begin joy anew—eya!
> And vex the jealous one—eya!
> The Queen has sought to show—eya!
> How much she is in love.

The concept of *joia* and its more complex masculine equivalent in Provençal, *joi*, is basic to the troubadour ethic, and was an effective reply to those ascetics in the Church for whom this world was a "vale of sorrows" and bliss was to be found only in the hereafter. The chorus of each stanza urges the jealous one to "begone, begone from here," and ends:

> *Lassaz nos, lassaz nos*
> *Ballar entre nos, entre nos.*

> Let us, oh let us
> Dance among ourselves.

In the fourth verse the unknown poet declares that the jealous king's efforts to thwart the young queen are in vain,

> For she heeds not the old man—eya!
> But gives ear to a sprightly "bachelor"—eya!
> Who knows how to hold sweet converse with her,
>   The delectable lady.

Apart from the theme of old age and youth which became a poetic commonplace, this *ballade* provides an interesting social note: around 1100 a gentler, more subtle type of conversation and wooing was required of any young man with knightly or courtly aspirations —a kind of gallantry that would have been incomprehensible in earlier times. The phrase describing the young Queen of April, *la domna saporosa*, can be translated as "the delectable lady" and is an homage to the physical beauty which delights the senses. Its French equivalent is *la dame savoureuse*, which shows that the *langue d'oc* has a more sensuous and rhythmic quality than the French and is a more singable language—akin to Spanish but softer and more melodious. Each consonant and vowel is given its full flavor.

One interpretation of this *ballade* of the Queen of April, given by Denis Saurat, a scholar from the Midi, is that it is a survival in legend of a matriarchal civilization preceding that of ancient Gaul—a period when a woman-queen was head of the people. The *jaloux*, the jealous old king, symbolizes the coming of the invaders, bringing with them another civilization in which the warrior was king.

Another type of song popular in Guilhem's time was the *aube* or *alba*—dawn song. Two lovers who have spent the night together are awakened by the watchman's cry and dread the coming of dawn, which must separate them. The most appealing of these anonymous *aubes* is the one beginning:

> *En un vergier sotz fuella d'albespi*

> In a fair orchard under hawthorn boughs
> The lady held her lover to her breast
> Until the watchman's cry that day was near,
> O God! O God! how early breaks the dawn!

The refrain *"Oy! Dieus! Oy! Dieus! de l'alba tan tost ve"* ends each stanza, and is a more primitive and naïve expression than Juliet's

> Wilt thou be gone? it is not yet near day:
> It was the nightingale, and not the lark . . .

There is a warm and candid eroticism in the medieval poem's fourth stanza, beginning *"bels doux amicx,"*

> Fair gentle friend, let us embrace each other
> In the green meadows where the sweet birds sing,
> Let us kiss well, despite the jealous one,
> O God! O God! how early breaks the dawn!

Like songs of a much later period, such as "It Was a Lover and His Lass," the words may seem overly simple without the music, and the "tang" of Provençal is hard to convey in English. One interesting point of difference between the lovers of the *Alba* and Romeo and Juliet is that the amorous passion in the medieval poem is illicit, in defiance of the *jaloux*. Romeo and Juliet, even though their nocturnal meeting is necessarily secret, have been married by a friar! Nor do Elizabethan lyrics ever suggest adultery, although a Shakespearean song warns that "old age and youth cannot live together." This does not mean that the Renaissance was more "moral" than the Middle Ages, but that "true love" and marriage were no longer seen as irreconcilable concepts.

Another popular anonymous genre stemming from Occitan folk-lore was the *pastourelle*, in which a lord meets a shepherdess tending her flock, and woos her, hoping to seduce her. The results vary, but as often as not she sends him on his way, saying, "Sir, you must be out of your mind!" or words to that effect!

Guilhem's poems have a variety, sophistication and wit which at times make them seem surprisingly "modern." He made no effort to conceal the contradictions in his nature. He had a lusty, reckless epicurean side which caused the English monk William of Malmesbury, writing some time after Guilhem's death, to describe him as "*fatuus et lubricus*"—foolish and lecherous. He also told of Guilhem's intention to found a "religious house" in Niort in Poitou to be devoted to the worship of Venus, an idea that was probably proposed in jest (as a mocking answer to Fontevrault?) rather than to be taken seriously. It may have been the subject of a lost poem. The most expert of the loose women was to be given the title of abbess! Orderic Vital called Guilhem "an enemy of all chastity and virtue" who "outdid even the most jocular in droll stories." In 1903 a *History of the Counts of Poitou* was written by Alfred Richard, who considered Guilhem's poems too salacious for publication.

Along with Guilhem's pagan delight in the beauty of women, there are hints of a more romantic approach to the loved one, and echoes of the code of chivalry which enjoins secrecy and discretion. Gallantry and the beginnings of *l'amour courtois* appear in his poems, although never expressed in such spiritual terms as in the works of later troubadours. The very fact that Guilhem, a powerful lord, used the language of feudalism to pay court to a lady whom he sometimes addressed by the masculine title of *midons*—my lord—is significant, as are his words "If my lady will consent to give me her love." This was new, the idea that love should be given by free consent, not demanded by the man as a right.

Guilhem's favorite verse form was the *canso*, an equivalent of the ode of antiquity which always had love as its theme. *Cansos* were sung as solos, often accompanied by the *vielle** (Fig. 29), played by another musician, usually the jongleur. The meter was variable and each stanza could contain from six to ten lines of verse, although the number was consistent within each poem. Guilhem was proud of his skill in versification and wished to be judged by professional standards. In one *canso* he called on his jongleur, "my friend

---

* The French term *vielle*, also spelled *viole* or *viele* and derived from the Latin *fidicula*, is used for two distinct types of instrument. As played by jongleurs and other musicians from the 12th to the early 15th century, it was a bowed instrument, usually oval in shape, having a box sound-chest with ribs. The type of *vielle* that originated in the 15th century, at a time when the Paris School was developing counterpoint and polyphony, is also known as the hurdy-gurdy. Its strings were set in motion by the friction of a wheel. Some writers have mistakenly had this later instrument in mind when dealing with the 12th, 13th and 14th centuries.

Fig. 29. Vielle player, from
the "Chansonnier Provençal"
MS in the Pierpont Morgan
Library, New York.

Daurostre," to "sing not shout" his verses to his lady, "for whom I
suffer cold and trembling."

In his best-known *canso* Guilhem gave a personal flavor to the
customary celebration of spring:

> *Ab la dolchor del temps novel*
> *Foillo li bosx, e li aucel*
> *Chanton chascus en lor lati*
> *Segon lo vers del novel chan;*
> *Adonc esta ben c'om s'aisi*
> *D'acho don hom a plus talen.*

> With the sweet coming of the spring
> When woods turn green and birds do sing,
> Each one in his especial tongue,
> The verses of his newest song,
> 'Tis fitting that each man should seek
> That which his heart does most desire.

Later in the poem he declared:

> The course of this our love, I vow,
> Is like the hawthorn on the bough,
> At night, on the tree's branches toss'd,
> It shivers in the rain and frost,
> But morning sunlight comes and then
> Shines on each leaf and branch again.

Although Guilhem's pursuit of love is presented as an ardent quest, closer to a pilgrimage than to a campaign, there is nothing very spiritual about the outcome:

> One happy morn in memory bless'd
> We laid our foolish war to rest.
> She granted me her greatest treasure,
> Her love, her ring—joy beyond measure!
>   Oh, would to God I live so long
>   To have my hands beneath her cloak!

Guilhem used the words *Sa drudari 'e son anel* for "her love, her ring." *Drudaria* and its derivatives in Provençal poetry nearly always imply physical love, less exalted than *fin 'amor*. A *dru* is sometimes a paramour. *Anel*, ring, like many of Guilhem's images, almost certainly has a double meaning. After all, the very act, hallowed by centuries of custom and ritual, of placing a ring on someone's outstretched finger could not have been more explicit as a sexual symbol.

The poem ends in a typically down-to-earth fashion:

> While others idly boast of love,
> We have the morsel and the knife.

In other words, we (the poet and his lady) have the real thing, all that is needed to enjoy love's repast!

In modern usage the word "libertine" has come to denote a profligate man, a rake, but it originally signified a skeptic, or one free from the discipline of religious faith. The term was not current in the Middle Ages, when one was either a believer, a heretic or an infidel, but there is a spirit of "libertinism," or at least a devil-may-care attitude, in Guilhem's fourth *canso*, his lighthearted and enigmatic poem about "Nothing."

It begins:

> *Farai un vers de drayt nien.*

This free translation captures the sense of the poem rather than its exact rhyme and meter.

> I'll make a verse about sheer nothingness;
> Not about me, not about other men,
> Not about love or youth
> Or aught besides;
> It came to me in my sleep
> Astride a horse.

I know not under what star I was born
For I am neither merry nor forlorn,
Nor peevish nor benign,
And 'tis no fault of mine
Being thus endowered by a fairy sprite
On a high mountaintop in dark of night

I know not if I sleep
Nor if I wake, unless men chance to tell me,
But oh, my heart is well-nigh bursting
With such a mortal grief;
But by St. Martial
I care no more than if it were a mouse!

Sick am I, and near death
But I know nothing of my malady
And seek a doctor for my fantasy . . .

I have a mistress, who she is I know not,
For, by my faith, I ne'er laid eyes upon her
And she has nothing done to give me pleasure,
Nor vex me neither; 'tis all one to me!

Though I have never seen her, yet I love her
And when I see her not, 'tis all the same,
For I know one more amiable and fair
Who's worth far more than she.

I've made my verse, I know not what about,
And I will hand it on to someone who
Will send it through another
To someone on the far side of Anjou,
And of its case send me the counterkey.

This final mention of a "counterkey" suggests that there could be hidden meanings in what is on the surface an inconsequential nonsense poem. The "counterkey" is the key to the interpretation of the poem. This particular symbol recurs many centuries later; in the 17th century, in one of Jan Steen's rowdy interiors, a key is painted on the floor to indicate that the knowing spectator will penetrate the picture's meaning or double meaning.

Guilhem's deliberate mystification of the loved one's identity or even existence has its parallel in the ritual of chivalry in which mysteries known only to the initiate were never revealed to the world at large. This also became one of the conventions of *l'amour courtois*, for troubadours would not name the lady who inspired the poet's passion—a form of discretion which did not always guarantee secrecy. Guilhem makes this concealment part of an elaborate game —but the mention of Anjou may be a reference to his mistress La Maubergeonne, who was born in that province. If this is so, the poem may have been written at the beginning of his passion for the beautiful viscountess, before he abducted her. In troubadour poetry, as in much medieval art, there is often "more than meets the eye."

In this same poem Guilhem casually invokes St. Martial, the apostle and patron saint of Limousin, the mountainous region bordering Auvergne and Périgord, where he himself was born. He describes himself as having been visited as an infant by fairies *sobr 'un pueg au*—on a high rocky hill, or *puy* in French (from the Latin *podium*), and gives this as the explanation of his waywardness. The *puy* is typical of Auvergne as well as the Limousin, and the mysterious hilltop city of Le-Puy-en-Velay is the most famous example.

Courtly love in Guilhem's view required a degree of equality between the partners, but it was still love among nobles. He wrote in one of the opening verses of his fifth *canso*:

> A lady commits a great and mortal sin
> Who does not love a loyal knight,
> But if she loves a monk or clerk
> She has lost her reason.

Later troubadour poetry was more democratic in spirit, and in the romance of "Flamenca," a highborn lady loves a young man of low birth, but worthy of her. In this same fifth *canso*, the most ribald of all of his poems, Guilhem apparently meant to satirize women who scorned the love of men of their own station and gave themselves to total strangers if assured of secrecy. As the poem progresses it turns into a "droll tale," no doubt in order to entertain the count's merry companions.

The story of Agnes, Ermessen and their cat was possibly adapted from some bawdy folk tale, but may also refer in a playful, oblique manner to Guilhem's own amorous adventures in Auvergne, on the other side of Limousin. The narrator, dressed as a pilgrim, is walking alone in silence when he meets "the wives of Sir Garin and Sir Bernard" (two absent knights), who are presumably sisters. They greet him without ceremony "in the name of St. Léonard" (a

Limousin hermit of the 6th century) and say that he seems to be a man of good breeding. The traveler slyly pretends to be dumb:

> Now pay good heed to my reply,
> No word, no "bah," nor "boo" said I,
> Nor spoke of handles or of tools
>   But merely said
> "Barbariol, barbariol,
>   Barbarian."

Encouraged by the stranger's gibberish, Agnes and Ermessen gleefully decide to give him shelter, "for he is really mute, and what we do will ne'er be told by him." They take him to their room, let him warm himself by the oven and feed him with capons. "No cook nor scullion was there, but just we three."

After a hearty meal washed down with good wine, the two women decide to put their visitor to the test, to determine whether or not he is shamming. The stranger has undressed and stands stark naked by the fire; meanwhile, Agnes brings in a fierce red cat with long whiskers and terrifying aspect. Agnes gives the cat's tail a sudden pull; it scratches the man's side, inflicting "over a hundred wounds" —but he utters not a word. The ordeal over, everyone relaxes. The women prepare a hot bath for their guest, who "stayed at least eight days in that warm room." In a typically male wish-fulfillment fantasy this illicit *ménage à trois* builds up to a steamy climax: *"Tant las fotei com auzirets"*:

> I tupped them both, as you shall hear,
> A hundred and eighty times and more
> 'Til straps and harness were well-nigh burst . . .

Guilhem ends by saying that this prolonged amorous bout did him grievous harm, but what the harm was he will not reveal! Even in this scabrous context, the idea of silence and secrecy, part of the code of chivalry, persists. Boccaccio, who knew and admired Provençal poetry, used this piece as the motif for one of the broadest tales in his *Decameron*.

The crude, frank, jovial carnality represented by this poem coexisted in Guilhem with an idealistic view of courtly love as a refining influence—a dualism found in other medieval and Occitan poets. He was not, like the scurrilous goliards, maligning women in general, but only those who debased the currency of love and were therefore "fair game." Guilhem and later troubadours speak of the *joi d'amor*, using the masculine noun, which implies an active, dynamic cult of love, whereas the feminine word *joie* describes a state or quality which could be translated as "joyousness." Charles Camproux, in his brilliant study *Le Joi d'Amor des Troubadours*, also points to the analogies between *joi* and *jeu*, meaning game. Love, like art, is a game on a very high level, played between two equal partners, as in those exquisite Gothic ivories in which a man and a woman face each other smiling across a chessboard (Fig. 30).

The *joi d'amor* had wider social implications, for it involved not merely one's feelings toward the loved one but also an attitude toward fellow human beings. In a stanza beginning *"Ja no sera nuils hom ben fis,"* Guilhem makes the following declaration, which, in

Fig. 30. Huon of Bordeaux playing chess with the Saracen admiral's daughter, who seems to be winning; 14th century ivory mirror-case. (Crown Copyright, Victoria and Albert Museum, London)

order to render its precise meaning, is best translated into prose: "No one will be truly perfect in the presence of love unless he submits to it, and unless he is as obliging toward strangers as to his neighbors, and unless he shows respect to those who dwell where his beloved resides: he who would love must show honor to many people: it is fitting that as a man of courtesy he refrain from speaking basely."

Guilhem's ideal lord was no arrogant feudal baron, bullying or exploiting his vassals and underlings, but a gracious, princely exponent of charity, tolerance, cheerfulness and civility, manifested to people of every degree—already the idea of the "gentle-man" was taking shape. In actual life Guilhem found it impossible to extend his benevolence to the clergy, except for those monasteries under his protection and the few churchmen on whose support he could count. But his unaffected cordiality and generosity toward the people in his domains won him their affection and loyalty, whatever his shortcomings as a ruler.

The exercise of power and the assertion of territorial rights were sometimes at variance with the harmonious ideal expressed in the poems. Bertrand, Count of Saint-Gilles, had caught the "Orient fever" like his father, Raymond of Toulouse. He abandoned his territories to carve out a principality in the Near East. Raymond had died in his castle near Tripoli in Syria in 1105. Bertrand, like his father, became Count of Tripoli, but he died in 1112, only three years after his departure for the Orient. His heir was his seven-year-old half-brother, Alphonse-Jourdain, who had been born in the Near East in 1103 during Raymond's campaign and as an infant was brought back to the Midi by his mother, Elvira of Castile. At the time of Bertrand's death the young heir was living in Provence under the tutelage of his mother's counselors. The lords of the county of Toulouse resented the authority of these men, and in 1113 appealed to Guilhem of Poitou to come south and take control. By papal decree the territories of a Crusader could not be violated during his absence, on pain of excommunication. After Bertrand's death the boy Alphonse-Jourdain could hardly invoke a Crusader's privilege; in any case, Guilhem was already excommunicated. He gathered an army and occupied the county of Toulouse a second time without a blow being struck. As in his previous occupation of Toulouse, Guilhem claimed only Philippia's patrimony, which consisted of the Toulousain, the Albigeois, Quercy and the county of Carcassonne. He made no attempt to trespass on Alphonse-Jourdain's private domains—the counties of Saint-Gilles and Provence and various regions along the Mediterranean coast. Guilhem gave generously to religious houses in Toulouse as if to show that excommunication had not affected his piety, and it was probably at this time that he presented to the Basilica of Saint-Sernin an extraordinarily fine Romanesque Christ on the Cross (Fig. 31), carved in wood and coated with gilded copper. He is said to have brought it back from his Crusade to the Near East, but it suggests Spanish workmanship. It is now in a small side-chapel in a setting which does not do it full justice. In the same chapel there is an unconvincing portrayal on a 19th century stained-glass window of Guilhem VII in his Crusader's armor.

Leaving Philippia in charge of Toulouse, Guilhem paid prolonged visits to Poitou on the pretext of maintaining order there. It was during one of these stays in the outer regions of his domain that he began his liaison with Dangerosa, the future La Maubergeonne, which had such fateful consequences, including a second excommunication. It is ironic that the only important visual memento of the epicurean, freethinking count-duke should be the powerful Christ image in Toulouse, in France's largest Romanesque basilica.

Anticlericalism in such strong-willed princes as Guilhem VII and William Rufus of England—a far less appealing character—did not necessarily mean complete absence of religious feeling. Given the climate of the time, they were bound to share to some degree in the common faith, even if they ignored it in their worldly activities. They were generous benefactors of their favorite monasteries, and in times of crisis they would suddenly become concerned about the state of their soul—after all, one could never be sure what the next world held in store!

Guilhem's encroachment on ecclesiastical property, his repudiation of Philippia, his refusal to give up La Maubergeonne and his sympathetic interest in various heretical movements had led twice to his excommunication. Even to a free spirit like Guilhem, this anathema, which he at first bore lightly, eventually became too hard to endure. It entailed ostracism from the Christian community and possibly grievous consequences in the hereafter. In 1117, Pope Paschal II lifted the ban in exchange for some concessions to the Church, and two years later Guilhem agreed to join King Alfonso I of Aragon in a crusade against the Almoravide Moors in Spain.

As always, Guilhem's motives were mixed. An unexpected complication had arisen in the person of his first wife, the proud and deter-

Fig. 31. Christ on the Cross, carved in wood and coated with gilded copper, in Saint-Sernin, Toulouse; late 11th century, said to have been brought back by Guilhem VII of Poitou from the Near East. (Reportage Photographique YAN)

mined Ermengarde, daughter of Foulques the Contrary, Count of Anjou. After the dissolution of her marriage to Guilhem in 1091, she had married Alain, Duke of Brittany. On his death she retired to Fontevrault, where she became the confidante of Guilhem's second wife, Philippia, who had embraced a monastic life. When Philippia died in 1118, Ermengarde left the abbey and claimed the title of Countess of Poitou and Duchess of Aquitaine. In October 1119 she stormed into the great council held by the new Pope, Calixtus II, at Rheims and demanded justice. She urged the Pope to compel Guilhem, on pain of a third excommunication, to reject La Maubergeonne and reinstate her, Ermengarde, as the countess. The Pope, a Frenchman, was Guilhem's first cousin and was not eager for a confrontation, and the clergy of Poitou did not welcome the prospect of the haughty Ermengarde being put in a position of authority, so the matter was not pursued. But the scandal caused by his first wife's appearance made Guilhem all the more willing to engage in a Crusade. Late in 1119, at the head of six hundred knights, he placed himself under the leadership of Alfonso I, King of Aragon and Navarre, known as the Battler.

Before leaving for this expedition Guilhem composed his most moving and personal song, one of the masterpieces of Occitan poetry. Wistful remembrances of past joys, thoughts of his own mortality—he was only forty-six, but that was considered an advanced age—the uncertainty of his return from the campaign and apprehension about the fate of his young son are simply but eloquently expressed.

The poem begins:

> *Pos de chantar m'es pres talenz,*
> *Farai un vers don sui dolenz:*
> *Mais non serai obedienz*
> *En Peitau ni en Lemozi.*

> Since now I do desire to sing,
> I'll put in verse my suffering;
> No more Love's servant will I be
> In Poitou or in Limousin.

He speaks of "going into exile" in great fear and danger. He grieves at leaving his beloved "seigniory of Poitou." Above all, he is afraid that his young son Guilhem, whom he has left in the custody of his cousin, Foulques the Younger, Count of Anjou, will be a prey to the aggressive designs of his neighbors in Gascony and Anjou, unless helped by Foulques and the King of France, "from whom I hold my fief." The French king was then Louis VI, the Fat, whom Guilhem, with unusual humility, here acknowledges as his liege lord. He craves forgiveness for any wrongs he may have done his fellow men, and to obtain remission for his sins:

> I pray to Jesus, King of Heaven,
> In my Romance tongue and in Latin.

He bids farewell to his old life:

> *De proeza e de joi fui,*
> *Mas ara partem ambedui.*
>
> My friends were Joy and Chivalry,
> But I from both must parted be.

It was typical of medieval thinking, especially in a poetic or symbolic context, to personify such qualities or conditions as "Joy" and "Prowess" or vices such as "Lust" and "Covetousness." The verse says literally, "I was *of* [that is, in the company of] Prowess and Joy." The poet goes to meet "Him in whom all sinners find peace." He had been "*cuendes e gais*," pleasure-loving and gay, but

> I find the burden hard to bear
> Now that I know my end is near.

The burden was presumably the constant threat of excommunication. Having submitted to God's will and abandoned all that he loved— "chivalry and pride"—he cannot contain his regrets:

> For Joy and Merriment were mine
> Both far and near and where I dwell.

In ending, Guilhem used the vivid imagery of furs to symbolize the princely style of living he must abandon:

> To Joy and Mirth I bid adieu,
> Gray squirrel, vair and sable too ...

Vair, a Russian or Siberian squirrel, ranked with ermine and sable in the Middle Ages as a precious fur for the nobility.

The Spanish campaign of 1119 was an unqualified success for the Crusaders. In the previous year Alfonso I had taken Saragossa from the Moors after a terrible nine-month siege, and made it the capital of his kingdom of Aragon. The Almoravide Moors had resumed their attacks, but were halted by the armies of the new Crusade. In the spring of 1120, Alfonso, with his chief allies, the Count of Poitou and the Viscount of Béziers, scored a sweeping victory over the Moslems at Cutanda. The Moors, led by seven emirs, sustained enormous losses. There were many captives, and according to one chronicler, over two thousand camels and other animals were taken by the victors. Guilhem VII distinguished himself in the fighting but, unlike many of his fellow Crusaders, did not enrich himself from the spoils of the wealthy Moorish strongholds. The thrill of adventure was more important to him than the accumulation of wealth.

There had been unrest in the Midi during Guilhem's absence; many powerful figures, among them the bishops of Toulouse and Albi, were rallying to the support of young Alphonse-Jourdain, whom they hoped to reinstate as Count of Toulouse. After his return to Poitiers in 1120, Guilhem was occupied with arranging the marriage of his eldest son, Guilhem, to La Maubergeonne's daughter Anor, and he ignored the threat to his domain in the South. The wedding took place in 1121, and is an indication of the hold La Maubergeonne continued to have on the count's affections. The future Eleanor of Aquitaine was born the following year. The attractive French form of her name is Aliénor, possibly a contraction of "Alia-Anor," the other Anor—the first Anor being, of course, her mother.

Fig. 32. Seal of Guilhem VIII, Lord of Montpellier, dated 1129. Here he appears as a troubadour. On the reverse he is represented on horseback in armor, brandishing a sword.

The revolt of the lords and higher clergy in the South increased—the clerics were particularly incensed at the marriage of the future Count of Poitou to the daughter of an adulteress (the count's adultery was not even mentioned!). In 1122 Guilhem's adversaries captured the main stronghold of Toulouse, the Château Narbonnais. The following year the twenty-year-old Alphonse-Jourdain was brought triumphantly by his supporters from Orange to Toulouse.

Guilhem VII made no further effort to claim Philippia's patrimony for his heirs. The last years of his life were comparatively uneventful; the chroniclers, at any rate, had few facts to report. As so often happened in the Middle Ages, the things most interesting to us today —how the count lived from day to day, whom he saw, what he thought about his career—all are wrapped in obscurity. There were no further scandals.

It was due to Guilhem that many great Occitan lords of the 12th century prided themselves at least as much on their *courtoisie* and cultural accomplishments as on their achievements in war and diplomacy. One of his vassals, Viscount Eble II de Ventadour, who lived in the Limousin, followed Guilhem's example in protecting troubadours at his castle in Corrèze, and wrote poetry himself. Several Counts of Toulouse composed verses and befriended troubadours on a basis of equality.

On a seal dated 1192, another Guilhem, Count of Montpellier, is represented seated on a richly decorated stool playing the harp (Fig. 32). The reverse of the seal shows him as an armed knight on horseback brandishing his sword. The Count of Forcalquier in Provence had a similar seal.

To an age steeped in religious imagery, a ruler playing a musical instrument would immediately have provided an analogy with the many representations of King David composing the Psalms, and accompanying himself with a viol, as in the expressive statue in the south porch of Santiago de Compostela (Fig. 33). As late as the 16th century, Henry VIII of England, proud of his accomplishments as a composer of love songs, was portrayed in a miniature as King David playing the harp!

Guilhem VII died on February 10, 1126, aged fifty-four, after a brief illness. He was buried in the chapter house of the Abbey of Montierneuf. The monks held a solemn Mass every year in his honor because of his many benefactions to the abbey. Due to the vicissitudes that have plagued Montierneuf over the centuries, among them the

Wars of Religion and the upheavals following the Revolution of 1789, the count's tomb has completely disappeared.

His real monuments were his poems, written for the delight of a wide audience, *"segon lo vers del novel chan"*—"with the rhythm of a new song"—and his humanistic belief in an age dominated all too often by fear and dogma, that life itself was precious and that it was important for men and women to enjoy it to the full.

Fig. 33. King David. Statue from the south porch of Santiago de Compostela, between 1075 and 1122. (Reportage Photographique YAN)

CHAPTER IV

Guilhem VIII: "The Toulousain," Last of the Count-Dukes

O N THE SUDDEN DEATH OF HIS FATHER the new Count-Duke of Poitou, Guilhem VIII, who was also Duke Guilhem X of Aquitaine, was twenty-seven years old. He was a man of gigantic stature, which for that period meant that he was over six feet tall, and he had the physical grace and charm of manner characteristic of his family, but he lacked his father's political flair, quick intelligence and broad human sympathies. He tended to make hasty, unreflecting decisions, adhere stubbornly to his chosen course, however unproductive, and then just as violently change his direction. His courtiers marveled at his Gargantuan appetite—at meals he would eat for eight men—and his more peace-loving vassals were dismayed at his readiness to pick quarrels with his neighbors and his inordinate love of fighting. Fortunately he did not renew his father's claims to the county of Toulouse, but having been born in its capital, he was proud of his nickname, the Toulousain.

During Guilhem VIII's eleven-year rule, Poitou-Aquitaine no longer enjoyed the unchallenged supremacy of previous years. The King of France, Louis VI, the Fat, was, in spite of his obesity, an able and energetic ruler. With the help of his lifelong friend and adviser, the great Abbot Suger, Louis VI resolutely strengthened royal authority and did not hesitate to demolish the castles of rebellious barons. Even the troubadour Guilhem VII, in the "fare-well" poem, had referred to the King of France as his liege lord, and his son and successor, however hotheaded, knew better than to challenge this powerful monarch.

The most serious problems of Guilhem VIII arose after the hur-ried election in Rome in 1130 of Pope Innocent II. Acting on the advice of his mother Philippia's former defender, the elderly Gérard, Bishop of Angoulême, Guilhem threw his support to a rival claimant to the papacy, Cardinal Pietro Pierleoni, who took the name Anacletus II. Pierleoni, or Pierre de Léon, a former Cluniac monk, was a member of a converted Jewish family which had played an important part in papal politics since the middle of the 11th century. Guilhem VIII's ardent championship of the Antipope Anacletus aggravated the schism in the Church and added to his own difficulties.

Bernard, the eminent abbot of Clairvaux and the most venerated churchman of his day, canonized as St. Bernard after his death, jour-neyed to Poitiers to urge Guilhem to change his policies. Bernard stayed at the Abbey of Montierneuf, where he conferred with the count for seven days. Guilhem listened attentively, and Bernard, thinking he had won him over, left Poitiers. Gérard, the Bishop of Angoulême, rushed to Poitiers to counteract Bernard's advice and confirm Guilhem in his support of Anacletus; he preached in the Cathedral so vehemently against the Antipope's enemies that angry passions were aroused and the dean of the Cathedral chapter house smashed the altar where Bernard had celebrated Mass. Guilhem VIII's militant partisanship fanned the flames and, egged on by Gérard, he drove out the Bishop of Poitiers, who supported the Pope, and replaced him with his own appointee. He violently opposed the elec-tion of any bishops whom he suspected of hostility to his policies. These and other acts of defiance led to the deposition and excommu-nication of Bishop Gérard of Angoulême by Pope Innocent II and to the excommunication of Guilhem himself.

Church bells were silenced in all the important sees of Poitou and Aquitaine. At the Council of Pisa in 1135, attended by Bernard, the Antipope Anacletus, abandoned by most of his supporters, was excommunicated and the schism in the Church was virtually at an end.

The stubborn resistance of Guilhem to Pope Innocent II's author-ity was finally broken by an extraordinary incident in 1135. Bernard returned to Poitou at the urgent request of the local clergy, and was celebrating Mass on a Sunday in the Church of Saint-Pierre in Parthenay-le-Vieux, an important stop on the pilgrimage route to Compostela. Count Guilhem, growing weary of the inconveniences of excommunication, decided to have a confrontation with his persistent adversary. He went with his escort to the church door during the ceremony. As an excommunicate he could not cross the narthex, but he planned to wait for Bernard's exit and threaten him with reprisals unless the ban was lifted. Bernard saw him standing in the doorway, and in a sudden burst of inspiration, he advanced toward Guilhem with the host held aloft in his right hand, urging him to repent of his sins, confess and restore the bishops to their sees. If the count could not come to God, God was coming to him! Guilhem was so overwhelmed by this dramatic gesture that he fainted, and his gigantic frame lay prostrate on the ground. The frail little Abbot Bernard had triumphed. When the count came to, trembling and perspiring, he agreed to recognize Pope Innocent and to make amends for the seizure of Church treasures and other sacrilegious acts. News of this miraculous event quickly spread in all directions. The bishops were restored and the church bells rang out once again. The proud Count of Poitou had been humbled by this experience.

A new star was rising among the French nobility: the young Count of Anjou, Geoffrey Plantagenet, known as le Bel, the Handsome. The surname Plantagenet was given him because of his habit of wearing a sprig of broom (*planta genista*) in his cap. In 1129 Geoffrey had advanced his fortunes by marrying Matilda, daughter of King Henry I of England and widow of the German Emperor. Geoffrey's shield, given him on the occasion by Henry I, bore the earliest-known armorial bearings—three golden lions.

Guilhem VIII had at first opposed the ambitious young Count of Anjou, but came to admire his energy and daring and attempted to model himself upon him. On the death of his father-in-law, Henry I, in 1135, Geoffrey undertook to conquer Normandy, which belonged to the English crown and which he claimed by his marriage to Matilda. In September 1136, Guilhem of Poitou and other important nobles joined forces with Geoffrey in an invasion of Normandy. After a few successes Geoffrey was wounded in the foot during a siege and was forced to withdraw, but the campaign laid the foundation of his conquest of Normandy six years later.

On his return to Poitou, the impressionable Guilhem was stricken with remorse at the memory of the bloodshed and devastation he had witnessed and participated in during the Norman campaign. He was reconciled with the Church, but he was eager to make his peace with his own conscience. In the winter of 1136 he resolved to go on a pilgrimage to the shrine of Santiago de Compostela. Some of his contemporaries, aware of his quarrelsome nature, doubted whether he was solely concerned with the salvation of his soul. Up to the time of his departure for Spain in March 1137 he was engaged in acrimonious dispute with some of his vassals, and it was said that he was going to Compostela only to invoke the aid of St. James against his enemies at home. His motives may have been mixed, but it seems likely that his fire-eating days were over. Guilhem crossed the Pyrenees with his retinue and planned to arrive at the shrine in Galicia by Easter, but he was taken mortally sick on the way. On his deathbed he showed deep concern for the future of his domain.

There was no male heir, only two daughters—Aliénor, who had just turned fifteen, and her younger sister, Aélith, also called Pétronille. A brother, Aigret, had died as an infant.

Aliénor, or Eleanor, still a child, was Guilhem's rightful heir. She needed protection against enemy vassals and unscrupulous neighbors. The count's younger brother Raymond, who could have acted as her guardian, was living in far-off Antioch. With a political acumen he had never previously shown, the dying Guilhem appealed to his Capetian overlord, King Louis VI of France, whose trustworthiness he respected, to take his daughter under his protection and find her a husband. Until that time the King would enjoy the use of all the lands inherited by Eleanor and watch over their safety. Whoever was chosen to be the young countess's husband would rule over vast territories.

The count's wishes were not set down in writing, but the words of a dying man had the authority of a will and testament. On Good Friday 1137, Guilhem VIII, last of the Count-Dukes of Poitou and Aquitaine, died at the age of thirty-eight. His body was taken to the sanctuary of Santiago de Compostela and was buried at the foot of the altar.

The tangled events of his brief reign would not be sufficient to win for Guilhem VIII a significant place in history. We remember him for two reasons—as the father of Eleanor of Aquitaine and as the generous patron of troubadours, who regarded him as the epitome of chivalry and mourned his passing. Although he himself was not a poet and had no intellectual pretensions, he had inherited his father's love of music and song. Whether holding court at Poitiers, Niort or Bordeaux, he not only welcomed troubadours of noble birth but gave his enthusiastic support to poet-singers of humble origin and exceptional gifts, the most famous being Cercamon and Marcabru. Given the count's restless, combative nature, it is not surprising that these poets sometimes sang of politics and war as well as of the joys, tribulations and ironies of love.

CHAPTER V

Cercamon: The First Jongleur-Troubadour

THE "PORTRAITS" OF POETS IN TWO RARE and beautiful manuscript volumes of troubadour poetry in the Bibliothèque Nationale, assembled in Italy in the early 14th century, are entirely imaginary, yet they convey something of the spirit of each poet. There is a delightful picture representing Cercamon in a short red tunic with a pack slung over his shoulders on a stick (Fig. 34). This is appropriate, as we know this early troubadour only by his nickname, Cercamon, which means "Scour the World."

He was born in Gascony of humble parentage in the closing years of the 11th century, and led a roving existence of which very little is known. He carried on the vagabond tradition of the earlier jongleurs, but unlike them he won prestige in his own right as an independent creator of verse. He assumed that his songs would be sung by others. In one of his poems he says that his verse is "plain," that he is constantly refining it and that it will be further improved if someone can be found who can perform it well. As in popular music today, much depended on the individual performer.

Whether or not Cercamon learned his craft at the Court of Guilhem VII, he was certainly influenced by the troubadour count's poems and by the rhythms of Hispano-Moresque song. But he added his own elegiac note, in which the poet seems to take a certain pleasure in his suffering. His poetic career did not begin until at least eight years after Guilhem the Troubadour's death, and most of his activity was in Poitou and the Limousin between 1135 and 1145. In a *planh*, or lament, written shortly after the death of his protector Guilhem VIII, and dedicated to Eble II, Viscount of Ventadour, there are allusions to the territories, once ruled over by the count-dukes, which had been entrusted to the King of France. Cercamon referred to Guilhem's "offspring" who had been put into the care of the French King. Just one month after Guilhem VIII's death, the fifteen-year-old Eleanor was married to Louis the Fat's son, the future Louis VII. References were also made to plans for the Second Crusade.

The seven surviving poems of Cercamon consist of two *cansos* on the theme of love; another poem couched in such ecstatic terms that it has to be a celebration of courtly love at its most exalted; two *sirventès*, that is, poems with a moral, political or satirical content; a *planh* for his patron Guilhem VIII; and a *tenson*, or lyrical dialogue, in which he alternates stanzas with another poet.

In his love poems Cercamon introduced a theme never used by the lusty, extroverted Guilhem of Poitiers—the "timidity" of the lover, and the severity or unattainability of the beloved, who holds the poet in her power with a smile or a frown. This concept can easily seem tedious and artificial to the modern reader, but it opened up an entirely new range of feeling in Cercamon's time and became part of the convention of courtly love. In his evocation of nature Cercamon created a mood of autumnal melancholy that is particularly his own. One of his *cansos* begins:

> *Quand l'aura doussa s'amaizis*
>
> When the soft breeze turns harsh and drear
> And leaves fall from the boughs above,
> When birds less sweetly strike my ear
> I sigh, and sing the pains of love;
> Love holds me captive in his lake
> And never have I made him mine.

Love is personified as a mysterious power who will always elude the pursuer. The poet laments that in the presence of the lady he is speechless and cannot reveal his feelings. He is willing to "serve" her

Fig. 34. Cercamon. Bibl. Nat. MS Fr. 854 fol. 133 r. (Bibliothèque Nationale, Paris)

for two or three years before he dares declare his love—here the attitudes of chivalry are evoked—and he seems to take a masochistic delight in his ordeal:

> 'Tis fine that she should make me mad,
> Cause me to stammer and to muse:

She has the power to make him

> Faithful or false, loyal or sly,
> Base churl or man of courtesy.

Love is seen in its dual aspect, as a power for good or evil, capable of turning the lover into an irrational beast or into a finer, more sensitive being. The *joi d'amor* cultivated in a patient, undemanding, yet persevering spirit, like a pilgrimage of the heart, can be an ennobling force. *Mesura*, or measure, a virtue constantly praised by the troubadours, means far more than the prosaic "moderation"; it implies self-awareness, restraint and consideration for the loved one.

Two expressive lines are in the same poem:

> *Quan totz lo segles brunezis,*
> *Delay on ylh as si resplan . . .*

> When all the world grows dark and dim,
> A light is shining where she dwells . . .

Beneath all the ethereal sentiments and tremulous hesitation an ardent sensuality bursts forth in places. Cercamon prays that one day he will see his loved one undressed for bed, and he longs to

> Kiss her and clasp her to my side
> All naked in a curtain'd room.

In later troubadour poetry the sensuality was still present—there was no bloodless Platonic sentiment—but its expression was less naïve and direct than in this troubadour "primitive."

In the *planh* composed soon after the death of Guilhem VIII in April 1137, Cercamon wrote that his valiant patron would be mourned by Normans, Frenchmen and his fellow countrymen, the "courteous and renowned Gascons." Their lands would now belong to the King (Louis VI), to whom Guilhem had left "his honor and his offspring." With some exaggeration Cercamon declared that "*despois muric lo Peitavis*"—"since the Poitevin died, Youth is laid low, Joy and the light of poetry have departed the world and Wickedness has been raised on high." He was referring in part to rebellious vassals in the Angoumois and Limousin whom Guilhem would have chastised had he lived—"they alone have cause to rejoice at his death!" Cercamon was in need of a new patron, for he addressed his poem to Eble II, Lord of Ventadour, known as the Singer, who had emulated his friend Guilhem VII as a poet and entertained on an even more lavish scale in his castle in Corrèze, where he maintained a school for troubadours. Cercamon also praised "Alfonso, who has conquered Joy"—Joy, like *Joven*, youth, was a manifestation of the dynamic life-giving spirit in which courtesy and poetry could flower.

From these words it has been assumed that Cercamon either went, or intended to go, to the brilliant court of Alfonso VII of Castile. Alfonso, who proudly claimed to be "king of the two religions" and had himself crowned Emperor in León in 1135, was a Christian, but his household was more than half Oriental. He was both a patron of the Church and a protector of the large number of Moslems who were his subjects. However, Cercamon could equally well have been referring to Alphonse-Jourdain, Count of Toulouse (page 227, Fig. 69), also a protector of troubadours. Much remains obscure about Cercamon, including the date of his death. An earlier biographer states that he was the master of Marcabru, a poet very different in temperament and style, but also one of the "primitives." Since they both frequented the same circles, they probably borrowed ideas from one another, and each developed them in his own way, but there is no proof that Cercamon was Marcabru's teacher.

CHAPTER VI

Marcabru: Idealist and Cynic

G UILHEM THE TROUBADOUR was an outstanding example of a man
fully aware of his uniqueness, and his high position made it
possible for him to exert a widespread influence. In the next generation the lowborn jongleur-troubadour Marcabru was no less sure of
his identity. Like his older contemporary Cercamon, Marcabru was
born in Gascony, around the beginning of the 12th century. According to the 14th century author of the *Vidas*, or the *Lives of the Troubadours*, his mother was "a poor woman who was called Marca la
Brune," no doubt because of her dark complexion. Nothing is known
about his father. Marcabru was a foundling, "left at a rich man's
door," and his adopted father, Aldric del Vilar, raised him and gave
him an education. His early years were difficult and produced a certain toughness and bitterness in his character. An illustration in one
of the troubadour manuscripts in the Bibliothèque Nationale shows
him with arms crossed and an ironic expression (Fig. 35).

He must have been in his twenties when he met the already mature
Cercamon, who became his model and rival and whom he later
influenced in turn. Marcabru began writing around 1129, and continued his poetic activity until about 1150, soon after the ending of
the Second Crusade. He was the favored poet of Count Guilhem VIII,
whose death distressed him deeply. Although in the course of his life
he was received at the courts of kings and nobles, he was always

proud of his humble origins—he remained "Marcabru, son of Marca-brune." This may account for his very personal treatment of the *pastorela*.

Throughout the Middle Ages the *pastourelle* or *pastorela* was a popular anonymous verse form in both the North and the South. Its northern *langue d'oïl* form could not be called popular in the sense of "of the people," for it was sung to entertain an audience of nobles and tended to emphasize the gulf between the *villeins* and the lords. In all *pastourelles*, a lord meets a peasant girl tending her flock and makes advances to her, hoping to dazzle her and seduce her. In the northern *pastourelles* the shepherdess was made simple-minded, slow-witted and gullible, and her surrender was inevitable. It was assumed that those who are serfs by birth must be servile in mind and feeling.

In the Occitan *pastorela*, sung to an audience of all classes, the peasant lass is unimpressed by the lord's blandishments, answers him wittily and bids him be on his way. The lord accepts his rebuff with good grace and realizes that the honors have gone to the *vilaine*.

In Marcabru's *pastorela* beginning "*L'auti 'ier jost 'una sebrissa*"— "One day beside a thicket green"—the narrative is in the first person, as if the poet himself were the lord, presumably adept in the *joi d'amor*. Walking in the countryside, he meets a young peasant girl "full of wit and gaiety":

Fig. 35. Marcabru. Bibl. Nat. MS Fr. 12473 fol. 102. (Biblio-thèque Nationale, Paris)

> In hooded cape and kirtle clad,
> Her shift of roughest cloth was made.

The lord decides to woo her by commiserating with her on her hard life, exposed as she is to wind and weather:

> "Good sir," the lass replied to me,
> "Thanks be to God and my good nurse,
> When blown by wind I'm none the worse;
> I'm blithe and hale as you can see."

He tries another line; seeing her all alone with many animals to tend, he feels that she needs companionship, but she will have none of it:

> "I know, whatever I may be,
> To tell good sense from foolery.
> And as for your fine company,
> Good sir," so spake the peasant maid,
> "Bestow it where it welcome be."

—that is, among those of his own circle. Let him go back to the fine lady he is so busy forgetting! The lord tries flattery, and tells her that she is so charming that she must surely be of noble birth. She takes this as an insult, as it assumes that her mother deceived her peasant husband with a knight who was passing by. She proudly retorts:

> "My father, mother, all my kin
> Work on the land year out, year in,
> With plow and sickle laboring.
> And, sir," the peasant maiden says,
> "He who puts on a knightly air
> Should to the fields like them repair
> And toil each week for six long days."

Then, turning "serious," the lord uses the language of the *joi d'amor* and assures her that, regardless of their different stations, they would be equal in the free and open partnership of love. She brings him sharply back to reality:

> "Possessed by love a man may be
> And swear eternal loyalty
> And words of homage offer me,"
> She answered me once more.
> "But for this modest entrance-fee

> I'll not lose my virginity
> To take the name of whore."

In a final ploy, the lord evokes the exuberance of nature, in which all living things joyously participate.

> "My dearest, every living creature
> Follows the promptings of its nature.
> Beside the meadow you and I
> By bushes hid can safely lie
> And taste the sweets of love."

She reminds him that in nature each creature seeks its own kind:

> "Perhaps, but reason tells us true
> That fools their folly will pursue,
> The courtier will a lady woo,
> The swain a peasant maid,
> For there is neither sense nor wit
> In him who knows not what is fit,
> So folks of old have said."

In her own way she is advocating *mesura*, which implies restraint and a sense of fitness. The lord realizes the lesson he has been given in *courtoisie* by a simple *vilaine*, who reminds him laughingly as he goes on his way that some, like himself, hanker after vain illusions, while others await the nourishing manna, the "true food of love."

Marcabru, who did not know who his own father was, may have been partly motivated in writing this *pastorela* by the desire to vindicate the reputation of his peasant mother. While the poem accepts the "class structure" of the day, his peasant girl is no comic rustic stereotype, but has her own individuality and pride—and she also has the last word!

A distinction is constantly drawn in Marcabru's poems between "true" and "false love." He has been called a misogynist, and the 13th century author of the *Vidas* wrote: "He made scurrilous verses and wicked *sirventès* and spoke evil about women and love." But Marcabru was by no means against all women, like so many medieval moralists, especially among the clergy. In one of his poems he hails *fin 'amor*, or delicate subtle love, as "fount of all goodness, light of the world." His attacks are aimed at "false love" based either on physical desire alone or on mercenary motives of self-interest. He reserves his angriest invectives for women who take lovers of a

higher estate than their own, virtually selling themselves for the sake
of material advantages. He rates them no better than *putanas*, whores.
True love is more likely to be found in honest peasant girls like the
shepherdess in the *pastorela* than in more privileged women who are
subject to many temptations and are full of wiles and deceit. To
follow "false love" is to make a pact with the Devil. He might have
agreed with the poet Marie de Ventadour that "a woman should give
herself to a lover as to a friend and not as to a master." Marcabru, no
doubt embittered by some painful experience, felt that such disinter-
ested love was extremely rare. In his poem beginning *"Ans que'l
terminis verdei"*—"Before the greening of the spring"—there is this
angry stanza:

> To sigh for love is nought to me,
> 'Tis full of lies and treachery,
> And so I tell you truthfully
> Love brought me no felicity,
> 'Tis my most hated enemy,
> I curse its very memory.
> Mad was I Love's poor slave to be,
> But now we've parted company.

When four centuries after Marcabru, the debonair King Francis I
wrote his charming but cynical couplet:

> *Souvent femme varie,*
> *Bien fol qui s'y fie,*

he must have known Marcabru's declaration that woman often
changes and *"ben es fols qui si fia"*—"who trusts her is a mighty
fool." The same sentiments are echoed in Verdi's "La Donna è
Mobile," in *Rigoletto*.

In all fairness, Marcabru blames the misdeeds of many married
women on their husbands who provoke them, either by jealousy or
by their own infidelities. Marcabru lashes out against all forms of
hypocrisy, deceit and egotism, whether in women, great barons or
lowly commoners.

There is an underlying sadness and disenchantment in Marcabru's
best-known poem, in which he rails against love, saying that neither
famine, pestilence nor war (*"Fams ni mortaldatz ni guerra"*) causes
more havoc in this world:

> The rites of love, I know them all,
> That blind one, devious and sly,
> Whose words like drops of honey fall.
>   Listen to me!
> If he but sting you less than a fly
> He fills your heart and soul with gall.
>
> Marcabru, son of Marcabrune,
> Was born, my friends, 'neath such a moon
> That he has heard love's every tune—
>   Listen to me!
> Never did he for women swoon
> Nor did a woman ever love him.

The refrain line—"*Escoutatz!*" "Listen!"—may have been sung in chorus. There is a theory that Marcabru composed this song in Spain during the summer of 1138, when he briefly joined one of King Alfonso VII's crusading expeditions against the Almohavide Moors. According to this view, Marcabru sang his poem to the soldiers to warn them against becoming involved with the harlots and camp followers who inevitably attached themselves to armies on the march. The rousing, vigorous rhythms would certainly be appropriate.

On the surface the sentiment of the last lines may recall the old English folk song of the miller on the river Dee who boasted that

> I care for nobody, no not I,
> If nobody cares for me,

except that Marcabru's sardonic temperament was far removed from the joviality of the "Jolly Miller" of the rhyme.

Like many of his colleagues, Marcabru was involved in the political events of his time; the troubadours led no ivory-tower existence. It has been possible to date some of Marcabru's forty-odd surviving poems on the basis of the contemporary happenings to which they refer. Since he was wholeheartedly devoted to Guilhem VIII, he was fiercely partisan in supporting the Antipope Anacletus against Innocent II, whose election in 1130 was so hotly contested. Marcabru addressed a scathing *sirventès* to the Holy Roman Emperor Lothair II, who had sworn an oath of allegiance to Pope Innocent and had promised to pay him annually one hundred silver pounds. Marcabru attacked Lothair's subservience to Rome and asserted that "*Proeza's franh et Avoleza's mura . . .*"

Prowess is dead and Evil reigns
And shuts out Joy from his domains.
Nor right nor reason can endure
When money's knave is Emperor.

These disputes have only a historical interest today, but it is significant that a poet of humble origin should dare in that period to use
such opprobrious language about the temporal head of the Christian
world. It is true that he was writing from a safe distance and enjoyed
the protection of a powerful prince.

Marcabru was genuinely grieved at Guilhem VIII's death in 1137.

Now that the Poitevin has gone
I am, like Arthur, all forlorn.

He looked around for another patron.

Everything had changed. Louis VI, the Fat, died in Paris a few
days after the celebration in Bordeaux of the marriage of the countess
Eleanor to his son who succeeded him as Louis VII. The serious and
devout seventeen-year-old monarch, who until the end of his life
was called Louis the Young, had no use for troubadours and in any
case was fully occupied in asserting his authority in his extensive new
lands.

Marcabru tried in vain to capture the attention of Louis and
Eleanor by striking a martial note in his celebrated "Song of the
Crusade." Around 1137 Alfonso VII of Castile formed an alliance
between some of the Italian republics, the French barons and the
cities of Catalonia, and was preparing to go on another Holy War
against the Almohavide Moors in Spain. Marcabru was convinced
that had his valiant and beloved protector, Guilhem VIII, lived, he
would surely have taken part in this noble enterprise.

The "Song of the Crusade" is also known as the "Song of the
Lavoir," or washhouse. The Crusade against the Moslems, whether in
Spain or in the Orient, was compared by the poet to a cleansing
pool in a bathhouse. All those of sound body who bathed in this
lavoir could expect salvation in Heaven—otherwise they would find
themselves in the hereafter "not above, but down below." Marcabru
opened his poem with a compelling rhythm and refrain:

Pax in nomine Domini!
Marcabru made this verse and song,
Listen to me!

Many troubadours, especially those who, like Marcabru, had grown up in the jongleur tradition, composed their own music, which was considered as important as the words. Marcabru's melody for the "Song of the Crusade" has been transcribed, and Spanish scholars have found in it a resemblance to the rhythms of both the Aragonese *jota* and the fandango. Since the notation of troubadour song provided no indication of the rhythm, the singer could probably vary it at will. Also the exact nature of the accompaniment is uncertain.

Characteristically, Marcabru began his poem in the earnest tones of a sermon, then quickly turned to invective:

> Lechers and sots and gluttons all,

and other idlers and laggards could huddle by the fire in their sordid hovels where Satan awaited them, but

> God bids the bold and humble too
> Be tested in his washing place.

King Louis was urged to follow the example of Alfonso of Castile, Raymond Bérenger, Marquis of Provence and Count of Barcelona, and "those of the temple of Solomon." This was a reference to the Knights Templars in Palestine who had been installed by King Baldwin II of Jerusalem in a palace adjoining the site of Solomon's temple. All these warriors, says Marcabru, have the sacred duty of saving Christendom from the "pagan pride of the infidels." He was more belligerent than persuasive in the poem's final stanza:

> Degenerate are those Frenchmen who
> Deny the cause of God, although
> > Summon'd by me!
> Antioch, Guyenne and Poitou
> Lament the death of chivalry.

The metaphor of the *lavoir* captured people's imaginations, and fifty years later Marcabru's "Song of the Crusade" was still being sung. It became almost as popular as "Onward, Christian Soldiers" in modern times.

People in the Middle Ages tended to think in moral absolutes and in symbols. Crusades and pilgrimages were regarded as purifying ordeals which would insure salvation and heavenly bliss in the next world. In Provence they were paralleled on an earthly plane by the *joi d'amor* of the troubadours, a sublimated erotic mystique, a difficult and ennobling quest, which, if cultivated in the right spirit, could raise the lovers to a state of ecstasy here below. Admittedly in this imperfect world, such ideal happiness was rarely achieved and difficult to sustain. "Perfect love is joy," said Marcabru, "but likewise it is unease and restraint."

Louis VII was in no position so soon after his accession to the throne to undertake a military venture in Spain. Ten years later he was to lead his own unsuccessful Crusade to the Near East.

After several brief and unsatisfactory visits to various courts in the Midi, Marcabru crossed the Pyrenees and joined Alfonso VII's army in Spain as a poet-soldier; taking part in an inconclusive campaign against the Almohavide Moors, he spent several years at Alfonso's court in León. Full of enthusiasm when he arrived in Castile, Marcabru wrote a poem in the language of the *joi d'amor* to the King-Emperor Alfonso, praising his expedition against the Moslems and adding:

> For Joy and Merit grace your court
> And keep you strong and light of heart.

Evidently Alfonso did not live up to the poet's expectations. Disillusioned once again, Marcabru left Spain in 1145. There is no record of where he went or what he did for the next few years.

In a spirit very different from his "Song of the Crusade," Marcabru wrote a *pastorela* in which for the first time the feelings of a young girl were portrayed as she lamented the departure of her lover for the Crusade. The girl, whom the poet-narrator found sitting all alone and disconsolate by a fountain in the shade of a fruit tree, was not a shepherdess, but a lovely damsel whose father was lord of a nearby castle. She tells the cause of her distress:

> Louis the king may ill befall!
> His calls to arms, his preachings, all
> Have plung'd my heart in bitter woe.

She admits that God may reward her in the next world for this sacrifice, but meanwhile the one source of her all too brief joy has been taken from her and has gone far away. In this poem Marcabru's latent tenderness is movingly expressed.

Marcabru was hostile to Viscount Eble II of Ventadour, the Singer, and described his work as "senseless," probably because it was too frivolous and lacked the idealism he cherished. He made no effort to seek his patronage. None of Eble's poems have survived. A chronicler of the times relates that Eble II "cultivated the art of light verse even in his old age."

Marcabru admired the courtly and spiritualized art of the highborn Jaufré Rudel, Prince of Blaia or Blaye, who sang so hauntingly of his mysterious *amor de lonh*, faraway love. Rudel belonged to a younger and more polished generation of troubadours than the archaic Cercamon and Marcabru. He went with Louis VII and the Counts of Angoulême and Toulouse on the Second Crusade, from which he probably did not return. Marcabru addressed a poem in praise of courtesy and *mesura* to Jaufré Rudel overseas.

> *Lo vers e'l son viroill enviar*
> *An Jaufré Rudel outra mer . . .*

> I'll send these words and melody
> To Jaufré Rudel across the sea,
> I want the French to hear my song
> And fill their hearts with gaiety.

Like modern wartime songs, but in a loftier vein, the purpose of these poems was to bolster morale.

It is not known if Marcabru had much contact with Eleanor of Aquitaine either before or after the annulment in 1152 of her marriage to Louis VII, and her marriage soon afterward to Henry Plantagenet. When Henry ascended the throne of England as Henry II, an anonymous poet, in the *romans de Joufroy*, tells of Marcabru, "a *trouvère* of great merit," visiting London and receiving a warm welcome from the King, "who recognized him, for he had seen him frequently at his court."

From what little we know about Eleanor's patronage of troubadours, she may have preferred less abrasive and more courtly and romantic songmakers. Marcabru's verse ranged from the blunt and coarse to the complex and abstruse, and he was probably a touchy and difficult person, not reassuring to have around. He had the disturbing faculty of seeing two sides of every question. If his medieval biographer is to be believed, "in the end he was killed by the castellans of Guyenne, of whom he had spoken much evil."

It is tantalizing not to have more details, but it is clear that the life of a polemical poet brought many dangers and few rewards.

CHAPTER VII

Pilgrims and Shrines of the Romanesque

THE LONG PERIOD OF INDEPENDENCE which ended with Eleanor's marriage to Louis VII in 1137 had been a glorious and exciting one for Poitou and Aquitaine. There was nothing "provincial" about these provinces, the richest and most powerful in all feudal France. People of all ranks of society were keenly aware of the outside world. The Crusades, in which the Occitan lords played so prominent a part, opened up new horizons to the East, stimulated trade and affected the whole quality of life, especially among the more well-to-do.

The vital message of the troubadours, of love as the guiding creative principle of the universe and a more civilized approach to human relationships, spread from castle to castle, through city and countryside, and appealed to a wide audience ranging from cultivated nobles to the illiterate peasantry. The troubadours were neither court poets nor folk singers, but had something of both. Their innovations in music and verse and their expressive use of the *langue d'oc* helped to create a dynamic and widespread cultural unity which survived even when the political unity was threatened by internal squabbles and outside threats.

Another factor contributed to the openness and liveliness of Provençal society—the constant stream of pilgrims on the dusty highways bound for Rome, Jerusalem and especially Compostela, and returning with wondrous tales of what they had seen. It is estimated that when pilgrimages were at their height, over five hundred thousand made their way each year to these venerated shrines. Very few of those who took the road to Compostela traveled under such relatively safe and comfortable conditions as Count Guilhem VIII had been able to maintain on the journey from which he never returned. In spite of the maximum amount of comfort available at the time, many died, and a harsh toll was paid by the poorer pilgrims, who suffered from sickness and exhaustion by the roadside.

People undertook pilgrimages for a variety of reasons. Some went spontaneously, moved by genuine religious zeal. Others went on the urging of their confessors, and hoped thereby to gain absolution from some grievous offense which threatened their salvation. There were those for whom it was an opportunity to escape an unhappy home life or a boring day-to-day existence. It was an excuse for taking a vacation, and it was well worth enduring the hardships of the road (if one survived) in order to see new places, meet people and enjoy fresh experiences with the added bonus of admission to Paradise at the end of life's journey.

Some dubious characters also donned the pilgrim's garb—thieves and assassins eager to escape from justice and ready to rob and even murder unsuspecting fellow travelers. Later in the Middle Ages pilgrims traveled in groups for safety as well as for enjoyment, like Chaucer's Canterbury pilgrims. By that time pilgrimages had become something of a social event, a chance to meet new and exciting people from all walks of life.

There were fewer women than men among the pilgrims—these journeys were not encouraged by either clerics or husbands—but Chaucer's convivial group included the mincing, aristocratic Abbess and that early feminist, the lusty Wife of Bath, whose visits to Jerusalem were almost as frequent as her trips to the altar. Occasionally, married couples went on pilgrimages; in a 14th century English manuscript in the British Museum (Fig. 36), the wife is carrying most of the luggage, including her husband's sword, helmet, and chain mail!

The pilgrim, with his wide-brimmed hat adorned with one or more cockleshells, his red cross sewn on a gray cowl fastened by a broad belt, and his sack or leather pouch slung over his shoulder and also decorated with a shell, his long staff and his gourd of water, was a familiar sight in medieval France. During his travels, the pilgrim's

Fig. 36. Pilgrim couple on the road, from a 14th century English MS in the British Museum.

beard was allowed to grow. Statues of St. James of Compostela (Fig. 37) show different forms of this costume. There is no agreement as to the reason for the choice of the scallop-shell as a symbol; its adoption by pilgrims cannot be traced before the 12th century. It has been suggested that an enterprising hawker selling shells near the Cathedral of Santiago may have called out that they came from the sea like St. James—but this is pure speculation.

In order to regulate the endless stream of pilgrims, the clergy, aided by various laymen, established a remarkably efficient system. There was an attempt to screen those who wanted to go on pilgrimages in order to test their sincerity, but this was an impossible task. Small leaden badges were issued which served as safe-conduct passes and which the pilgrims were required to show along the way whenever necessary. In theory, pilgrims depended on charity, and the faithful everywhere were urged by the Church to give them alms and shelter.

Fig. 37. Fifteenth century statue of St. James of Compostela in the Church of Saint-Jacques, Châtellerault (Vienne).

In practice, the clergy, especially the monks of Cluny, set up hostels and almshouses in every town and village along the way, and there were monasteries equipped to receive the weary travelers. (Over the doorways of many old buildings in Poitou the traditional cockleshell of St. James can still be seen, carved in the worn gray stone.)

In many ways the organization regulating the pilgrimage routes anticipated the modern travel agency, but its activities were on a larger scale. The monasteries that took in pilgrims were the "luxury hotels" of the period. Many travelers preferred the informality of the local inns, although these were often dirty and dangerous. Jongleurs, whose songs and antics relieved the tedium of the journey, were more likely to put up at the inns than in the monasteries. A popular pilgrim's song in France went:

> My gourd and staff for company,
> I tread the pilgrim's road.
> Taverns my guiding lanterns be,
> The hostel, my abode.

A wealth of information is provided in the curious guidebook for pilgrims, the *Liber Sancti Jacobi*, compiled between 1140 and 1160 by Aimeri Picaud, a monk from Parthenay in Poitou. In addition to outlining the various itineraries to Compostela and enumerating the churches and shrines where pilgrims should stop to pray along the way, the author gave revealing details and helpful hints about fresh water, food and the character of the inhabitants of each region. He warned that beef and pork in Spain and Galicia made most foreigners ill. He was full of praise for his native Poitou and its people, "full of life, good warriors, free in speech, elegant in dress, handsome, sprightly of mind, generous in giving, lavish in their hospitality and living in a fertile, very beautiful country." Neighboring Saintonge was "the best country in the world, 'but there were' wicked people ready to steal our money." The Bordelais region, he wrote, "lacks everything, bread, wine, meat, fish, water and fountains; villages are few." Gascony, "rich in white bread and an excellent red wine," provided a welcome change from the aridity of the Bordelais, but the Gascons, he warned, were "garrulous and mocking, lecherous, drunken and gluttonous." Aimeri was appalled by the table manners of the Basques, "whose language is as barbarous as their souls are black!"

The author provided a map and described in detail the four roads to Compostela. One, beginning in the ancient city of Arles in Provence, went through Saint-Gilles, Montpellier, Saint-Guilhem-le-Désert and Toulouse. Another started from Vézelay in Burgundy and went from Saint-Léonard in the Limousin to the city of Périgueux. Pilgrims from the Ile-de-France and the North set out from Paris or Orléans; after stopping at Tours in the Loire Valley to pay homage to the relics of St. Martin, they entered Poitou, passing through Châtellerault to Poitiers, where the churches of Sainte-Radegonde and Saint-Hilaire were the obvious stopping places. Aimeri noted that the tomb of St. Hilaire was profusely decorated "with gold, silver and precious stones." The pilgrims then continued on through Aulnay and Saint-Jean-d'-Angély to the Basilica of Saint-Eutrope in Saintes, then on to Bordeaux. At Saintes they would cross the bridge over the Charente, passing under the Roman Arch of Germanicus, which in the middle of the last century was moved to the right bank of the river for its greater protection. The pilgrims would then proceed through the fortified gate on the left bank into the walled city, which in medieval times was full of churches and shrines. The most arduous route began in Le Puy in mountainous Auvergne, went to Sainte-Foy in Conques, one of the most majestic of all Romanesque pilgrimage churches, and continued southwest to Moissac in the Garonne region. All these roads came together in Ostabal, southeast of Bayonne, and "from there," wrote Aimeri, "one single road leads to St. James." (See maps.)

Detours were recommended for those extra-zealous pilgrims who wished to visit other venerated shrines not on the direct routes.

The popularity of pilgrimages contributed to the extraordinary architectural inventiveness displayed by the builders of the many churches, large and small, constructed along the roads to Compostela. The most spectacular of the French churches of the Southwest was Saint-Sernin in Toulouse (Fig. 38), which, with its long nave and spacious transept and ambulatory, was designed to accommodate huge throngs of pilgrims and lay worshippers. The grandiose scale of Saint-Sernin, unusual in Romanesque architecture, and the vast, cold, overrestored interior of Saint-Front in Périgueux, roofed by five massive domes, are less moving than some of the smaller churches.

Poitevin churches are rivaled only by those of Burgundy in their abundance and variety. In Poitiers, where in the late 11th century there was intensive building activity, the spell of the Romanesque is

Fig. 38. Basilica of Saint-Sernin, Toulouse. Begun in 1060, completed in the middle of the 12th century. (Copyright YAN)

Fig. 39. Notre-Dame-la-Grande, Poitiers. West Facade ca. 1140. (Photo Bernard Biraben)

present in the peaceful, dim interior of Saint-Hilaire with its forest of pillars and in Sainte-Radegonde and Saint-Jean-de-Montierneuf. Pilgrims rarely left Poitiers without visiting the city's most popular church, Notre-Dame-la-Grande, with its magnificent west façade carved with Biblical episodes (Fig. 39), which were once painted and gilded and must have resembled a magnified page from a missal. The church housed a venerated Madonna, whose miraculous intervention was credited with saving the city from destruction.

The luxuriance of sculptural decoration is also found in other parts of Poitou and in neighboring Saintonge, a province which was one of the most important fiefs of the duchy of Aquitaine. Unmistakable Arab elements in the carvings reflect the part played by the Counts of Poitiers in the Spanish Crusades. Even the pointed arch, associated in most people's minds with the Gothic period, but making a tentative appearance in Romanesque architecture, had been used by the Arabs in the Near East.

The arches of the large blind arcades on either side of the west portal of Notre-Dame-la-Grande are not the pure rounded forms typical of the Romanesque, but are pointed. By the time this façade was completed around 1140, the Gothic style, a Northern creation, was taking shape at Saint-Denis, near Paris, under the auspices of Abbot Suger, chief adviser to Louis the Fat and to his son Louis VII.

Even in small market towns and villages in the time of the last three Counts of Poitou, fine churches were built, often on a scale which might seem incongruous in such modest surroundings. There was a real "frenzy of stone," part of the creative ferment of an age which also produced the first troubadour poetry. Byzantine and Arab influences can be seen; Moorish motifs, as well as lively imagery inspired by everyday life and the forms of nature, were incorporated into carefully planned sculptural programs. The main purpose of these programs was the exposition of Christian doctrine, but they also summed up the thoughts and feelings of the age in a naïve and forceful manner. The builders of these churches, with their massive walls and sturdy pillars, were prepared to sacrifice elegance to strength. The bell towers, however, were extraordinarily varied in their design, and served as landmarks to travelers.

Among the hundreds of churches of this period in Southwestern France there is one masterpiece—Aulnay-de-Saintonge in the Charente region. Aulnay was easily reached from both Saintes and Angoulême. It was built in a small market town on the main road that

Fig. 40. Aerial view of the Church of Aulnay-de-Saintonge (Charente-Maritime) from the southeast, built 1119–1135. (Photo R. Henrard)

went from Tours through Poitiers to Santiago de Compostela. Like many of the smaller pilgrimage churches, it was erected on the outskirts of the town as a symbol of removal from the world. Pilgrims were not encouraged to linger amid whatever comforts or pleasures the towns and villages might provide. In Aulnay the sense of isolation is all the stronger because of the large, quiet cemetery (Fig. 40) separated from the road and the fields by a low stone wall. The tall spire, echoing the verticality of the cypress trees, is Gothic, and was rebuilt in the 18th century. The rest of the church, completed around 1135, represents the final, consummate phase of the Romanesque in Poitou and Saintonge. The so-called "lanterns," the turrets flanking the façade and pierced with arcading, once contained actual lanterns to guide the pilgrims and other wayfarers overtaken by nightfall. The church was dedicated to St. Peter.

As in so many Romanesque churches, the fine proportions of the exterior can best be appreciated from the east, especially when the warm gray stone is lit by the morning sun. The graceful forms of the round apse and the two round side chapels are admirably related to the extended arms of the transepts. Within the overall simplicity of the structure the decoration has an unparalleled richness. The intricately patterned bands of carving over the central window of the apse are quite Oriental in feeling. On the door of the south transept, the innermost of the four stone rings, or *voussoirs*, has monsters carved in low relief within an interlacing pattern of branches. The linear, two-dimensional effect is similar to the marginal decorations of Romanesque manuscripts. The second ring, carved in higher relief, has saints standing, or moving, with the crossed legs also found in the ecstatic prophets of Souillac and Moissac. In the third ring, seated frontally, are thirty-one elders of the Apocalypse, each holding a cither and a vial. The outermost ring, in very strong relief, contains an amazing bestiary in stone, a swarming and often grotesque pageant of animal and semi-animal life (Fig. 41).

Included in this bizarre menagerie are a harp-playing donkey, two

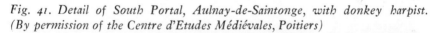

Fig. 41. Detail of South Portal, Aulnay-de-Saintonge, with donkey harpist. (By permission of the Centre d'Etudes Médiévales, Poitiers)

beasts aping the singing of monks, a siren with a knife, a centaur shooting an arrow, and a bearded man astride a rearing lion. The theologically minded may have seen in these mythological creatures embodiments of the powers of evil who were to be subdued by the Apostles and Prophets, but they were also expressions of the sculptor's wild, restless and fantastic imagination.

It is not wonder that the austere Bernard of Clairvaux (later St. Bernard), whose Cistercian order shunned all vain decoration, attacked the "monstrous" stone carvings of Cluny when he was abbot of that great monastery. In a letter written in 1124, he expressed his indignation: "And further, in the cloisters, under the eyes of the brethren engaged in reading, what business had there that ridiculous monstrosity, that amazing misshapen shapeliness and shapely misshapenness—those unclean monkeys? Those fierce lions? Those monstrous centaurs?" (Fig. 42) After enumerating the carvings, which he had obviously studied attentively, Bernard concluded: "In fine on all sides there appears so rich and so amazing a variety of forms that it is more delightful to read the marbles than the manuscripts, and to spend the whole day in admiring these things piece by piece than in meditating on the law divine."

Fig. 42. Centaurs, from a capital in the cloister of Notre-Dame-du-Puy.

Fig. 43. *The Month of March, miniature by Pol de Limbourg and his brothers, in the* Très Riches Heures du Duc de Berry, *1413–1416. In the background is the Castle of Lusignan (Vienne). (Musée Condé, Chantilly. Reproduced by permission of the Bibliothèque Nationale, Paris)*

Above: Fig. 44. Virtues and Vices. Detail of archivolts over window of the south transept, Aulnay-de-Saintonge. (Bildarchiv Foto Marburg)

Right: Fig. 45. Tympanum, archivolts and capitals from portal of west facade of Aulnay-de-Saintonge. (Photograph by Sue Marks)

Bernard's observations are an involuntary tribute to the demonic potency of art and to the intensity of the Romanesque sculptor's vision. His pungent phrase "misshapen shapeliness and shapely misshapenness" shows that, in spite of himself, he responded to the formal mastery of these carvings.

Aulnay, like many other churches on the pilgrimage routes, was influenced by the workshops of Cluny, although there are many regional variations of style. But whether primitive, as in Auvergne, or more refined, as in the Toulouse region, Romanesque church carving has an organic quality and is never "applied decoration."

Even the most grotesque and vigorously modeled figures are firmly contained within the space they occupy, whether it is the narrow frame of a *voussoir*, the compact block of a capital (Fig. 42) or the flat surface of a wall. The most ingenious example in Aulnay of adaptation of figures to an architectural setting is to be found in the archivolts over the window of the south transept: warriors in coats of mail are almost entirely hidden behind their tall, Norman-type shields, with the center of each shield bent to conform to the sharp angle of the molding (Fig. 44).

The western door of Aulnay, through which the pilgrims passed, contains the clearest moral lesson of all, pertaining to man's salvation —the triumph of the Virtues, all female, over the Vices, who are placed under their feet. Above them is the parable of the Wise and Foolish Virgins, and in the last curve, much mutilated, are the signs of the Zodiac and the Labors of the Months. These carvings, more refined in execution than those of the south transept, are probably from the same large workshop, but may be slightly later in date. The *voussoirs* of the side-portals of the west façade have a lacy, almost Moorish elaboration (Fig. 45), contrasting with the simplicity of the tympanum figures.

Once the pilgrim's eyes became accustomed to the dim light of the interior, he could "read" the varied and elaborately carved capitals. He could marvel at birds sailing in a boat, fierce Assyrian-looking griffins, a Philistine armed with an enormous pair of scissors about to cut the hair of the sleeping Samson, who is being tied to his bed by the treacherous Delilah, and a capital with a procession of elephants of the same peculiar species as those of Montierneuf. The unknown sculptor helpfully carved above them in large letters: *"Hi sunt elephantes"*—"Here are elephants."

Among the many hybrid creatures that haunted the imagination of Romanesque sculptors, none were more intriguing than those siren figures with the head and upper body of a young woman and the tail of a fish or serpent. These seductive half-humans who insinuate themselves into the margins of devotional manuscripts, and into church and monastery carvings, are sometimes given the generic (but inaccurate) name of "Mélusine." It is impossible to travel in Western and Southwestern France without hearing many references to "Mélusine." According to a popular legend, in ancient times a Count of Poitou called Raimondin, who had accidentally killed his uncle during a boar hunt in the forest of Coulombiers near Lusignan, was wandering alone through the woods when he saw, standing on a rocky promontory near a stream, three women clad in white. One of them was the fairy Mélusine, whom Raimondin fell in love with and married.

After her marriage Mélusine retained her supernatural powers. At night she would cause dream castles to arise miraculously on beautiful sites with a wave of her wand. It was in this way that she founded the Castle of Lusignan, raised on the very spot where she had met Raimondin. She was said to be the ancestor of the illustrious Counts of Lusignan, some of whose members, in the time of the Crusades, were destined to rule as kings in Jerusalem and Cyprus. But Mélusine had a jealously guarded secret. She had murdered her father, and as a punishment she was doomed every Saturday to change into a serpent from the waist down. Her husband and all who served him had to promise never to look at her on that day.

One of the count's retainers (a *lauzengier*, or slanderer, in troubadour parlance) hinted to Raimondin that she must be meeting a man in secret. One Saturday the count, unable to contain his jealous curiosity, burst open the door of the room into which she had retired, and saw her in her siren form, bathing herself and combing her long golden hair.

As Raimondin gasped in horror, Mélusine fled through the window—this moment is shown in a quaint woodcut illustrating a late 15th century printed version of this tale (Fig. 46). She changed into a huge dragon and flew three times around the city and Castle of Lusignan, uttering terrible shrieks, then vanished into thin air. Forever afterward her appearance or her howling were said to foretell the death of the lords of the castle.

The historic, as opposed to the legendary, Castle of Lusignan, southwest of Poitiers, was founded by Count Hugues II of Lusignan, the Well-Beloved, around 950 and was enlarged and modified by his descendants. It appears in all its splendor in the illustration to the month of March in the famous *Book of Hours*, the *Très Riches Heures*, of the Duke of Berry, who ruled in Poitou in the early years

Fig. 46. "How Mélusine flew away from Raimondin in the form of a serpent from the Castle of Lusignan through a window." From a woodcut in L'Histoire de la Belle Mélusine *by Jean d'Arras, published by A. Steinschaber, Geneva, 1478.*

of the 15th century and was fascinated by the Mélusine legend. In this delightful illumination, Mélusine is given the form of a golden dragon (Fig. 43) and hovers over one of the castle towers. Amid the signs of early spring, her ominous presence may be a reminder of the uncertainty of Fate. She also must have represented to the medieval mind what was regarded as a "feminine" principle of willful movement and change. The castle was indeed doomed; in 1575 it was razed by the Duke of Montpensier and only its ruins remain.

Contributing to the mystery and glamor of the Mélusine legend was the fact that around 1151 the historical Hugues VII, Count of Lusignan, married a Saracen girl called Sarazanne after his return from the Second Crusade. She became identified in the popular imagination with Mélusine, and thus there was the added lure of the exotic, the Orient.

The popularity of the Mélusine legend indicates that the forces of nature, worshipped as deities by the pagans, were regarded in the Middle Ages as enticing, mysterious and at times malevolent —God's creation, but also a possible instrument of the Devil. In medieval bestiaries animals were given both benign and malign qualities. Woman was regarded as "closer to nature" than man, and aroused the same dualism, or ambivalence—the Madonna-Eve antithesis in its many variations, including the mother-harlot dichotomy, which still exists in many minds.

In a more subtle way the troubadours often proclaimed the dual nature of love. It could be the source of the highest joy and excellence, or it could become, as in Marcabru's song, a wild runaway horse, wrecking all in its path, and hurtling madly to destruction with its panting rider on its back, "dying of hunger, dying of thirst."

A siren of the Mélusine type appears on an elaborately carved corbel in the choir of the collegiate church of Saint-Pierre at Chauvigny, just east of Poitiers (Fig. 47). This church, a splendid example of early Romanesque, is on a high ridge of rock overlooking the picturesque *ville basse*, or lower town. The houses of the upper town, on its steep promontory, are grouped around the Church of Saint-Pierre. Nearby are the imposing ruins of five feudal castles. In medieval times one of these castles was owned by the Bishops of Poitiers, who were also lords of the region. (It was to Chauvigny that the irate Guilhem VII exiled Bishop Pierre II, who had dared pronounce the sentence of excommunication on him.)

Below: Fig. 48. "Luxuria" (Lust), from the Porche du For, *Notre-Dame-du-Puy (Haute-Loire).*

Above: Fig. 47. Corbel with Siren and geese, from the Church of Saint-Pierre, Chauvigny (Vienne). (Photograph by Sue Marks)

The capitals on the pillars in the apse of the church, in which the figures are offset by a red-ocher background, are unforgettable, although the interior as a whole is marred by garish 19th century painted "reconstructions." Many of the carvings show the wild, even nightmarish vision of the sculptor, who, in this instance, is known by name. Above one of the more serene groups, an Adoration of the Magi, is the inscription *"Gofridus me fecit"*—"Gofridus made me."

The monsters of Gofridus' lurid imagination are given vaguely female characteristics. The most sensuous and least alarming of these apparitions is the siren figure on the corbel (Fig. 47). She holds a goose by the neck in each hand. Could this, like the siren with the knife at Aulnay, correspond to an unconscious castration fear? As far away as the Basilica of Notre-Dame-du-Puy in Auvergne, in a cloister whose polychrome richness recalls the Mosque of Cordova, a carved siren reminds the faithful of the temptations of the flesh, and in one of the same cathedral's porches a shameless twin-tailed damsel with long

braids and a crown on her head is a symbol of *luxuria*, or lust
(Fig. 48).

According to a local tradition, the fairy Mélusine is represented in
one of the curved arch stones above the central portal of the fine
Romanesque Church of Saint-Pierre in Parthenay-le-Vieux, in Poitou.
This was the church where Bernard triumphed over the formidable
Guilhem VIII. Mélusine, with her magical powers, was the legendary
founder of Parthenay and its citadel, which were considered impregnable. Now only a few of the old town walls remain.

The Larchevêques, the lords of Parthenay, were a branch of the
Lusignan family, who claimed to descend from Mélusine. In the 14th
century Guillaume VII of Larchevêque had a poem composed in
honor of his fairy ancestor:

> She founded Vouvant, Mervent too,
> And then the town of Parthenay,
> And raised our castle, fair and gay.

The lords of Parthenay were called Larchevêque because they once
had an Archbishop of Bordeaux in their family. The Horseman of
Parthenay-le-Vieux, in the typanum over the left portal of the Church
of Saint-Pierre (Fig. 49), has a falcon on his wrist and a coronet on
his head; a vanquished foe lies before him on the ground. Tradition-
ally these riders on the façades of Poitevin churches, many of them
badly damaged by time and vandalism, represent the Emperor Constantine triumphing over paganism and setting out to deliver the
Church from her foes, just as St. George had rescued the princess
from the fearsome dragon. But the Parthenay cavalier, with his bold
demeanor and his cloak fluttering in the breeze, could serve equally
as an image of the spirited and independent Occitan lords, especially
the Counts of Poitou and Dukes of Aquitaine, and the gallant, life-
loving spirit that produced the first troubadour.

In the Middle Ages the women of Parthenay were renowned for
their beauty and charm. Parthenay was an important station on the
pilgrimage route to Santiago de Compostela. The weary bands of
pilgrims would first stop at the infirmary, or Maison-Dieu—its chapel
is still standing—and leave those who had been taken sick on the
journey. Then they would cross the narrow bridge and pass under
the great towered gate, the Porte Saint-Jacques, that led to the center
of town. Having visited the prescribed sanctuaries, the worldlier
among them would disperse into the various taverns, where some may

Fig. 49. Horseman, on tympanum of lateral portal of Church of Saint-Pierre, Parthenay-le-Vieux (Deux-Sèvres), 12th century. (Centre d'Etudes Médiévales, Poitiers)

have joined in rousing drinking songs, celebrating the beauty of Parthenay women. One popular ditty began:

> *A Parthenay y avait*
> *Une si belle fille . . .*
>
> In Parthenay there lived a maid,
> So blithe and fair was she . . .

CHAPTER VIII

Enter Queen Eleanor

Eleanor, sole heiress of the county of Poitou and the duchy of Aquitaine, and successor to eight generations of male rulers, was barely fifteen when she learned of her impending marriage to Prince Louis, son of Louis VI, the Fat. The King of France, grievously ill and knowing that he could not survive, hastily summoned five hundred knights and dignitaries to escort his son to Bordeaux in the scorching summer of 1137 and to bring the young bride to Paris. After stopping at Limoges to celebrate the feast of St. Martial and passing through Périgueux, the cavalcade crossed the Garonne and arrived in Bordeaux in early July.

In the richly furnished palace of the Ombrière in Bordeaux, Eleanor, surrounded by her ladies in waiting, met her future husband. Louis, only a year older than Eleanor, was tall and well proportioned, gentle and courteous in manner. In appearance he was typically northern. His long blond hair fell to his shoulders, and his pale blue eyes had a mild expression. As the second son of Louis the Fat, he had not been expected to succeed to the throne. His elder brother, Philip, had been trained for kingship, and Louis had been raised in Paris by monks in the secluded atmosphere of the cloister of Notre-Dame. It was expected that he, like many younger sons of royalty, would occupy an ecclesiastical office.

In 1131 Philip was accidentally killed by a fall from his horse, and

Louis, at the age of ten, suddenly became the heir apparent of the Capetian dynasty and was duly anointed by Pope Innocent II in Rheims Cathedral. Six years later, Louis still had the solemn, unworldly air of the monastery about him, even though he was to have a splendid royal destiny and was about to marry a brilliant and beautiful young countess. Eleanor's fabulous dowry included Guyenne and its great capital, Bordeaux, Périgord with its abundant forests and fertile valley, the Limousin, gateway to the South, Poitou, the Angoumois, Saintonge and Gascony as well as suzerainty over the mountainous province of Auvergne. The administration of these vast territories so unexpectedly added to his kingdom was a task that would have proved challenging to the ablest ruler. No one could have foreseen how disastrous Louis' narrow religiosity and chronic indecisiveness would be to the exercise of royal power and to Louis' own growth as a man.

On his arrival at the court of Bordeaux, Louis was dazzled by the young bride selected for him by his astute father. Eleanor was tall and slender and bore herself proudly. She had the clear, gray-green eyes of her family, a fair complexion and delicate features. Some years later troubadours and chroniclers were to describe her as *"avenante"* (charming, welcoming) and *"vaillante"* (gallant), but these qualities were already apparent at the age of fifteen. The 13th century English historian Matthew Paris, although hostile to Eleanor, praised her "admirable mouth, gentle but amiable expression, and her consummate beauty" which delighted all who saw her. Having grown up in the vital and cultivated courts of Poitiers and Bordeaux, where the French and Normans were regarded as barbarians, Eleanor was accustomed to stimulating conversation and the delights of music and song. She had traveled with the ducal family through her father's varied and prosperous lands and had gained a direct experience of life and people; she had a keen critical sense which some found disconcerting. Later, as the wife of Louis, and even later as the queen of Henry II of England, she always thought of herself as Countess of Poitou and Duchess of Aquitaine, and was determined to keep her patrimony intact.

Whatever Eleanor's feelings may have been on first meeting Louis, she was bound to accept the purely political view of marriage held by all of her contemporaries. The young couple had only fifteen days to become acquainted before their wedding, which was celebrated with great pomp in the domed Cathedral of Saint-André. As the handsome bride and groom rode in procession through the streets of Bordeaux, hung with banners and tapestries and festooned with garlands, the marriage must have seemed to the cheering populace a romantic as well as a political event.

After much festivity, the royal escort began the long homeward journey. In early August they reached Poitiers, where Louis and his bride were lodged in the fabled Maubergeon tower. This was the first time they shared the nuptial bed. Louis was crowned Count of Poitou and received the none too eager homage of the local vassals. Then the news arrived from the royal hunting lodge of Béthizy near Paris of the death of Louis the Fat. His sixteen-year-old son became Louis VII, the Young, and it was as Queen of France that Eleanor entered Paris in late August 1137.

The Parisians, who have always appreciated feminine beauty, were delighted with the young queen, but Eleanor, accustomed to the green and smiling vistas of Poitou and Aquitaine and the luxurious courts of her childhood, was anything but enchanted with the somber palace at the west end of the Ile de la Cité that had once housed the Merovingian kings. The narrow, dank streets surrounding her new residence were a poor substitute for Bordeaux, with its bustling harbor, lush gardens and tiled fountains.

Paris was at that time a famous center for theological and philosophical dialectics, and its schools on the left bank of the Seine attracted students from all over Europe. Peter Abélard (this was long after his passionate love affair with Eloïse) had returned from his long exile in Brittany; his controversial teachings had led to his enforced absence from Paris. Abélard was such a masterful logician that he was in great demand as a teacher and his eloquent lectures were attended by women as well as men. Under his guidance animated discussions of the fine points of theology and philosophy took place in the schools of the city and on certain days in the royal garden by the Seine.

Bernard of Clairvaux, the very embodiment of orthodoxy, regarded Master Abélard's belief in rational inquiry as dangerous and heretical.

Eleanor had an inquiring mind, but there is no record that she met or listened to the teachings of Abélard. However, she was probably aware of what went on about her.

Louis' sober court was made up of hard-faced barons and solemn clerics who scorned new ideas and condemned such idle frivolities as music and poetry. They criticized the debonair ways and colorful attire of the young members of Eleanor's household, and a Frankish chronicler wrote that the Poitevins were better "feeders than fighters." The Norman Raoul de Caen made similar remarks about the men of Provence: "The Franks to battle, the Provençaux to the table."

The outstanding personality at Louis' court was the great Suger, Abbot of Saint-Denis, who had been the close friend and counselor of Louis the Fat and continued as mentor to his son. Suger, a self-made man of small stature but tremendous energy, had been brilliantly successful in forging an alliance between the Capetian monarchy and the Church. The new Gothic style was emerging under his inspired direction in his rebuilding of the Abbey of Saint-Denis, the burial place of the French kings. But Suger, well on in years, was busy with the affairs of state and could not be a companion to a young queen.

Eleanor quickly mastered the *langue d'oïl* of her new home, but she was unable to master the boredom that surrounded the serious, solemn and dull associates of her young husband. Long prayers and periods of lonely meditation were not for her.

Although Louis was enamored of Eleanor and was anxious to please her, she was not in love with him. They were in every way incompatible; he did not attract her physically, and the more she came to know him and observe his actions, the less the proud, intelligent and passionate Eleanor could respect him as a man. Eager to assert his authority, this apparently timid and gentle young king was capable, when under pressure, of acts of needless cruelty, in itself a symptom of weakness.

In 1137, the citizens of Poitiers, unhappy at the transfer of power to the French king, began to make plans to turn their city into a free commune along the lines of the Italian city-republics. They attempted to persuade other cities of Poitou to follow their lead. Louis suppressed the uprising with great brutality at the head of his own army. He himself hacked the hands off several rebellious vassals in lower Poitou who resented the "French" interference in local affairs. But Louis had been crowned Count of Poitou, and in Eleanor's capital of Poitiers he forced the leading citizens to assemble their heirs in the square before the palace with their baggage packed, ready to go into exile as hostages. Only the entreaties of Eleanor and the urgent intervention of Suger prevented Louis from carrying out this reckless and vindictive project.

Every one of Louis' political initiatives was disastrous. He was so carried away by his love of Eleanor that at one point he even dared to defy the Church to advance her interests. In 1141 he tried to assert her right to appoint the Bishops of Aquitaine and Poitou and came into violent conflict with Pope Innocent II, who imposed an interdict on him—less serious than excommunication, but terrifying to a man with Louis' agonizing religious scruples. However, this did not prevent him from offending the Church in yet another matter. He allowed his cousin Count Raoul of Vermondois, Seneschal of France, to repudiate his wife, the niece of Louis' chief vassal, Count Thibault of Champagne, and marry Eleanor's younger sister, Pétronille. Eleanor was eager for the marriage, and some complaisant bishops were found who asserted that Raoul's previous marriage was invalid on the grounds of blood relationship. Bernard of Clairvaux, a friend of the first wife's family, immediately appealed to Rome and threatened Louis with excommunication. Bernard regarded Eleanor as an evil influence on Louis and urged her to "put an end to your interference in affairs of state." But it was too late to turn back. Louis became involved in a two-year war with his proud and angry vassal Thibault and invaded Champagne. The occupation of the province by the royal army culminated in a horrible incident in the summer of 1144. Louis set fire to the town of Vitry on the Marne. The inhabitants fled in panic from their thatched wooden houses that were going up in flames and took refuge in the church. The fire spread to the church, the burning roof collapsed and over a thousand people, men, women and children, were burned and suffocated.

Although his armies continued to pillage the countryside, Louis suffered agonies of remorse and was convinced that Heaven was showing its displeasure and punishing him for his sins. Dangers were arising on all sides. Geoffrey Plantagenet, the bold and handsome Count of Anjou, had conquered Normandy and was an additional threat to Louis' royal domains. In his desperation, Louis went to extremes of penitence and fasted and mortified his flesh.

Bernard of Clairvaux was moved by the King's contrition. Chroniclers noted Louis' "dove-like simplicity." The interdict was lifted. But Eleanor found this self-abasement contemptible, and is said to have remarked some years later, "I thought to have married a king, but found I had married a monk." After seven years of marriage she was childless. Bernard obtained an audience with Eleanor and besought her to exert a moderating influence on her husband. The pious, ascetic abbot was shocked, but at the same time fascinated in spite of himself, by Eleanor's proud femininity and love of display. He wrote an epistle to the nuns of his Cistercian order in which he warned them against the pernicious example of fashionable ladies who "furnish and adorn themselves as only temples should be, and drag after them a trail of precious stuff that raises a cloud of dust." He described in detail their cloaks lined and bordered with costly fur, their arms loaded with bracelets, and jeweled pendants hanging from their ears. "For headdress they have a kerchief of fine linen which they drape about their neck and shoulders, allowing one corner to fall over the left arm. This is their wimple, ordinarily fastened to their brows by a chaplet or fillet, or a circle of wrought gold." Bernard's description of their dress and "everything that pertains to queenly splendor" shows that the unworldly abbot had studied these fashionable ladies as attentively as he had scrutinized the reprehensible carvings in the cloisters.

In spite of the tedium and drabness of the Paris court a more gracious life style was emerging as Eleanor and her entourage developed a new sense of fashion and elegance. There is no authentic portrait of her at this time. The statues of the period provide clues to the feminine ideal that she inspired and reflect a style of dress far more flattering to the figure than the shapeless and monastic fashions of the 10th and 11th centuries. It is not too farfetched to suppose that one or another of the splendid statues of Biblical queens adorning the so-called Royal Portal of Chartres Cathedral may bear some resemblance to Eleanor (Fig. 50). The elongated forms echo the rigid cylindrical shapes of the columns to which they are attached, but the heads of these kings and queens are more individualized than anything in Romanesque sculpture. Each figure has a grave and gentle presence that heralds the humanism of the Gothic style. The Royal Portal was completed around 1150, shortly after the return of Louis and Eleanor from the Second Crusade. The sculptural theme, strongly influenced by Abbot Suger's program at Saint-Denis, was intended to stress the harmony of secular and spiritual rule. The purpose in representing the kings and queens of the Bible was to proclaim the rulers of France

Fig. 50. Jamb statues from central porch of west front, Chartres Cathedral, ca. 1150. (Archives Photographiques)

as the spiritual descendants of David, Solomon and other Old Testament royalty.

It is easy to imagine Eleanor in the guise of one of the queens of Judah in the Chartres portal who is dressed in the height of early medieval elegance. Her hair, parted in the middle, is hidden under a small rectangular veil, surmounted by the royal crown, and she wears a tightly laced bodice, richly bordered and adorned with a massive brooch. Her close-fitting gown, exquisitely pleated, is girded very low. For certain occasions Eleanor would have worn a long, semicircular mantle, as in the statue of the Queen of Sheba on the same portal.

It has been suggested that one of the solemn kings on the portal may represent Louis VII, who wore his hair long and had a short blond beard. He is certainly portrayed on the tympanum of the portal of Sainte-Anne in the Cathedral of Notre-Dame-de-Paris, kneeling in homage to the enthroned Virgin (Fig. 51). This portal was carved soon after 1163, by which time the early Gothic style was fully developed. Louis was then in his forties and no longer married to Eleanor. Allowing for the fact that the sculptor's realism did not extend to an exact representation of age, he is still convincing as "Louis the Young."

In 1145 Eleanor gave birth, not to the long-awaited male heir, but to a daughter, who was named Marie. On Christmas Day of that year Louis announced to his court assembled at Bourges his intention of going on a Crusade. He wanted to redeem himself in the eyes of Bernard of Clairvaux, and also, no doubt, to impress Eleanor by assuming a heroic role. He decided to take the Queen with him on this expedition so that she could witness the great deeds he hoped to accomplish.

One chronicler suspected that another motive for taking the Queen along was jealousy—the King, knowing the impact of Eleanor's beauty, charm and intelligence, was afraid to leave her for so long a period. Throughout 1146, Bernard, although frail and ailing, untiringly preached the Second Crusade in Vézelay and elsewhere, and Louis himself went around to monasteries and almshouses to plead for the prayers and active support of even the humblest of his subjects. These were the "calls to arms" and "preachings" referred to disparagingly by the young girl in Marcabru's poem. There was far less enthusiasm for this Crusade in the Midi than in other parts of France, although Alphonse-Jourdain, Count of Toulouse, decided to join the King, and so did Guillaume Taillefer, the powerful Count of Angoulême, and Hugues VII, Count of Lusignan.

Fig. 51. King Louis VII and his guardian angel, from the tympanum of the portal of Sainte-Anne, Notre-Dame, Paris, soon after 1163.

Among Eleanor's many vassals from Poitou and Aquitaine who took the Cross and set out for the Orient in the summer of 1147 was a gifted troubadour of noble birth, Jaufré Rudel, Prince of Blaye and lord of Pons and Bergerac. Rudel's strange and melancholy songs had moved even the cynical Marcabru, and have haunted the imagination of later poets from Romantics like Heine to the modern Surrealists with their "nostalgia of the infinite."

CHAPTER IX

Jaufré Rudel: The Quest for the Ideal

Very little is known about Jaufré Rudel, even though one of the most frequently quoted phrases in all Provençal poetry is his *amor de lonh*, or "faraway love." There must have been an aura of romance about this highborn troubadour during his lifetime which would account in part for the posthumous legends. The little town of Blaye on the Gironde, where Rudel was lord of a stately castle, was the reputed burial place of the hero Roland after his death at Ronce-vaux. According to legend, Roland was buried in the former Abbey of Saint-Romain on the site of the citadel and was joined in death by his betrothed, La Belle Aude. Today Blaye, thirty-five miles north of Bordeaux, is noted mainly for its boatbuilding and its fine red wine. A few ruined walls are the only reminders of Blaye's importance as a stronghold in medieval times.

The Jaufré Rudel legend was romantic rather than epic. On the basis of a few enigmatic verses on the theme of *l'amor de lonh*, the Provençal author of the *Vidas* devised a charming but completely fictitious biography of Rudel. The Prince of Blaye fell passionately in love with a lady whom he had not seen; he had heard accounts of her beauty from some pilgrims returning from Antioch. The lady, Odierne, Countess of Tripoli, was the wife of Raimon I, a kinsman of the Counts of Toulouse. The biographer says that Rudel wrote many verses in her honor, and it was in the hope of seeing her face to face that he embarked for the Crusade in 1147. He became ill on the sea voyage, and on the ship's arrival in Tripoli (the Syrian, not the North African Tripoli), he was thought to be dead and his body was taken to an inn. This was reported to the countess, who asked that he be brought to her bedchamber. She took him in her arms, whereupon he regained consciousness. He had just time to thank God for granting him the sight of his beloved before he expired in her arms.

The brief and dramatic meeting is represented in the illuminated initial in one of the manuscripts in the Bibliothèque Nationale (Fig. 52). The countess gave Rudel a stately burial in the Templars' head-quarters in Tripoli and, grief-stricken by his death, retreated to a convent.

All that is known for certain is that Jaufré Rudel departed for the Holy Land in 1147 with Louis VII, Count Alphonse-Jourdain of Toulouse and other lords, and probably never returned. The actual identity of the mysterious "faraway lady" is not really important, nor where she was living. It is the theme of distance and the elo-quence and poignancy with which it was expressed that make the songs memorable.

Fig. 52. Jaufré Rudel and the Countess of Tripoli. Bibl. Nat. MS Fr. 851, fol. 121 v. Note written in Petrarch's hand. (Bibliothèque Nationale, Paris)

The *canso* beginning *"Quan lo rius de la fontana"*—"Where the spring's waters clearer flow"—was certainly composed before Rudel left for the Crusade. The second stanza:

> *Amors de terra lonhdana,*
> *Per vos totz lo cors mi dol.*
>
> Beloved in a far-off land,
> For you my heart is full of woe.

The dream of union with the loved one "in orchard or in curtained room" haunted Rudel. He showed an awareness of other races characteristic of the Midi in the third stanza:

> God has not willed that there be seen
> More beauteous Christian here below
> Nor Jewess nor fair Saracen.

Religion and class were more important than race. Hugues VII, the Brown, to whom Rudel dedicated his poem, married a Saracen girl after his return from the Orient. In the concluding stanza Rudel used a convention common among troubadours and advised his jongleur, Filhol, to carry his song by word of mouth to the Count of Lusignan, who may have been his patron. Rudel rejoiced at the widespread popularity of his poems.

> My words I'll not on parchment write,
> But send these verses to be sung
> In plain and simple Romance tongue
> By my Filhol to Hugh the Brown.
> It likes me well that Poitou men
> And those of Berry and Guyenne
> And Bretons in my songs delight.

Rudel's masterpiece is the *canso* celebrating his faraway love, in which the words *de lonh* constantly recur as a melodious and obsessive refrain. It begins: *"Languan li jorn son lonc en May. . . ."*

> In May when the days longer grow
> I hear birds sing from far away,
> And as I journey to and fro
> I think of my love far away.
> So wracked with longing am I now
> That song, or hawthorn on the bough,
> Please me no more than winter's cold.

The Lord will let me see, I know,
This love of mine so far away,
For this one boon, a double woe
I bear; my love's far, far away.
Were I a pilgrim in her land
In woolen cape, my staff in hand,
Her lovely eyes would me behold.

For the sake of this love the poet declares that he would gladly endure captivity among the Saracens. The next stanza has two lines that contain the essence of the troubadour ethic:

> *Dieus que fetz to quan ve ni vai*
> *E formet sest' amor de lonh . . .*

> God who made all that comes and goes
> And shaped this love so far away . . .

The *joi d'amor* was seen by Rudel and other troubadours of the 12th century as a manifestation of the divine rhythm animating all creation—flowers, orchards, streams and fountains, the song of birds, the changing seasons, and all human thoughts, feelings and activities. The idea of movement was always present in the Middle Ages; there was constant travel both by land and by sea, and in addition to pilgrimages and Crusades, there were trading expeditions—the most extraordinary one being Marco Polo's incredible voyages to the Far East.

All this contributed to a vision of the world that was anything but static, even if the earth was thought to be flat. The great lords were constantly traveling from castle to castle within their domains, and troubadours and jongleurs were always on the move. The wayfarer was a typical medieval figure. In the margin of a Provençal *chansonnier* in the Morgan Library, a ship is drawn in full sail and on the same page are two figures: the man represents the "troubadour's troubadour," Guiraut de Borneilh, conversing with his lady while seated at her feet (Frontispiece). Two stags have been drawn on the bottom of the page.

The melodious beauty and relative simplicity of Rudel's poems give his verses a strong emotional quality, however skeptical one may be today about the nature of such a spiritualized, sublimated and inaccessible love. Today these sentiments have become trite through centuries of repetition, but for Rudel's audience they were fresh and new. Poets have always been fascinated by the idea that "distance lends enchantment" and have yearned for the perfect love. In the work of some of the later troubadours the unreality of the situation was compounded by the artifice of the language, which alienates the modern reader. Rudel's brief life and his poetry achieved a unity that enhanced the legend.

The young Edmond Rostand took the theme of his second play, *La Princesse Lointaine*, produced in Paris in 1895, from the story of the troubadour Rudel and the Lady of Tripoli. Rostand interpreted the poet's adventure as a symbol of the aspiration of the human soul toward an ideal which may be unattainable but which, like Goethe's Eternal Feminine, "draws us on." Sarah Bernhardt played the "faraway princess" in her own theater, which was named after her. As described by Cornelia Otis Skinner in her book, *Madam Sarah*, the actress was "crowned with silver lilies, sumptuous and sad like one of Swinburne's early poems." The play was a financial failure, but Bernhardt more than recovered her losses with a revival of the ever-popular *Dame aux Camélias*.

All that is known about Jaufré Rudel after his arrival in the Near East is that Marcabru addressed a poem to him "across the sea." He may have died during the disastrous Second Crusade, or he may have entered a monastery in Antioch and died there.

His songs, which gave a new dimension to the ideal of courtly love, must surely have been known to Eleanor of Aquitaine, and would have been more congenial to her than the archaic bluntness of Cercamon and Marcabru. In poetry as in art, the primitive vitality of the Romanesque gradually yielded to early Gothic grace and majesty and to a new kind of human awareness.

CHAPTER X

Adventure and Discord in the East

ELEANOR WAS AS EAGER as her husband to leave for the Orient, but for very different reasons. The expedition provided a welcome escape from the long Parisian winter and the opportunity to see new lands and share in an exciting adventure. Sometimes Crusaders did take their wives with them, but Eleanor was no ordinary traveler. To the indignation of the English chronicler William of Newburgh, the Queen's example led other noble ladies to take the Cross and join a campaign where their presence could be only an encumbrance and a dangerous distraction, especially in hostile territory. Like the Queen, the ladies had to take along their retinue and their belongings, and consequently the crusading army was swollen by a cumbersome array of baggage wagons full of clothes, as well as litters, mules and gaily caparisoned horses.

With an instinctive sense of the dramatic, Eleanor and her ladies are said by one chronicler to have dressed up as Penthesilea, Queen of the Amazons, and her warriors at Vézelay in order to stimulate recruiting for the Crusade. This may be apocryphal, but it is in character, and Byzantine historians made several references to the presence of "the Amazons" in describing the Frankish army during the Second Crusade. One Byzantine chronicler, Nicetas, described the leader of one feminine group as "the lady of the golden boots." The ladies may well have worn distinctive and spectacular costumes with glittering pieces of chain mail added to their flowing gowns, tightly fitted at the waist. Peter the Hermit would have been scandalized at such worldly display!

Since these Crusades were a combination of military expedition, pilgrimage and grand tour, all kinds of people—cutthroats and vagabonds as well as humble pilgrims—attached themselves to the armies. Bernard of Clairvaux had every reason to lament that "it was not faith alone that drove that multitude to the East." The presence of troubadours, concubines and other hangers-on had been expressly forbidden by a papal bull at Vézelay, but such regulations were impossible to enforce. Jaufré Rudel, being a noble, would have traveled not as a minstrel, but as a knight with his own retinue. There may well have been troubadours and jongleurs in Eleanor's motley entourage to entertain her and her Poitevin ladies with songs sung in their familiar *langue d'oc* and to discourse with her on the *joi d'amor*.

The German king Conrad III, first of the Hohenstaufen line, had been persuaded by Bernard to join the Crusade, but he distrusted Louis VII's military skill. He set out with his own army of one hundred thousand men, going through Hungary and the Balkans into Asia Minor. The miscellaneous and poorly organized French forces followed the same route, at the astonishing speed of twenty miles a day, through the Danube Valley to the Bosporus.

In September 1147, Louis wrote in a letter to Abbot Suger that his army, after "intolerable hardships and infinite dangers," had "come safe and joyful to Constantinople." The French were received with great pomp by the Byzantine Emperor, Manuel I Comnenus, whose commanding presence and gorgeous brocaded robes encrusted with jewels formed a striking contrast to Louis' meek bearing and modest attire. Manuel was willing to provide the two crusading armies with guides, supplies and equipment in order to be rid of them. The German and French armies, in passing through his Balkan domains, had pillaged the territory. The French distrusted the Greeks, and there had been numerous clashes for which both sides were to blame. Louis VII had been warned by Bernard to be "like a sparrow with careful watchfulness," to avoid the snares of Byzantium, and he was anxious to reach Jerusalem.

Eleanor was enchanted with the exotic splendor of Constantinople —its domed churches and gleaming mosaics, its sumptuous palaces and luxurious gardens by the Bosporus, its squares and obelisks and marble columns, and the ritual splendor of the imperial court. The Byzantine Emperor's flowery compliments were not unwelcome, and compared to the magnificence surrounding Manuel and the Empress Irene, with whom Eleanor had previously corresponded, her own Merovingian palace in Paris seemed drab and primitive. Even her father's castles at Poitiers and Bordeaux had no comparable luxury. Louis was seemingly oblivious to all this beauty, and with his fasting, his penances and his daily visits to the sacred relics, he cut a poor figure in the glamorous setting. The common experience of the Crusade, instead of bringing Louis and his queen closer together, was driving them further apart.

In October the French army set out for Syria, and in January 1148 they were toiling through the rugged mountain passes of Pisidia in southern Asia Minor. Because of the difficult terrain the army had to split into two parts. One branch, the vanguard, was commanded by Eleanor's Poitevin vassal Geoffroy de Rançon, who was entrusted with the protection of the Queen and her ladies. The other branch, led by Louis and his knights, brought up the rear. Geoffroy had orders to pitch his tents and plant the royal standard on a certain high and spacious plateau and wait for the rest of the army to arrive. On closer view the plateau seemed depressingly bleak and bare. When they passed the crest of this elevation Geoffroy and his knights saw a green and inviting valley below. Geoffroy took it upon himself to disregard the royal orders and led his contingent down into the valley, with terrible consequences.

The Queen's enemies among the French later blamed Eleanor for what happened and claimed that it was at her insistence that Geoffroy disobeyed his orders. All that can be said for certain is that, had Eleanor wished, she could have exerted her authority to prevent her vassal from making this move, but after the long and arduous journey through the barren mountain passes, she probably welcomed the more pleasant encampment and trusted Geoffroy's decision.

The vanguard were separated from Louis' forces. When the King and his contingent arrived in sight of the place where Geoffroy and his army were to await them, they searched in vain for them. Because of the heat, some of the men had removed their armor. Suddenly, without any warning, Turkish horsemen who had been hiding in the ravines came charging at the French from all sides, uttering terrible cries. It was almost a repetition of Guilhem VII's disastrous experience forty-eight years earlier. There was a furious mêlée in which the French knights were routed. Louis, on this occasion, showed great courage and fought valiantly, but his army sustained heavy losses. Ironically, the German forces of Conrad III had been the victims of a similar Turkish ambush some weeks before.

When the survivors joined the Queen's camp in the valley there were violent recriminations. There was talk of hanging Eleanor's vassal Geoffroy de Rançon as the cause of the catastrophe. The Queen's intercession, combined with the fact that the King's uncle, the Count de Maurienne, had also been in charge of the vanguard, saved Geoffroy's life. But he was deprived of his command, and Eleanor's prestige suffered a severe blow. The remnants of the army made their way to the port of Adalia, the modern Antalya (known as Satalia to the Crusaders), on the southwestern coast of Asia Minor, and after the leaders paid exorbitant fees to the Greek sea captains for their passage, the French set sail for Antioch.

The tension between Louis and Eleanor was aggravated after the arrival of the French in Antioch in the spring of 1148. They were eagerly awaited by Eleanor's uncle, Raymond of Poitiers, who, after a brilliant and adventurous career, was Prince of Antioch. Raymond was thirty-four at the time, and he had many of the characteristics of his father, the troubadour Count Guilhem VII. He was tall, handsome, charming and outgoing, a brave and skillful warrior as well as a lover of hunting, gambling, festivities and luxurious surroundings. He enjoyed songs and tales of chivalry and the company of learned men. Although Raymond attended Mass regularly, he had his father's skeptical wit. He also showed some of the more dangerous traits of his family, being headstrong, given to violent rages, and not overly scrupulous in pursuing his ends.

Raymond had prepared a lavish reception for the French and was relieved that his niece, whom he had not seen since she was a child, had survived the ordeals of the disastrous expedition. He tried to detain his guests amid the pleasures of Antioch, the exciting and colorful meeting place of East and West. He hoped to enlist Louis' support in retaking Edessa, Aleppo and Caesarea from the Turkish sultan, but the French king refused to fall in with his plans. His one thought was to fulfill his vow and go to Jerusalem.

Louis' followers could not fail to notice that there had been an immediate rapport between Eleanor and her vital and attractive uncle. In Raymond's stimulating company she revived happy memories of her early youth at the court of Poitiers. She was delighted to converse in her native *langue d'oc*, barely intelligible to the French. Rumors circulated among the French knights, and were repeated by the hostile chronicler William of Tyre, that the young queen had become Raymond's mistress. There was no evidence to support this view of what was probably no more than a gallant flirtation, given added zest by the subtle and ambiguous language of troubadour poetry and the daring repartee and verbal interchanges that had been customary at the court of Poitiers.

The chronicler Matthew Paris went even further in his charges. There were Arab lords who had chosen to be Raymond's allies, staying at the palace in Antioch, and others living there as honored captives. As in Spain, there was much "fraternization" between Christians and Moslems in the peaceful interludes between wars. Matthew Paris, writing in the following century, reported that Eleanor "was accused of adultery with an infidel from a race of devils," meaning a Saracen prince. He accused her of having "abandoned herself to the voluptuousness of the Levant." About the same time the monk Alberic declared that in Antioch "she behaved not like a queen but like a common harlot."

Eleanor was no doubt indiscreet and in a frivolous mood and was "making a spectacle of herself." This high-spirited and beautiful young woman was certainly enjoying the flattering attention she received on all sides, but her enemies—especially the eunuch Thierry Galeran, one of Louis' confidants—were determined to present her as a Messalina and an evil influence on the King.

For Louis, Antioch was the cradle of the Christian faith, blessed by memories of St. Paul and other evangelists, and he assiduously visited the holy shrines. He soon became aware of the disturbingly hedonistic and semipagan atmosphere of the city, and he could no longer ignore the fact, long evident to his advisers, that Eleanor was under the spell of her charming uncle Raymond.

Realizing that his niece was discontented with her life as Queen of France, Raymond suggested to her that there might be a way of dissolving the union on the grounds of blood relationship. This was stretching a point, for one had to go back nearly two centuries to discover marriage ties between the Capetians and the house of Poitou. In the late 10th century Adelaide of Poitiers, the daughter of Eleanor's ancestor Guilhem II, Proud Arm, had married Hugues Capet, founder of the royal dynasty of France. Louis VII was unaware of these discussions, but he became angry and suspicious when he learned that Raymond was using his influence over his niece to induce the French to remain in Antioch in the hope of enlisting them as his allies for the reconquest of Edessa from the Moslems.

Incensed, Louis ordered his army and retinue to leave Antioch at once and proceed to Jerusalem, the goal of his pilgrimage. Eleanor loved the easy life in Antioch and the courtly badinage of the *joi d'amor* with Raymond and his lords. As Queen of France she had no power to defy her husband's orders, but as Duchess of Aquitaine she expressly forbade her vassals who had taken the Cross to leave Raymond's principality. While Louis was still devoted to his queen, this could not be tolerated. He threatened to compel her to leave Antioch, and it was then that she voiced for the first time doubts about the validity of her marriage according to canonical law. She announced her wish to sever all ties with the house of Capet and proceed no further with the Crusade.

Louis, seeing all his hopes and plans imperiled, followed Thierry Galeran's advice and resorted to force. The Queen was seized, Louis had the gates of Antioch opened at midnight, and the whole army headed southward to Jerusalem.

They were received with great fanfare and celebration by the populace of the Holy City and by the half-Armenian Queen Mélisende, who was acting as regent of the Latin kingdom of Jerusalem during the minority of her son King Baldwin III. Little is reported of Eleanor during her stay in Jerusalem. She was under a cloud and probably biding her time. It is known that she and Louis, the latter in humble pilgrim's garb, visited the Holy Sepulcher. After leaving Antioch, Louis sent a letter to Abbot Suger in Paris expressing his resentment and chagrin at the Queen's behavior. The old counselor wrote back advising patience.

Louis debated with the Latin princes and with his unreliable ally, Conrad III, who was then in Jerusalem with his German barons, how best to pursue the Holy War and guarantee the safety of the sacred shrines. They decided on a joint attack on Damascus, which failed because of jealousy, and possibly treachery among the leaders. The Second Crusade, begun with such high hopes, ended in dismal failure. It was obvious that the Christian princes were no longer capable of effectively defending their hard-won conquests in the Holy Land. Conrad III became Louis' bitter enemy and returned home. Many of Louis' weary and homesick Crusaders left for France by sea.

But Louis was as reluctant to leave Jerusalem as Eleanor had been to leave Antioch—for very different reasons. Whether or not he made a tour of the Holy Land, the long stay on this hallowed ground provided a respite from his burdensome duties as King of France.

Abbot Suger sent an impassioned letter urging the King's speedy return, but Louis and Eleanor prolonged their stay and celebrated Easter in Jerusalem in 1149. Soon afterward they sailed from Acre. Louis and his knights embarked on one ship, and Eleanor and her ladies on another. Eleanor was pregnant, and the hope of a male heir made her safe arrival in France all the more important.

Their troubles were not over. During the voyage the vessels were separated by a storm. In late July, Louis and his companions finally landed on the coast of Calabria in southern Italy, exhausted and still ignorant of the Queen's fate. Louis was received by Roger of Sicily, who, to his immense relief, gave him news of Eleanor. Her ship had been driven by unfavorable winds toward the dangerous "coast of Barbary" but had eventually arrived in Palermo in Sicily. It took three weeks for Eleanor and her ladies to reach the Calabrian mainland and rejoin her husband. They traveled up the Italian peninsula and were welcomed at Tusculum, southeast of Rome, by Pope Eugenius III, who tried to bring about a reconciliation between the royal couple.

After a visit to Rome, Louis and Eleanor pursued their homeward journey across the Jura Alpine passes of Eastern France. They were met by Suger at Auxerre, and arrived in Paris in November 1149. They had been gone two and a half years.

Although saddened and bewildered by the failure of the Crusade, the French people were happy to have their king back home. After her exciting experiences overseas, Eleanor found life in Paris during the severe winter of 1149–50 intolerably dull, depressing and constricting. She remained bitter about her forcible abduction from Antioch. Outwardly there was no breach with the King. The venerable Suger, at this time a very old man, who had capably administered the realm during Louis' absence, advised against any hasty action, knowing the complications that would arise from a divorce.

Early in 1150 a second child was born to Eleanor, a daughter named Alix. Had the Queen given birth to the long-awaited heir, the course of events would have been very different. Louis thought that the marriage was under a curse. The malicious rumors about the Queen's conduct abroad flared up again, and Louis may have had agonizing doubts about the paternity of Eleanor's new baby. But he was still reluctant to dissolve the marriage.

In 1151 Abbot Suger, the great statesman and foremost historian of his time, died at Saint-Denis, where he had presided over the splendid beginnings of the Gothic style and shaped the destiny of France. He had been the faithful counselor and chronicler of two kings, and was called the "Father of His Country." He was unlike the other outstanding churchman of his time, Bernard of Clairvaux, in every way.

The austere Bernard had asked: "What has gold to do with the sanctuary?" He opposed the cult of images, and his own Cistercian order favored bare, unadorned architecture. In rebuilding the Church of Saint-Denis, Suger arrived at the ultimate visual splendor, which was achieved through the glowing radiance of stained glass, the painting and gilding of statues, and the golden richness of vestments, crosses and reliquaries. Suger declared that reliquaries should be adorned "with the most precious materials we can possibly obtain." This was not display for its own sake, but because Suger believed that "it is only through symbols of beauty that our poor spirits can raise themselves from things temporal to things eternal."

Suger, the son of a serf, was a self-made man, and with his stocky build, heavy features and pendulous cheeks, looked more like a manual laborer than a priest. He was proud of his achievements and had himself represented no less than three times in the stained-glass windows of Saint-Denis.

Bernard of Clairvaux was small, frail and humble in manner. His father was a knight and his mother a member of a noble family. Suger, the practical statesman, had not favored the Second Crusade, which Bernard fervently advocated.

In the matter of the Queen's divorce, Suger, who had constantly sought to strengthen the royal power, feared the consequences of the loss of Eleanor's far-flung territories. For this and other reasons he had opposed any plans for the annulment of the marriage. After Suger's death, the King's relatives and supporters who detested Eleanor questioned her fitness to be Queen of France and blamed her for the failure of the Second Crusade.

Bernard had always distrusted Eleanor, and thought her to be responsible for the King's weakness and indecision. He sincerely believed that he was swayed by moral, not political, considerations when, fourteen years after the royal marriage, he raised the problem of consanguinity. Bernard declared that it was a mortal sin for cousins, however far removed, to live in a state of matrimony. Louis, painfully scrupulous in all things religious, appears to have taken this to heart, and he was also distressed by the lack of a male heir. On March 21, 1152, a council assembled at the King's castle of Beaugency on the banks of the Loire, presided over by Louis and attended by eminent churchmen, pronounced the dissolution of the marriage on the grounds of blood relationship. Eleanor was to retain full possession of her domains as they were before her marriage; at the same time the two royal princesses were declared legitimate and "awarded" to Louis.

The chronicler from Aquitaine, Jean Bouchet, writing five centuries later, gave a dramatic description of Eleanor fainting away on hearing the verdict and remaining unconscious for over two hours. When she came to, she looked with her clear green eyes on the two prelates and two barons who brought her the news, and in anguished tones proclaimed her innocence. There was probably more fantasy than fact in this account, written so long after the event. Separation after fourteen years of marriage was no trivial matter, but Eleanor was certainly weary of the bigoted, self-torturing Louis and longed for a less confining existence. No sooner had she heard of the council's decision, and was assured of her titles as Duchess of Aquitaine and Countess of Poitou, than she took her leave of the melancholy king and, escorted by a few faithful vassals, set out on horseback for her own capital city of Poitiers.

CHAPTER XI

The Rise of Henry Plantagenet

EVERY EVENT IN ELEANOR'S LIFE was attended by drama. News of her divorce spread with lightning speed, and twice on her hurried journey to Poitou she narrowly escaped capture by adventurous young feudal lords who were eager to acquire such a valuable prize. Near Blois she and her party were ambushed by the sixteen-year-old Geoffrey of Anjou, younger brother of Henry Plantagenet, Duke of Normandy. Eleanor's men-at-arms fought off this attack, but when she learned that Thibault of Blois, second son of Louis' vassal the Count of Champagne, was waiting to capture her as she and her escort crossed the Loire, she foiled this plan by taking a different route and reached the safety of her palace stronghold in Poitiers.

In those troubled times Eleanor and her domains urgently needed a protector, but he would be of her own choosing, and her mind was already made up. Her second husband would be no ambitious younger son seeking aggrandizement, but, if all went well, Henry, Duke of Normandy, son of Geoffrey Plantagenet, Count of Anjou, and Matilda, daughter of Henry I of England. In 1150 Henry was invested with the duchy of Normandy by his father, Geoffrey. At eighteen he seemed destined for a brilliant future.

But Eleanor's interest in Henry was not entirely political. When, as a girl of fifteen, she had been chosen as Louis Capet's bride, she had never seen him. Henry Plantagenet was no stranger to her. In August 1151, he had accompanied his handsome father, aptly nicknamed Geoffrey the Fair, to Paris to pay homage to their nominal overlord, the King of France. Eleanor had been impressed both by the strong-willed Geoffrey and by his son, who although almost twelve years younger than herself—she was nearing thirty—was already a mature man, able, intelligent and self-assured. Henry was not exactly handsome; he was a sturdy, thick-set, muscular youth, bull-necked, clean-shaven, with keen gray eyes and close-cropped reddish hair. He was quick to anger and would not brook opposition, but he had great personal charm and winning ways. He had received a good education and knew several languages, including English, which he had learned in Bristol. It has been said that his hands were never empty; they held either a book or a bow.

Henry's virility and strength of purpose were far removed from Louis VII's unstable temperament, forever oscillating between abject despondency and irrational bursts of activity born of frustration and rage. Louis' clerical advisers and those hostile chroniclers, always ready to put the worst possible construction on everything Eleanor did, implied that there had been a secret agreement between Henry and the Queen of France, whose discontent was obvious to all. The most malicious of these historians hinted that Geoffrey had persuaded her to betray her royal husband. Gossip aside, there was an evident compatibility between the young Duke of Normandy and Eleanor, and she may well have seen a possibility of changing her unhappy situation.

On the return journey to Angers from Paris in September 1151, Geoffrey Plantagenet was suddenly seized with a fever while bathing in the Loire and died three days later. Henry became Count of Anjou as well as Duke of Normandy. The news of Eleanor's divorce in March of the following year opened up even more splendid prospects.

In May, Henry and his Angevins rode into Poitiers; it is not known whether his visit was at Eleanor's invitation or on his own initiative, but there was clearly a strong mutual attraction, as well as a community of interests. The differences in their ages was no obstacle; at thirty Eleanor was as beautiful as ever, and her quick mind, her worldly experience, the glamor of her travels in Byzantium and the Orient, the homage paid her by troubadours, and the admiration and sympathy she aroused, made her all the more precious and desirable in Henry's eyes.

They were married on May 18, 1152, in the Cathedral of Saint-Pierre in Poitiers, only eight weeks after the divorce at Beaugency. By an incredible stroke of fortune Henry had won not only a brilliant and beautiful consort but also her fabulous inheritance—the Limousin, Gascony, Poitou and the duchy of Aquitaine. He was master of a realm extending from the English Channel to the Pyrenees, and with the chaotic situation in England, there were even greater prospects ahead. Like Eleanor's ancestors, the Dukes of Aquitaine, Henry had grown more powerful than the King of France. Eleanor's speedy remarriage and its fateful consequences caused stupefaction and fury in Paris. Louis VII's prestige sunk even lower than before, and the resentment caused by this sudden transfer of power and territory caused dissension which eventually led to the Hundred Years' War.

But in Poitiers, in the spring of 1152, there was rejoicing. Even the wording on Eleanor's official proclamations in the first months of her marriage had a triumphant ring and reflected her new-found happiness:

I, Eleanor, by the Grace of God, Duchess of Aquitaine and Normandy, united with the Duke of Normandy, Henry, Count of Anjou . . .

One of Eleanor's first visits after her marriage was to the Abbey of Fontevrault. The abbess in charge was the widow of Prince William Atheling, the English king Henry I's only son, who had drowned in the *White Ship* over twenty years earlier. The people of Poitou were happy that their countess had escaped from the realm of the Capets. But many of the barons wondered whether she or Henry would be the real ruler of their province. Henry, a skillful politician, flattered the burghers of Poitiers and confirmed many of their privileges that Louis VII had tried to suppress twelve years earlier.

Louis was in no mood to let the couple enjoy their happiness. Not only had he suffered a personal humiliation, but Henry and Eleanor had committed a serious breach of feudal law by marrying without their suzerain's consent. At the urging of his counselors, Louis persuaded Henry's younger brother Geoffrey, who had tried to abduct Eleanor on her way to Poitiers, to take up arms against the insolent Duke of Anjou. Louis himself invaded Normandy, but Henry retaliated with such deadly effectiveness that Louis, once again defeated, had to sue for peace and swallow another hurt to his pride.

In the autumn Henry and Eleanor made a triumphant tour through the Limousin, Poitou, Saintonge and Gascony, but all the time Henry was keeping closely informed of events in England. His mother, Matilda, and her cousin Stephen had for several years been battling for the throne of England in a complicated succession of thrusts and victories and counterthrusts and defeats. Finally Matilda abandoned her claim, and Stephen ruled over England. The clergy refused to confirm Stephen's son Eustace as his successor. Seeing his opportunity, Henry Plantagenet sailed for England with twenty-six vessels and was able to extort from Stephen the recognition of his claim through Matilda. Stephen died on October 25, 1154, six months after Henry's return to Normandy, and Henry was crowned at Westminster as King Henry II. He was twenty-one years old.

During her husband's absence, Eleanor had the choice of many residences, but preferred the Castle of Angers, for two centuries the seat of the powerful Counts of Anjou. A seal struck by Eleanor in 1152 just after her marriage and commemorating her donations to Fontevrault points to the significance of her title of Countess of Anjou.

Although the workmanship is simple and the frontal pose is rigid, there was an attempt to make the figure on either side of the seal convey Eleanor's slender majestic presence. On the obverse side she is bareheaded and holds a falcon on her left hand and a fleur-de-lis in her right. On the reverse an ample veil or mantle is draped over her head and sweeps down in graceful folds. In both representations she wears a clinging gown with tight-fitting sleeves falling from the cuff to the ground in long narrow bands. The inscription on the obverse reads ALIENOR · DUCISSE · AQUITANE · —the rest is obliterated. On the reverse her titles NORMANORUM DUCISSA and ANDEGAVIS COMITISSA (Countess of Anjou) are given.

The Castle of Angers was completely rebuilt in the 13th century, and in Eleanor's time it was less imposing than it now appears. It provided a worthy setting, however, and the young duchess and her ladies had the freedom to lead the kind of life they had long desired. In addition to lively young nobles of both sexes from Poitou and Aquitaine, poets and musicians flocked to Angers, full of praises for their patroness's beauty, charm and generosity. The colorful *langue d'oc* was heard far more frequently than French or Latin, and, according to 14th century biographers of the troubadours, it was at this time that the most gifted and tender of all these poet-singers, Bernart de Ventadour, first visited Eleanor's court.

CHAPTER XII

Ventadour and the School of Song

THE GRANDIOSE RUINS of the Castle of Ventadour—or Ventadorn, as it was called in the Middle Ages—are high on a rocky promontory overlooking the wild and densely wooded gorges of the Corrèze Valley in the heart of the Limousin. It was once the seemingly impregnable stronghold of the Viscounts of Ventadour, who, with their kinsmen the Viscounts of Turenne and Comborn, controlled all the surrounding country. Their overlord was the Duke of Aquitaine. The original castle was built by Viscount Eble I, in the late 11th century. It was remodeled in the 15th century, although elements of the Romanesque structure were preserved. During the Renaissance the viscounts found their massive feudal fortress too austere and abandoned it for an elegant mansion they built in Ussel. Even in its ruined state the castle is a proud reminder of the past. The huge cracked walls are overgrown with ivy and weeds, and the narrow winding path that climbs up the steep precipice is covered with vegetation.

The Limousin Archeological Society is excavating the site and the lush greenery is being cleared away; the extraordinary shapes of the ruins, including the round master tower which was part of the original castle (Fig. 53) and the tall square 15th century donjon, are

Fig. 53. The ruins of the castle of Ventadour (Corrèze). (Archives Photographiques)

clearly revealed. Experts have established the position of the postern gate and other entrances to the fortress. The Great Hall, where the lord administered justice and received his guests, was given handsome Gothic vaults in the 15th century and part of the molding has been found. The Hall was paved with square bricks. In the center of an area identified as the kitchen, a circular hearth of fireproof terracotta tiles marks the place where soups and ragouts were kept warm before being taken in to the viscount's table. A drain was hollowed out for discarded water.

Eble II, the Singer, who became Viscount of Ventadour around 1106, presided over a famous "school" of troubadours and jongleurs for over forty years when the castle was one of the great centers of

Provençal culture. Eble prided himself on his lavish hospitality and on his practice and patronage of poetry and song. He was the friendly rival of his overlord, Guilhem VII of Poitou.

There is no way of judging Eble's merits as a troubadour, as none of his works have survived. From Marcabru's vehement lines:

> Never will I practice song
> In Lord Eble's school . . .

and his scornful remark that the viscount's ideas were "senseless" and "against all reason," it may be assumed that he regarded Eble II as an aristocratic dilettante. The genial viscount and his friends were leisurely nobles for whom *trobar* was a pastime and a pleasant mental exercise. Much of their verse may have been in the style of the lighter poetry of Guilhem VII, without the Count of Poitou's professionalism and finesse, but the enthusiasm of this privileged group for music and song attracted a number of jongleurs and poets to Ventadour, where they had the opportunity to cultivate and refine their art. Some were of humble origin, yet they pursued the courtly ideal with a delicacy and subtlety unknown to their aristocratic patrons. Among this younger generation, none were more gifted than Bernart de Ventadour (a member of the viscount's household, not of his family), whose sensitivity and power of expression made him one of the greatest poets of the Middle Ages.

CHAPTER XIII

Bernart de Ventadour:
The Many Faces of Love

U NLESS A TROUBADOUR was a great lord like Guilhem VII of Poitou
or Count Raymond V of Toulouse, the events of his life were
not likely to be recorded by contemporary chroniclers. For this reason the identity of many of the troubadours remains vague. The
anonymous early 14th century author of the *Vidas* tended to recon-
struct the poet's biography on the basis of the often ambiguous references in the poems—the most obvious example being his treatment of
the life of Jaufré Rudel. But it does not follow that all the information in these brief biographies should be rejected as "unhistorical" or
that the oral traditions on which the author partly relied were necessarily false.

The appealing account in the *Vidas* of the lowly beginnings of
Bernart de Ventadour (Fig. 54), the son of humble domestics in
Eble II's castle, is confirmed by some rather patronizing verses by
the troubadour from Clermont, Peire d'Auvergne, who was Bernart's
contemporary. In a satirical *sirventès* on twelve of his fellow poets,
perhaps the earliest-known attempt at literary criticism, Peire places
Bernart slightly lower than Guiraut de Borneilh, whom his contemporaries considered the "master troubadour," the favorite of connoisseurs. After humorous and somewhat mocking descriptions of two
poets, Peire Rogier and Guiraut himself, Peire d'Auvergne went on:

> To Bernart of Ventadour I come,
> Less then Borneilh by the breadth of a thumb!
> His father, worthy of his hire,
> Wielded a stout laburnum bow.
> His mother made the oven glow,
> And gathered twigs to light the fire.

This indicates that the father, employed as a servant, was a trained archer, ready to help if necessary in the defense of the castle. A long subterranean passage has been discovered at Ventadour adjoining the guard room—it was used by archers for "target practice." Laburnum, a hard, dark wood, was much in demand for bows in the Middle Ages. Bernart's mother worked in the kitchen bakery. Peire d'Auvergne, the son of a well-to-do burgher of Clermont, and originally destined for the Church, may have felt superior about Bernart's origin—and yet owing to the open and mobile character of Occitan society, Bernart was picked out at an early age by Eble II, and taught the art of poetry. He was able to sing as an equal with the powerful lords of Ventadour, who were legally his masters.

The date of the death of Eble II is not known, but by 1147 he

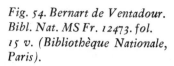

Fig. 54. Bernart de Ventadour. Bibl. Nat. MS Fr. 12473. fol. 15 v. (Bibliothèque Nationale, Paris).

had been succeeded as viscount by his son Eble III. The new lord of
Ventadour was not himself a poet, but, like his father, he presided
over a large school of troubadours and jongleurs. Eble's court
gained luster in 1148 when he married the beautiful Marguerite de
Turenne, the widow of the Viscount of Limoges. No portrait of her
exists, but a sculptured head of a lady with a heart-shaped face, wearing a coronet, was discovered among the ruins of the castle. It probably formed part of a capital, and although mutilated it suggests the
kind of feminine ideal that captivated the troubadours. The lady
Marguerite is said to have inspired a burning passion in the susceptible
Bernart, then in his early twenties.

As Bernart was to discover several times in his life, the theory of
the perfect *joi d'amor* and the ardent homage to a loved one from a
distance was less arduous and dangerous than its practice when the
lady in question was near at hand. Twelfth century noblewomen,
most of whom had been married at an early age to a husband not of
their own choosing, were flattered and thrilled by the romantic aura
created around them by the troubadours, who praised their beauty
and charm and who saw them as desirable but probably unattainable
lovers. The husband was supposed to accept this adoring homage to
his wife gracefully; if he resented it, he became a *jaloux*, lacking
"courtesy." In the close quarters of a castle, where there was very
little privacy and where the lord was often away for long periods,
this situation was at best ambiguous and at worst full of danger.

When strong emotions were aroused on either side or both, the
patterns of tender gallantry—which at that period were perfectly
genuine—could easily be upset, and violent passions could take over,
with sometimes disastrous consequences. Bernart believed in absolute
sincerity, and his frequent use of "I," the first person, underlined
the subjective nature of his poetry. In his fifteenth *canso*, beginning
"*Chantas no pot gaire valer*," he says:

> It is of no avail to sing
> Unless the song spring from the breast.
> The song cannot from the heart spring
> Unless the heart with love be blessed.
> My song surpasses all the rest
> Because, to serve my love's great joy,
> I lips, eyes, heart and mind employ.

According to tradition, Bernart, unable to keep his love on the
sublimated plane required by the *joi d'amor*, made ardent advances to

Marguerite, who, although she rejected them, was obviously moved by the young poet's passion. Viscount Eble, who had at first encouraged his father's protégé and admired his talent, evidently decided that the situation was not to his liking. The proud motto of his house was *"inania pello"*—"I reject vain things"—and the overzealous poet was one of them!

Bernart was banished from the castle, and several of his poems contain poignant allusions to his sad plight. Whatever questions may have been raised about the authenticity of this story, it is a fact that Eble repudiated his wife in 1152, only four years after their marriage, so something must have been seriously amiss. Both Marguerite and Eble lost no time in remarrying—the viscount's new wife was the daughter of the Count of Montpellier. Little is known of Eble after his remarriage, except that in 1170 he died in the monastery of Monte Cassino in central Italy, after returning from the Holy Land.

Tempting though it is to speculate on the autobiographical elements in the songs of Bernart de Ventadour, it is the poems themselves that are important. Like all true poetry, their meaning is inseparable from their sound. Even without the musical accompaniment, the sheer melodiousness of such lines as

> *Lo tems vai e ven e vire*
> *Per jorns, per mes e per ans . . .*

especially the alliteration of the "v" sounds in the first line, poses a difficult problem for the translator. The literal meaning is:

> Time goes and comes and turns
> Through days and months and years . . .

and Bernart constantly played with the idea of time. Here the rhythm is protracted to convey the feeling of endless, hopeless waiting. Later in the same poem he says wistfully:

> No longer will I sing
> In Eble's school of song . . .

where he had served his apprenticeship and mastered his art, if not his emotions.

One of Bernart's most personal poems has been preserved with its music, which is as moving as the words. The *canso* begins, *"Can vei la lauzeta mover"*:

> When I behold the lark on high
> Beat joyous wings to greet the sun
> Then drift in sweet oblivion
> So filled with rapture is her heart,
> Alas, how I do envy those
> Who find their pleasure in this sight.
> I marvel that my heart does not
> Melt and dissolve with my desire.

The equation of "joy" with the freedom of flight and the exhilaration of open space is beautifully expressed, and Bernart always saw love as involving the entire being, emotional, physical, spiritual and intellectual. Two of his most moving lines follow:

> *Ai, las! tan cuidava saber*
> *D'amor e tan petit en sai!*

> I thought I knew so much of love
> Alas! how little do I know!

Dante paid Bernart de Ventadour the tribute of virtually paraphrasing his song "*Can vei la lauzeta mover*" in Canto **XX** of his *Paradisio*. One of the few classical allusions to be found in troubadour poetry occurs in a later stanza.

> All power over myself was gone
> And I was helpless from the hour
> When she allowed me to behold
> The lovely mirror of her eyes,
> And when therein I saw myself
> My sighs were heralds of my death.
> As surely will I perish now
> As fair Narcissus in the pool.

He concluded his *canso* with a sad farewell:

> Tristan, I'll trouble you no more!
> I leave you, to go who knows where?
> All song I sadly will forsake
> And hide me now from Joy and Love.

It has been suggested that Tristan was the *senhal,* or surname before marriage, of Marguerite, but it was also customary for troubadours to use a male form of address in order to "conceal" the lady's identity. Both Guilhem VII and Bernart in another poem use the term *midons*—my lord—like a vassal paying homage to his suzerain.

When he was still in favor at the castle, Bernart had written, "Never will Ventadour without her singers be." Eble III's second wife, Alaïz, daughter of the lord of Montpellier, was a patron of troubadours, although presumably more discretion was shown on all sides, and the "game of love" was played according to the rules.

What makes Bernart de Ventadour especially interesting to the modern reader is the tension between the demands of *l'amour courtois*, which he himself accepted and helped to perpetuate, and the turmoil of his own instincts and emotions. The split between the ideal and the reality is at the heart of what centuries later was called the Romantic spirit. Only in the discipline of his verse—and Bernart was a consummate artist—could he experience the ideal state of love and "joy" so fragile and elusive in real life.

After leaving Ventadour in disgrace, Bernart, according to his medieval biographer, paid brief visits to several courts in the Midi, and then made his way to Angers. It was probably sometime in 1152 that "he came to the Duchess of Normandy" (Eleanor), "who was young and of great worth, and she had understanding in matters of value and honor, and cared for a song of praise."

Eleanor was no doubt charmed by Bernart's pleasing appearance and exceptional poetic talents, and the young troubadour fell completely under her spell. Accents of genuine emotion constantly break through the conventions of courtly love in the work of this sensitive and vulnerable poet. While there is every reason to believe that Bernart fell in love with the green-eyed duchess, who was about his own age, one would have to have an incurably romantic imagination to assume that she returned his passion or that she showed him more than sympathy and admiration. Eleanor was in the first thrill of her marriage to the young and virile Henry Plantagenet, and was expecting a child. At the same time it was gratifying to be adored and appreciated as a woman after years spent in the cloistered monotony of Louis VII's court in Paris.

In the winter of 1153 Henry was in England engaged in the difficult negotiations which led to his recognition by King Stephen as the rightful heir to the English throne. Henry, who was kept well informed of everything that happened across the Channel, was possibly aware of the circumstances of Bernart's dismissal from Ventadour. Unwilling to take chances, he summoned the poet to England. Bernart, who always interpreted the moods of nature in relation to his own emotions, was depressed by the fog and snow on the banks of the Thames, and was sustained only by his passion for his "*bonna domna jauzionda*," his good and joyous lady, and his longing to see her once again, in the gracious and welcoming atmosphere of her court. Unlike many of his fellow troubadours, Bernart had no interest in politics and war; love and nature were the only realities, with nature providing a background and at times a counterpoint to the emotions.

The most famous of the poems generally assumed to have been addressed to Eleanor from England is the *canso* beginning:

> *Can la frej'aura venta*
> *Deves vostre pais,*
> *Veyaire m'es qu'eu senta*
> *Un ven de paradis . . .*

> When the cool breeze blows hither
> From the land where you dwell,
> Methinks I do feel
> A wind from Paradise . . .

The poet praises her "lovely eyes and noble countenance"—description of the lady is nearly always vague—he quotes her words to him counseling patience and perseverance, and in the sixth stanza, he takes comfort in her enjoyment of his verse:

> I am not one to scorn
> The boon God granted me;
> She said in accents clear
> Before I did depart,
> "Your songs they please me well."
> I would each Christian soul
> Could know my rapture then,
> For all I write and sing
> Is meant for her delight.

Finding the stay in England burdensome, Bernart crossed the Channel and made his way back to Eleanor's court. Then it seems that Henry returned to Anjou and took Eleanor away with him, first to Normandy and later, in December 1154, to England for his coronation in Westminster. Because of the references to wintry chill, it is sometimes assumed that the poem beginning, "*Tant ai mon cor plen de joia*," was written in London, but the poet clearly said:

> My spirit yonder flies,
> My body here remains,
> In France, far from my Love . . .

The opening of the poem shows how Bernart's delight in words and imagery was ultimately linked with his whole philosophy of the joy of love and creation.

> My heart is so filled with joy
> All nature is transformed,
> A flower, crimson, yellow and white,
> So seems the wintry frost.
> Come wind and pelting rain,
> My happiness soars on high,
> And higher grows my worth,
> My song is purified.

Joy, an active force, has the power to work miracles and change winter into a many-colored flower. *Fin 'amor*, or true love, is "purified" both in form and in content; anything which does not express the essence of emotion is removed. Even if the lover suffers as much as Tristan for "fair-haired Iseut," he is uplifted by this quest and sustained by hope. Love becomes a pilgrimage of the heart, with its ecstasies as well as its ordeals.

The romance of Tristan and Iseut was of predominantly Celtic origin, although there are parallels in the Arabic love story of Kars and Lobna. It was already a well-known romance in Occitan and Anglo-Norman circles, and even across the Rhine, long before the appearance around 1185 of the earliest extant version, written in the *langue d'oïl* by the courtly Anglo-Norman poet Thomas of Britain. Thomas refers in his poem to an earlier version by one Bleheris, or Bleri, a professional poet-singer of Welsh origin who apparently recited the tale to a Count of Poitiers at some time between 1100 and 1137. This span of years includes part of the reign of Guilhem VII and all of the short reign of Guilhem VIII; if it was the latter, Eleanor may well have heard the romance of Tristan and Iseut at her father's court from Bleheris himself. The story of how Tristan was sent to Ireland to bring Iseut the Fairhaired back to Cornwall to be the bride of his uncle, King Mark, and how a potion that Tristan and Iseut unknowingly drank bound them in eternal love, was admirably suited to the theories of courtly love prevalent in

Fig. 55. Tristan and Iseut(?) meeting in a garden, from an ivory jewel-casket, ca. 1200, possibly from Cologne. This and other scenes on the casket may be the earliest known illustrations of the Tristan legend. (Courtesy of the Trustees of the British Museum)

Southern France. It was a glorification of love and at the same time a rejection of the claims of feudal marriage. Around 1170 Eilhart von Oberg wrote a poem on the same theme in the Rhineland. Representations in art of this and other Arthurian legends are extremely rare before the late 13th century. The earliest known illustrations of the Tristan romance are to be found on a small ivory casket of around 1200 in the British Museum, probably intended to contain a lady's jewelry (Fig. 55). It may have originated in Cologne, where there was a school of ivory-carvers that produced many reliquaries. Its secular theme makes it a great rarity for the period. One of the scenes shows a tryst of the lovers in a garden. It is not known which episode is represented nor which version of the tale was followed by the designer. It is not the rendezvous often depicted in 14th century Gothic ivories in which King Mark is spying on the lovers from a tree and is reflected in the waters of the spring below. The scene on the casket may represent a parting of the lovers as told by Thomas of Britain.

It was natural that Bernart de Ventadour should have been moved by this passionate tale of a transcendent love, and referred to it in his poems.

There is no indication that Bernart joined Henry and Eleanor in England after the coronation. Completely taken up with the challenge of her new life and her new crown, Eleanor, who had just borne her first son, had little time in the ensuing months for "silken dalliance" with troubadours. It was sixteen years before she would hold her celebrated court at Poitiers, and by that time Bernart had found other patrons.

Leaving Eleanor's depleted household at Angers, Bernart traveled south and later became the protégé of another remarkable woman, Viscountess Ermengarde of Narbonne. This able and popular ruler was renowned for her beauty and gentleness and entertained many troubadours in her palace. She did not inspire in Bernart the kind of passion he had felt for Eleanor. However, his fellow poet Peire Rogier became enamored of the viscountess, and Rogier's biographer says that Ermengarde, feeling herself about to reciprocate his love, regretfully dismissed him from the court.

Bernart's last patron was Count Raymond V of Toulouse, who had married Louis VII's sister Constance. The count was an amiable and tolerant ruler who wrote poetry himself and befriended several troubadours on a basis of easy equality. For Bernart, then in late middle age, Raymond's court in Toulouse was more of a comfortable retreat than a spur to creation. He wrote nothing after 1180, and on the death of Raymond V in 1194 he became a monk in the Cistercian Abbey of Dalon in the Dordogne, where he died.

Bernart de Ventadour raised the Limousin dialect of the *langue d'oc*, first given literary form by Guilhem VII, to great heights, and his spontaneity and sincerity transcended the ritualistic patterns of "courtly love." Just as poetry bridged the gap between lord and commoner, the love sung by the poet was intended to create a spiritual and emotional equality between the highest-born lady and the singer who paid court to her. Even if they were not destined to become lovers in a physical sense, the ideal of reciprocity and mutual enrichment was stressed:

> In full agreement and consent,
> 'Tis thus true lovers' love must be.
> Two wills can only find content
> In absolute equality.

But the troubadours were no strangers to physical desire, and it is a mistake to think of their attitude as "Platonic." Even Bernart, who is considered an ethereal poet of love, had a sensual strain. In one poem, after listing the loved one's many attributes, he wrote:

> Her body slender, fresh and fair,
> Her beauty, worth and subtle wit,
> Her virtues, more than I can tell . . .
>
> . . . And I can find no fault in her
> If she but graciously consent
> One night, while shedding all her clothes,
> To set me in some chosen place
> And make a necklace of her arms.

Elsewhere there is a real cry of passion:

> And I will kiss her mouth a thousand times,
> That one month hence the traces can be seen!

CHAPTER XIV

Eleanor's Court at Poitiers

THE FIRST TEN YEARS of Eleanor's marriage to Henry were full of excitement, but they were not idyllic. Henry was a man of restless and overpowering energy. Although he was well read and enjoyed the conversation of intelligent and learned men, his was the active, not the contemplative, temperament. Deeply involved in politics and administration, and faced with the urgent necessity of controlling territories covering much of present-day France and all of England, he had less time than he would have liked for the more leisurely world of poetry and the arts. He willingly shared his power with Eleanor; traveling sometimes together, and sometimes on separate expeditions, they were constantly on the move.

One striking memento of the progress of the royal couple through their domains is the capital in the Cloisters in New York from the Church of Notre-Dame-du-Bourg at Langon, near Bordeaux, carved with two crowned heads which almost certainly represent Eleanor and Henry (Fig. 56). There is all the more reason to accept these beautifully carved heads as portraits, as similar pairs, less finely executed, have been found in the Cathedral of Saint-André in Bordeaux, in a small church near Saintes, and in England in Oakham Castle in Rutlandshire. Henry and Eleanor are known to have visited the

Fig. 56. Eleanor of Aquitaine and Henry II. Engaged capital from the Church of Notre-Dame-du-Bourg, Langon (Gironde), French, 12th century. (The Metropolitan Museum of Art, The Cloisters Collection)

abbey church at La-Sauve-Majeure near Bordeaux in 1155, and the church at Langon was a dependency of the La Sauve monastery to which they had made a donation. The two heads in the Cloisters in New York, although they each have the same conventional treatment of the eyes, are far more lifelike in a realistic sense than most sculptures in the 12th century. The head of Eleanor has fine intelligent features with an expressive mouth; that of Henry has a broader, squarer face with high cheekbones. The emphasis on simple planes is satisfying esthetically and the restrained decorations of the moldings are in keeping with the strong forms of the carving.

In the earlier years of his reign Henry spent much time on the Continent, but he was at the same time concerned with restoring

order in an England ravaged by civil wars. He subdued the English
barons and established a strong centralized royal authority. In spite of
giving birth to eight children in an almost unbroken succession,
Eleanor was incessantly moving from Normandy to Poitou and from
Poitou to Aquitaine, and crossing and recrossing the English Channel,
at all seasons of the year in the far from luxurious ships of the period.
In addition to the royal palace at Westminster, she had residences in
Oxford, Salisbury, Rouen, Angers and Poitiers.

As Queen of England, Eleanor was the first to break that country's
tight cultural insularity. She invited poets and writers to London and
introduced them to the English court. She encouraged the *langue
d'oïl* as well as her native *langue d'oc*. The Arthurian legend, the
story of Tristan and Iseut, and other romances became as popular in
London as they had been at the court of Anjou. Philippe de Thaün,
in dedicating his Bestiary to Eleanor, called her "the arbiter of honor,
wit and beauty." Her fame spread across the Rhine, where court
poets, predecessors of the Minnesingers, praised her in their verse.
One anonymous poet wrote:

> Were all the lands mine
> Between Elbe and Rhine,
> I'd deem them little worth
> If England's fair queen
> Lay my arms between.

Dress and manners in England were strongly influenced by
Eleanor's stress on civility and courtliness, and several English chroniclers were indignant at what they considered the baleful effects of
the newfangled and "effeminate" ways on stalwart Englishmen. In
spite of the frequent visits of troubadours, the demanding ritual of
fin 'amor never had the same success in England as across the Channel.
Nevertheless, the oldest English lyrical poetry was derived from the
Provençal songs, either in their original form or in French versions.

Of all Eleanor's residences, her ancestral castle at Poitiers was
undoubtedly her favorite. Henry realized the strategic value of
Poitou and its capital, which was on the main road to the Midi, and
rebuilt the city's ramparts. He also erected a massive fortress at
Niort. Like his ancestors the Counts of Anjou, Henry had a passion
for building, and Eleanor was eager to take advantage of Poitou's
growing prosperity and enhance the beauty and prestige of her
capital. The two most important monuments of their joint rule in

Poitiers, the Cathedral of Saint-Pierre and the Great Hall of the Palace of the Counts, are in the style known as Angevin, or Plantagenet, Gothic. One characteristic feature is a domed vault over a crossing of pointed arches, but the style is distinguished above all by a sense of spaciousness and luminosity rare in buildings of that period.

The Cathedral was begun in 1162 to replace the previous church destroyed by fire. Eleanor was determined that it should be larger than any church she had ever seen (she had never been to Toulouse to see the immense Saint-Sernin). Behind the altar, in the axis of the great central nave, one of the finest examples of medieval stained glass shows the Ascension, the Crucifixion and the Martyrdom of St. Peter, to whom the Cathedral is dedicated. The Crucifixion panel is the largest in scale; just below it is the scene of the Martyrdom of St. Peter, crucified upside down according to his wish, and immediately underneath, but hidden by the altar, are the kneeling figures of Eleanor and Henry holding up a ground plan of the Cathedral.

In 1144 Eleanor and her first husband, Louis VII, had assisted at the solemn ceremony of the consecration of Saint-Denis, in which under Suger's inspiration the splendor of the Gothic style had first been revealed. Eighteen years later, through the joint initiative of Henry II and herself, the Angevin Gothic, severe yet elegant, was introduced into Poitou. The influence of the Cathedral of Saint-Pierre can be seen in the basilica of Le Puy in Auvergne, and even across the Rhine, in some of the *Hallenkirchen* of western Germany. The Cathedral took many years to build, and its flamboyant towers were added at the very end of the Gothic period.

Eleanor made the castle in Poitiers more livable. The vast Hall, or Grande Salle, with its beautifully proportioned arcaded walls (Fig. 57), dates from the later years of her reign. The dominant feature of the palace was the Maubergeon tower, built by Guilhem VII for his mistress; smaller rooms were added to it to give greater comfort and privacy for Eleanor and her ladies. Still further alterations were made over a century later by Jean, Duc de Berry, who favored a luxurious style of living.

The Maubergeon tower itself is a massive rectangular donjon. Later four large round towers were built at each corner of the palace and adorned with statues and carvings. The whole structure was truncated in the 17th century because of Richelieu's systematic policy of "decapitating" the castles of nobles in the provinces in order

Fig. 57. The Great Hall of the Palace of the Counts in Poitiers, facing south. The side and north walls, in the Angevin Gothic style, were built in the time of Eleanor of Aquitaine. The monumental chimney-piece and the "flamboyant" window tracery were added in the late 14th century under Jean, Duc de Berry. The exterior of the south wall is seen in Fig. 27. (Photograph by Hélène Plessis, Poitiers)

to assert the central royal authority. (See illustration on page 67.) The ruins of Les Baux bear witness to the deadly effectiveness of his cannons, which were fired point-blank at the structure to destroy it. In Poitiers no cannons were used, only pickaxes and similar instruments.

Eleanor did not set up her own court at Poitiers until around 1170, when she was nearly fifty. Much had happened to cool her relationship with Henry. In England, Henry became involved in the long and bitter conflict with his one-time favorite, Thomas à Becket, whom he had himself raised to greatness and made Archbishop of Canterbury and for whose murder in Canterbury in 1170 he was indirectly responsible.

In 1168 Henry returned from England in haste to crush a revolt by rebellious vassals in the Angoumois, Marche and Limousin headed by Guy de Lusignan. Skillful and tenacious in war, Henry succeeded in maintaining order where Louis VII had failed miserably. Even the Count of Toulouse acknowledged Henry as suzerain. But there was tension in the realm, and if the populace of Poitou and Aquitaine remained generally loyal, it was more out of devotion to Eleanor than out of any strong allegiance to the King of England.

The struggle with Louis VII was by no means over. Two years after divorcing Eleanor, Louis had married the gentle Constance, daughter of the King of Castile. A chronicler wrote that the French king was "better married than he had been." Constance died in 1160, and there was still no male heir. Louis' third wife, Adèle of Champagne, finally presented him with a son in 1165, the future Philip Augustus. The birth of a son improved the strategic position of the French monarchy, and for several years there was recurrent warfare between Louis and Henry, followed by uneasy truces.

When Eleanor's many children were born, almost yearly, it was hoped that the Plantagenet dynasty would be strengthened. No one could have foreseen the terrible conflicts and rivalries that would embitter Henry's last years. The eldest son, Guillaume, born before Henry's accession to the English throne, died in infancy. Then came Prince Henry, a daughter Matilda, and the future Richard Coeur de Lion, who was born in Oxford in 1157. Richard was designated as Eleanor's heir to the county of Poitou and the duchy of Aquitaine, and he always remained his mother's favorite. The fourth son, Geoffréy, was born in 1158 and given the title of Count of Brittany, a province of which Henry had gained control. A second daughter, named Eleanor like her mother, was born in Normandy in 1161, and the following year Joanna was born in Angers. The youngest of all of Eleanor's children, John, born in Oxford in 1166, was the prince on whom his father placed great hopes and whose reign as king was to leave bitter memories for his subjects.

In spite of this growing family, Henry's frantic activities kept him away from Eleanor for long periods. She had complete freedom of action, and at first found this stimulating, especially as she could indulge her taste for books, music and poetry and enjoy the lively companionship of her Poitevin friends. But after some years it became obvious that Henry was no longer greatly attached to his wife, and after 1166 the notoriety of his relationship with Rosamond Clifford, the "Fair Rosamond," was one of the causes of their estrangement.

The flaxen-haired Rosamond, renowned for her beauty, was the daughter of Walter de Clifford, a Norman knight who had served Henry during his Welsh campaign in 1165. It was probably then that Henry first met this "faire and comely dame" (to quote the "Ballad of Fair Rosamond"). During her husband's absence Eleanor was his vice-regent in Angers. If Rosamond was in fact residing in the King's palace at Woodstock near Oxford at the time of Eleanor's arrival in that city in 1166 shortly before Prince John was born, the Queen's outrage is understandable. The chronicler Giraldus Cambrensis informs us that Henry "had long been a secret adulterer" and "now flaunted his paramour for all the world to see."

Legends arose concerning Rosamond, invented by later chroniclers and writers of ballads and romances. Henry was said to have built a wondrous tower and maze in the densely forested park of his palace at Woodstock to hide the "Rose of the World"—"*rosa mundi*"—from the Queen's jealous fury. The story that Rosamond was poisoned by Eleanor first appeared in the *French Chronicle of London* in the 14th century. In other versions she was stabbed to death or beheaded at the Queen's command. The romantic details of the "clue of thread" which guided Henry to her bower were even later inventions. The real Rosamond died young, around 1177 (at a time when Eleanor was in captivity), and was buried in the nunnery church of Godstow in the upper reaches of the Thames, where she had been living in pious retreat. She could not possibly, by reason of age, have been the mother of Henry's natural son William Longsword, Earl of Salisbury, as was once believed.

There had been earlier infidelities which Eleanor, as was customary at the time, had chosen to ignore, but Henry's callous parading of his amour with Rosamond in the royal halls and palaces was a terrible affront to Eleanor's pride and to her deepest feelings as a woman. Shortly after her marriage to Henry she had begun a letter to the Pope with the words "I, Aliénor, by the wrath of God, Queen of the English." There was no overt break with Henry, but Eleanor was "terrible in her wrath," and the estrangement was all but complete. There are indications that her sons shared their mother's resentment, and this, combined with their nascent political ambitions and individual grievances as they grew to manhood, boded ill for the future.

With the intention of strengthening his dynasty and at the same time delegating some of his royal power, Henry II, in a solemn assembly at Montmirail in January 1169, confirmed his eldest son and namesake Henry as heir to Maine and Anjou, and also confirmed Eleanor's favorite Richard in the titles assigned him at birth, those of Count of Poitou and Duke of Aquitaine. Henry II little suspected how much this corresponded to Eleanor's desires, for the outraged queen saw the possibility of Richard, under her guidance, governing those rich provinces in a manner quite independent of Henry's autocratic policies. Louis VII, as titular overlord of the princes Henry and Richard, was present at Montmirail, and Henry II's third son, the nine-year-old Geoffrey, for whom his father had conquered Brittany, paid feudal homage to the French king. Louis agreed to Geoffrey's marriage to the Countess Constance, heiress of the province. In the following year 1170, young Henry was crowned at Westminster by Roger of York, a move his father would have cause to regret. The handsome, spoiled, much-favored heir apparent, always known as the "Young King," was to be the source of terrible discord. The situation was made even worse by the excessive indulgence that Henry II showed to his youngest born, Prince John.

Around 1170 Eleanor decided to remove herself as far as possible from the King's immediate authority and to assert her independence in her own inherited domains. Henry's prestige in Poitou and Aquitaine had been severely damaged by the murder of Becket, for which the clergy held the King responsible. There was also resentment of the abuse of power by some of Henry's deputies. Eleanor's strength and popularity in her own territories had never been greater, and her favorite son, Richard, was by her side as count-duke. It was then that she established her court in the palace of Poitiers, which had long been neglected and which for the next few years was a brilliant center of culture as well as political power.

There was constant coming and going in the Great Hall. Restless and exuberant younger sons of the Poitevin nobility, scholars, troubadours, artists and musicians mingled with attractive young chatelaines and worldly and cultivated clerics. The *langue d'oïl* was heard almost as frequently as the *langue d'oc*, especially after the arrival of Marie, Countess of Champagne, the elder daughter of Louis VII and Eleanor. Marie had not seen her mother since her childhood, and had received a strict upbringing at her father's court in Paris. When she was nineteen Louis had married her to his vassal Henry, Count of Champagne, who was nearly twice her age. She was in her late twenties when she arrived at the court of Poitiers, and the importance given to women in Eleanor's entourage must have been a welcome change from the male-dominated palaces and castles of the North, where women, to quote her father, were "the meaner sex."

There were strong bonds of sympathy between mother and daughter, and together they presided over splendid festivities, tournaments, animated musical and literary gatherings and the curious, much misunderstood "Courts of Love," which need some explanation.

Not all of those who frequented the palace at Poitiers were paragons of courtliness. Some of the young knights were quite unruly, especially the Poitevins, of the same stock as those whom a Frankish chronicler at the time of the Second Crusade had called "an unrestrained and incorrigible people."

Eleanor and Marie set the fashions in dress and behavior. Everything these intelligent and charming women did captured the imagination of those who saw them. They created a code of civility within the framework of the "courtly love" sung by the troubadours.

In 1174 Marie commissioned the cleric André Chapelain—Andreas Capellanus was the Latin name under which he wrote—whom she had known in Paris, to write a treatise on love, roughly based on Ovid's *Ars Amatoria*. Chapelain, described as *sapientissimus*, most learned, produced *Tractatus de Amore et de Amoris Remedia— Treatise on Love and the Remedies of Love*—in which the differences from his Roman model are far more striking than the resemblances. But this was certainly Marie's intention in commissioning the work. For Ovid love was entirely a sensual pastime, and he presented it either as an ardent pursuit, like the hunt, or as a war of the sexes with no holds barred. "The bird catcher knows the groves and the fisherman the waters teeming with fish. You who are in search of love, find out where all the prettiest girls are." His cynical conclusion was: "All women can be seduced"; since all is fair in love and war, every kind of scheme and stratagem was discussed with mock-seriousness; it was a handbook, a how-to-do-it book for the young Roman roué! At one point Ovid declared, "When it comes to love, I am no longer a civilized man, but a savage beast."

The work of Ovid was well known in the Middle Ages, but medieval values were very different from those of Augustan Rome. Even the hearty paganism of Guilhem VII was restrained by the code of chivalry and, despite his anticlericalism, by the Christian concern for the human soul. In André Chapelain's *Tractatus* the erotic element was still present, and illicit passion and elaborate strategies of seduction played an important role, but it was radically transformed by the new cult of women. In Ovid's instructions as to how to acquire and keep a lover, the male was always the dominant figure. Chapelain, at Marie de Champagne's urging, drastically altered the spirit of the original by giving women the supremacy and the power of decision. The lover was to devote all his ingenuity to pleasing her and winning her favor. The attitude of the aspiring lover toward his mistress in Chapelain's treatise parallels that of the troubadour toward his *domna* or the knights of the Arthurian legend toward their ladies.

In an age in which both extremes, unbridled sensuality and monastic asceticism, were common, and in which marriage might be based on mutual interests but very rarely on mutual attraction or affection, the complicated code of *fin 'amor* posed many problems. It was to arbitrate on these delicate matters, and in a wider sense to re-evaluate the whole relationship between men and women, that the so-called Courts of Love were held in the palace of Poitiers and in other castles further south. Nostradamus, or Jehan de Nostredame, who in 1574 published *Les Vies des Poètes Provençaux* in Aix, gave a highly romanticized account of these gatherings, making them seem more solemn and ritualistic than they actually were. On the basis of contemporary references, including letters written by Marie, it appears that all "petitioners" who had "questions of love" to raise would assemble in the Great Hall and one by one present their problem to a jury of ladies, sometimes as many as sixty, seated on a dais. Other participants in the "court" would be seated on the stone benches that ran along the walls on either side of the Hall. There were probably long horizontal strips of tapestry hung over the benches to provide "backs" to these stone seats and relieve the severity of the walls. Although the gaily clad assembly presented a colorful spectacle, there was little physical comfort by modern standards. Presiding over the panel of noblewomen were Eleanor and Marie, sometimes joined by Constance (Countess of Brittany, who was betrothed to Eleanor's son Geoffrey), Emma of Anjou (Henry II's lovely sister), Henry's natural sister Marie de France and other high-born ladies. Occasionally there would be such distinguished visitors as Ermengarde, Viscountess of Narbonne, who was about Eleanor's age and held similar gatherings in her own palace. Most of the ladies were young, between twenty-five and thirty years of age.

A typical question was whether a lover who, in defending his mistress—presumably a married lady—against slanderous tongues, had in the heat of the moment revealed her identity, should forever be banished from her presence, or whether she should "reinstate" him in her favor. The court recommended leniency, since it was the young man's ardent devotion that had led to his indiscretion.

One petitioner wanted to know whether love could survive marriage. Marie, in the spirit of Chapelain's *Treatise*, expressed her doubt that "ideal love" could ever exist between a married couple. This remark caused quite a stir. Queen Eleanor was consulted, and is quoted as saying that she could not contradict her daughter, whose "verdict" was now law, but that she would find it admirable *if* a wife were able to reconcile marriage and true love. She did not, of course, say that, having experienced two very different but equally disillusioning marriages, she could hardly be expected to have an exalted view of the institution.

Similar Courts of Love were held in Narbonne under Ermengarde, as well as in Gascony and other parts of the Midi. Troubadours would have been present, and possibly the sentiments expressed in their songs were discussed, since they dealt with these very same matters. To the modern mind these gatherings may seem to have been idle and artificial society *divertissements*, but this would be a misunderstanding of their real significance. Not only were they the ancestors of the literary salons of a much later period, but in an age of chain mail, massive stone walls and cruel punishments, an age when warfare and hunting were considered a man's proper pursuits, they contributed to a refinement of manners and a cultured spirit that spread far beyond the confines of Aquitaine and Provence.

The troubadours' ideal of love, with its combination of physical desire and chastity, a sublimated love in which the moment of consummation was constantly deferred, may seem painfully unrealistic today, and yet what the French call *l'attente amoureuse*—love's expectant waiting, the eager anticipation—was the expression of a very real and human condition unacknowledged until then and which greatly enriched the language of the emotions, especially in France. More important than any of these considerations is that in these "courts" judgments were passed independently by women on matters directly concerning them; this was a challenge not only to the whole authoritarian structure of the old-fashioned feudal system, but also to the inferior role accorded by the Church to all women except nuns— and even the nuns had less prestige than the male monastic orders (Fontevrault being the great exception). The fact that some women in these gatherings had political power of their own made their ideas seem all the more "subversive" to the upholders of feudal authority —including Eleanor's estranged husband, Henry Plantagenet.

Bernart de Ventadour's songs were in great favor at the time, but it is not known if any troubadours of comparable stature resided at Eleanor's court at Poitiers. Many must surely have passed through, as there was a great deal of traveling to various courts, shrines and towns. However, Eleanor's main interests were political. Her daughter Marie was more directly involved with poetry and literature.

Marie de Champagne contributed to the spread of the courtly ideals of Poitiers to the North and to their dissemination in the *langue d'oïl* by her patronage of the French poet Chrétien de Troyes. Like her other protégé, André Chapelain, Chrétien wrote an imitation of Ovid, but his pious spirit was even less attuned than Chapelain's to the cynical hedonism of the Roman poet. Chrétien's greatest achievements were his Arthurian romances in verse, the first important literary treatment of the Arthurian legend. It was at Marie's behest that he composed the romance of Lancelot. The haunting story of Sir Lancelot of the Lake, the gallant knight of King Arthur's court who became the lover of his sovereign's queen, Guinevere, was already well known, and through Chrétien's poem it became even more popular in the courts of France and England. It had all the elements of *l'amour courtois* with the added appeal of a very real, flesh-and-blood love affair. Chrétien de Troyes later wrote a didactic treatise, *Cligès*, in which he condemned the doctrine of a "higher love" that at Marie's bidding he had put into the Lancelot story.

The art of Eleanor's time was almost entirely at the service of religion, and whatever secular decorations there were in palaces and castles have disappeared. Except for the ivory casket mentioned previously, the earliest illustrations of the Arthurian legend, including the romance of Lancelot, appeared in 13th century manuscripts.

Sculpture and mural painting of the 12th century provide several examples of the influence of Eleanor, Marie and their friends on female fashions. Adorning the façade of the Church of Saint-Hérie

in the little township of Matha in Saintonge there is a proud and slender figure of a woman wearing a close-fitting, finely pleated dress with long sleeves falling over the wrists (Fig. 58). Her hair is plaited into long braids, of the kind which were sometimes weighted to keep them hanging straight. Similar female figures, less finely executed, are found on other Romanesque façades in Poitou and Saintonge and may possibly personify the Church. They are usually paired with the figure of a horseman. On the façade of the church at Matha only a fragment remains of an equestrian figure which is thought to represent the Emperor Constantine, as a valiant knight delivering the Church from oppression. The two grotesque animal heads beneath the pedestal on which the lady stands may symbolize heresy which has been subdued but which, like Satan, is always lying in wait to devour the faithful.

Local folklore spun legends around the "Lady of Matha." Whatever her symbolic meaning, she has the aspect of a fashionable noblewoman of Eleanor's time. The head is a later restoration, but the overall image is that of a gracious, civilized and triumphant femininity surmounting the forces of ignorance and barbarism.

A similar fashion is shown even more vividly in the figure of a female saint (Fig. 59) in a fresco in the crypt of the Church of Notre-Dame in Montmorillon, a prosperous little town on the river Gartempe, southeast of Poitiers. These murals date from the late 12th century or the earliest years of the 13th, and are in the belated Romanesque style sometimes called "Romanesque-Baroque"—a rare phenomenon in a period dominated by the Gothic. The saint is part of a scene representing the Mystic Marriage of St. Catherine. Her dress is in the style that aroused the anger of hostile clerics and chroniclers; the narrow upper body of her long garment, or *bliaud*, is laced tight, blousing around the waist to stress the belly, jutting abruptly over the hips and cascading in generous folds to the ground. She wears the same elongated sleeves as the lady in Matha, but bordered with a

Fig. 59. Saint, from a fresco of The Mystic Marriage of St. Catherine, *in the crypt of the Church of Notre-Dame, Montmorillon (Vienne), late 12th or early 13th century.*

dramatic cuff. Since she is a virgin saint, her hair is allowed to flow over her shoulders from under a little pillbox cap. Married women were expected to conceal their hair under a wimple, as hair was thought to be irresistible to the Devil, a trap in which he could be snared. This, it is said, is the reason women are required to cover their heads in churches, so that they cannot bring the Devil inside the building.

It has also been claimed that the cult of women by the troubadours and the prestige they acquired in the time of Eleanor of Aquitaine were responsible for a change in the rules of the game of chess. Hitherto the King had been the most important piece; in the 12th century the Queen became the most powerful piece on the board, with far more freedom of movement. However, the capture of the King continued to be the object of the game.

Some female fashions were even more extreme than those represented in the art of the time. The chronicler Geoffroy de Vigeois wrote of certain extravagant ladies: "You might think them adders, if you judged by the tails they drag after them." All kinds of expensive items are mentioned in the documents of the period—furs, fine clothes, handkerchiefs, jewelry, gloves, combs and little boxes for powder and cosmetics. The merchants who supplied these luxuries grew wealthy, and sumptuary laws had little effect.

The art of Eleanor's day is less helpful in revealing male fashions. Men also wore a form of the *bliaud*, a long tunic, and it is reported that the elegant attire of the Southern nobles made them seem effeminate in the eyes of the rough, bearded, unkempt and often unwashed barons of the North. The French monastic chronicler Raoul Glaber described his amazement on first seeing a company of richly dressed Provençal lords mounted on Arab steeds and carrying elaborately inlaid weapons—another example of Oriental influence. Glaber commented that "they shaved their faces and wore their hair parted," and this, he wrote, "caused them to look like mummers," or mountebanks. Geoffroy de Vigeois complained that "youths affect long hair and shoes with pointed toes." Even people of lesser rank wore "clothes fashioned of rich and precious stuffs," sometimes snipped or slashed to show the lining "so that they look like the devils that we see in paintings."

If the art of the 12th century had shown the same concern with realistic description as that of the 14th and 15th centuries, we might have a clearer idea of these colorful fashions. Henry II and his Anglo-Norman court appeared niggardly to the lavish and extravagant lords of the Midi, especially to Raymond V, Count of Toulouse, who would entertain on a magnificent scale and distribute large sums among his knights. Henry at this time was in no mood for such frivolities, and was becoming increasingly angered at the course of events in Eleanor's domains.

While campaigning in Ireland in 1171, Henry II received disturbing reports of seditious activities in the Castle of Poitiers. It was obvious that Eleanor, in addition to encouraging "subversive" ideas in the lively gatherings in the Great Hall, was playing a dangerous political game. In order to avenge her honor as wife and queen, and also to control her sons and protect them from their father's domination—Henry was an affectionate but possessive, suspicious and close-fisted parent—Eleanor had become the center of a powerful confederation.

Not only had she rallied the Counts of Lusignan and Angoulême and other disaffected vassals against Henry's rule; she had enlisted his three eldest sons, Henry, the Young King, Richard, whom his father had confirmed as hereditary Count of Poitou and Duke of Aquitaine by the Treaty of Montmirail in 1169, and Geoffrey, Count of Brittany. This rebellious coalition was supported by Henry's cousin Philip of Flanders, whose countess had visited Eleanor's court in Poitiers.

Eleanor was not motivated by personal feelings alone. She was protecting the interests of her Poitevin subjects, and she shared their love of independence. In a tactical move which must have infuriated Henry, she took advantage of the fact that as Duchess of Aquitaine she was technically Louis VII's vassal and proposed a political alliance with her former husband!

To complicate the situation still further, the Young King had been married in infancy to Louis' daughter Marguerite—this posed an additional threat to Angevin supremacy.

Henry decided that it was time to strike. In 1173 he returned to Normandy and, after promising the Church to do penance for the death of Becket, he moved south. He was determined to remove his eldest son from the pernicious influence of the court of Poitiers, where the spoiled and handsome prince had a devoted following of reckless young nobles and troubadours who sang his praises. Henry was alarmed to see in the Young King signs of *instabilitas*, the rash, impulsive, unpredictable nature of which the Poitevins and their rulers had always been accused. He compelled his son to accompany him to his castle at Chinon on the banks of the Loire. Henry would not allow the Young King out of his sight, even forcing him to occupy the same bedchamber. Young Henry escaped while his exhausted father was asleep and, instead of returning to Poitou, he went directly to the court of his father-in-law, Louis VII, in Paris.

The French king declared young Henry to be England's rightful sovereign and referred to his father as the "former King of England." Before Henry could retaliate, Eleanor sent Richard and Geoffrey into Louis' safekeeping. Louis knighted Richard and promised him and his brothers his full support against his old Plantagenet rival.

In a raging fury Henry descended on Poitou, sacking and burning the castles of rebellious vassals between Tours and Poitiers. He stormed the manor of Faye-la-Vineuse, whose lord, Raoul de Faye, was Eleanor's kinsman and trusted friend, but Raoul could not be found. Henry's scouts found a small band of Poitevin knights on their way to Paris, but Raoul was not among them. Instead, they found Eleanor in male disguise! At fifty-two this still beautiful woman had lost none of her venturesome spirit. Her escort, all members of her household, were taken prisoners. While it is not recorded, Eleanor was probably taken to the castle at Chinon until she was sent to England.

Her daughter Marie de Champagne presided over one last courtly gathering in Poitiers in the spring of 1174. At Pentecost, at the close of Eastertide, the vengeful Henry arrived at the castle and dispersed the last remnants of Eleanor's household. Marie returned to her county of Champagne, and in its capital, Troyes, continued to support Chrétien and André Chapelain. She enlivened her sober northern province with some of the gracious and festive spirit of the Poitiers court. Eleanor's niece Isabelle, Countess of Flanders, was less fortunate. One year after her return to Arras, in 1175, her husband, Philip, had one of his vassals drawn and quartered for addressing impassioned love poems to the countess. Arras, already a flourishing center of banking and trade, was no place for aspiring troubadours!

Eleanor, whose feelings for Henry had changed in the course of twenty tumultuous years from love to indifference and from indifference to active hostility, was taken to England and imprisoned in Salisbury Tower. She remained there for nearly ten years, not too strictly guarded and provided with every comfort, but with no outlet for her restless energy. Henry subdued his enemies one by one and exacted homage from his sons. The stern feudal world seemed to have triumphed.

Even if many of the events of Eleanor's life read like a novel, it would be a mistake to romanticize or idealize her. It was not a question of "good" Queen Eleanor against "bad" King Henry. They were both complex human beings in which "positive" and "negative" qualities were combined. At the very same time that Eleanor's ladies were discoursing on love with troubadours, she was plotting and counterplotting and inciting her sons against their father. It is true that she had ample provocation and that Henry played the power game with even less scruple.

Henry's rule could be considered despotic in his French territories, but in England it was on the whole beneficial, and he laid the basis for English law. He was capable of strong affections, but in human terms he and Eleanor were ill suited to each other—once the initial attraction had passed. However questionable Eleanor's political actions might appear, she represented a more subtle and civilized way of life than Henry and his barons, whose values were shaped by the feudal code.

Even if *l'amour courtois* was an unattainable ideal, the fabric of society was enriched by a greater understanding of the role of women. Never again could the doctrine of "the meaner sex" be accepted as absolute truth.

CHAPTER XV

The Rebellious Princes

HENRY II'S TROUBLES were by no means ended with the imprisonment of Eleanor, and the baronial revolt of 1173 had dealt his
Anglo-Angevin empire a blow from which it never quite recovered.
His son Henry the Young King had joined the rebellion because in
spite of his title he was allowed no power and an inadequate revenue.
Having crushed the revolt, Henry II could afford to be magnanimous
and in a treaty signed in 1174 he gave his sons generous terms. Eleanor and Louis were blamed for all the unrest. The Young King was
granted an annual stipend and two castles of Henry's choosing;
Richard was pardoned and reinstated as Count of Poitou and Duke
of Aquitaine, and Geoffrey was confirmed as heir to the Duchy
of Brittany. Nevertheless, Henry continued to keep a close watch on
the Young King, whom he dearly loved but whose character gave
him cause for alarm.

Henry Fitz Henry, the Young King, was also called Henry Curtmantle because of the short cloak he often wore. He was handsome
and charming, with all the personal fascination of the Poitevin side of
his family. His openhandedness won him many friends, but one
chronicler observed that "he was less generous than prodigal." He
attracted an enthusiastic following of young knights, some of whom

were willing to serve him without pay for the honor of being associated with his exploits in jousting and war, although these feats were greatly exaggerated by his admirers. Troubadours who enjoyed his patronage praised him as the flower of chivalry; this was not self-serving flattery, for they were genuinely dazzled by his fair outward appearance. Yet he was unstable, fickle and often treacherous, and the chronicler William of Newburgh described him as "a restless youth born for many men's undoing." Young Henry continued to intrigue with Louis VII, and many of his actions were motivated by his jealousy of his younger brother Richard, who surpassed him in strength and daring and who, as ruling Count-Duke of Poitou and Aquitaine, had far more political power and greater revenues.

Richard, the future Coeur de Lion, was only seventeen in 1174, three years younger than his brother Henry. He had grown to manhood very quickly and was fully prepared to exercise his authority—which he did with more energy than wisdom. Although Richard and his father were often in conflict, they seem to have had genuine mutual affection, and he was always Eleanor's favorite. He resembled his father in his sturdy build and florid complexion, and also in the violence of his temper when aroused, but he had more physical grace and charm. Richard lacked Henry II's abilities as an administrator, and while his exceptional bravery and strength won him the nickname the Lion-Hearted, he could be ruthless in warfare and capable of acts of needless cruelty. His most attractive qualities were his love of poetry, music and romance. He had grown up in the stimulating atmosphere of Eleanor's court, and his literary tastes had been formed at an early age by his mother and his half sister Marie de Champagne. His own lyrics, written in the *langue d'oïl* with Marie's encouragement, show real poetic gifts. He also composed in the Poitevin dialect, and his strongest attachments, like those of Eleanor, were always with his county of Poitou.

Richard considered himself one of the brotherhood of troubadours. Like his elder brother, but with somewhat more justification, he became the hero of poets and romancers, even if in reality he was far from being the embodiment of the virtues of chivalry. With all his faults Richard was the most gifted, accomplished and versatile male member of this extraordinary family.

In 1175 Richard distinguished himself by crushing a formidable revolt by disaffected vassals in Poitou, the Limousin and Aquitaine. These nobles had hoped that Richard would uphold their interests instead of acting on behalf of the English king, and they resented Richard's despotic rule. Aided by Henry II's mercenaries, Richard scored a series of rapid victories over the Count of Angoulême, the Viscounts of Limoges and Ventadour and other rebellious lords, and even exacted homage from the Count of Toulouse.

Richard was so powerful that young Henry became seriously alarmed and demanded, as heir apparent to the English throne, that Richard, as Duke of Aquitaine, pay him homage. Richard scornfully rejected this irrational demand, and a fratricidal war ensued. Young Henry, allied with his brother Geoffrey, put himself at the head of the rebellious vassals in a desperate effort to dispossess Richard of his duchy of Aquitaine.

The Anglo-Angevin empire was threatened as never before. To add to King Henry's woes, the ineffectual Louis VII died in 1180, after a rule of forty-two years, and was succeeded by his son, Philip II Augustus, a man of very different caliber. Philip was destined to become one of the greatest of the Capetian kings: he was determined to take full advantage of Plantagenet weaknesses and, if possible, to gain the English possessions in France for himself.

By the spring of 1182 the feud between the brothers had become so fierce that there was every likelihood of King Henry's taking the field in aid of Richard. Young Henry persisted in his reckless course. Among the many nobles he rallied to his banner was one who gloried in the clash of arms and bloody encounters of the battlefield—the troubadour Bertran de Born.

CHAPTER XVI

A Warrior-Troubadour: Bertran de Born

Bertran de Born belonged to the petty nobility. In his outlook he was more the daredevil soldier of fortune than the chivalrous aristocrat. He was not a viscount, as erroneously stated in his biography. He was born around 1140 in the modest manor of Born de Salignac, on the confines of Périgord and the Limousin, near the valley of the Dordogne. His birthplace is now in ruins. By marrying into the Limousin family of Lastours, Bertran and his brother Constantin came into possession of the Castle of Hautefort, which had been built by the Lastours in the previous century. Bertran married the sister of the Viscount of Lastours, and Constantin married the daughter, which gave him the stronger claim to the castle. But Bertran found it intolerable to share the seigniory with his younger brother and they became bitter rivals. Finally Bertran drove Constantin out of Hautefort. In a poem he stated that while he would willingly share his last penny or even an egg with a kinsman, he would never surrender what was rightfully his. Constantin bore his grudge and planned his revenge, but Bertran became sole lord of Hautefort.

Hautefort, as its name suggests, was a powerful fortress, but it was

[*192*]

not the center of an important seigniory, nor was it a source of revenue. As Bertran complained some years later:

> No Lusignan or Rancom do I own,
> To have the means to fight in far-off lands.

He was to find many outlets for his bellicose inclinations nearer home, and an illustration in the troubadour manuscript in Paris shows him most appropriately on horseback and in full armor (Fig. 60).

One of the few remaining traces of the original Castle of Hautefort that Bertran knew is part of a Romanesque column with a lozenge pattern embedded in the wall of the handsome 17th century château near the postern gate (Fig. 61). The château, with its domes, Baroque towers and vast court of honor, commands a splendid view of the valley of the Auvézène.

It is not known when Bertran de Born began to compose poetry or where he learned the art of *trobar*, widespread throughout the Midi at the time of his birth. Of all forms of troubadour poetry, the topical *sirventès* was best suited to his forceful, concrete and realistic style. His few love poems, though not without interest, are somewhat brusque and perfunctory. War, or the possibility of war, inspired his most eloquent verses. His preoccupation with this violent theme was due partly to an enjoyment of battle for its own sake, partly to his

Fig. 60. Bertran de Born. Bibl. Nat. MS Fr. 12473, fol. 160. (Bibliothèque Nationale, Paris)

Fig. 61. Romanesque column preserved in the wall of the entrance facade of the chateau of Hautefort (Dordogne), the sole remains of Bertran de Born's 12th century castle. (Photograph by Sue Marks)

constant need of money and partly to his desire to settle personal grievances. Gifted and colorful though he was, he is the least likable of the troubadours.

Bertran differed from barons of his type in the North in two respects—in his poetic talents and in his admiration for the reckless, extravagant generosity and festive display of the southern lords, a style of living he himself could not afford but welcomed in others. He used the troubadour term *largueza* to describe this liberality, opposing it to *cobeïtat*, meaning miserliness and greed, and he equated this carefree lavishness with *joi* and its inseparable companion *joven*, youth. Bertran used the words "young" and "old" symbolically, not to describe chronological age. "I hold him to be young when he spends generously on his guests; very young when he commits sweet extravagances. Young when he burns his chests and cupboards, young when he wants to hold court and combats; young when he wants to gamble lavishly; and very young when he knows well how to woo the ladies."

The "old" man, according to Bertran, was the very opposite, the incarnation of cold-blooded avarice and egotism. He wrote that he is "old when he wants to stay one day without fighting, old when he can slip away without paying."

These were typical exaggerations, but in their flamboyant way expressed an ideal of generosity and independence that Bertran found lacking outside the Midi.

Before becoming actively involved in politics and warfare, Bertran, according to his 14th century biographer, fell in love with a lady named Maheut de Montagnac, daughter of the Viscount of Turenne. Maheut was married to Talairau, brother of the Count of Périgord, and her sister was the troubadour Marie de Ventadour, of whose work practically nothing remains. Bertran's love songs have none of the subtlety and tenderness of those of Bernart de Ventadour; one always senses the rough chain mail under the long tunic. However, his verses describing Maheut's charms are a little more specific than is usual in troubadour poetry and have a lively rhyming pattern. He addresses the poem to "Rassa," which is either an imaginary name for the lady or, it has been suggested, a pseudonym for Geoffrey, Count of Brittany.

> *Rassa, domna es frescha e fina*
> *Coinda e gaia e meschina;*
> *Pel saur ab color de robina*
> *Blancha pel corps com flors d'espina.*

> Rassa, my lady is sprightly and fair,
> Gracious and gay, in the pride of her youth,
> Her rosy complexion a joy to behold,
> Her body as white as the hawthorn flower,
> Her dimpled elbow, her breasts so firm,
> Her shoulder as smooth and soft as down,
> Her coloring fresh and delicate;
> I praise her worth and her high renown.
> He who my verses understands
> Will easily know what I most adore.

This does not mean that he was actually her lover, but the ladies enjoyed the most daring compliments and were very free in their speech, however circumspect in their actions. Bertran rejoiced in the fact that, although Maheut had been courted by such wealthy and powerful princes as Richard, Count of Poitou, Raymond V of Toulouse and King Alfonso II of Aragon, she rejected them all to favor him, an indigent baron:

She craves not Poitiers nor Toulouse
Nor Brittany nor Aragon,
But worthily bestows her love
Upon a poor and valiant knight.

He implies that a great lord would enjoy her love only to dishonor her. Bertran's devotion to Maheut did not prevent him from singing the praises of another lady, Guicharde de Comborn, in the Limousin, whom he called "melhz-de-bé"—"better than good." This led to a quarrel with Maheut; but they were later reconciled by yet a third recipient of Bertran's verses, Tibour de Montausier, a chatelaine of Saintonge. Obviously his emotional attachments to women were not very deep, and his love poems were more a pastime than a vocation. His truly personal expression was the *sirventès*, which he made into a potent propaganda weapon, wielded with little scruple and often fatal results.

Bertran's earliest-known *sirventès* dates from 1181 and was addressed to Raymond V, Count of Toulouse, who exemplified the qualities he admired and who welcomed troubadours at his court. At that time Toulouse was being threatened by an alliance of the King of Aragon and some of the chief lords of Languedoc. Bertran wrote a strident *sirventès*, urging Raymond to battle, describing tents and standards in martial array and implying that he himself was eager to join the count's army. This was largely bluster and a way of bringing himself to Raymond's attention, for Bertran had urgent matters to attend to nearer home.

His brother Constantin, driven out of Hautefort, had appealed to the Viscount of Limoges and to Richard as Duke of Aquitaine and had won them to his cause. Richard and his forces laid siege to Hautefort and pillaged the surrounding country. Hautefort was impregnable, and Richard soon abandoned Constantin—in the kind of *volte-face* which won him the nickname Richard Yea-and-Nay.

It was partly to be revenged on Richard for this attack that Bertran embraced the cause of the Young King. Moreover, young Henry, handsome, affable, headstrong and generous to the point of prodigality, seemed the very embodiment of Bertran's ideal of gallantry.

In a series of fiery *sirventès* sung throughout the Dordogne and Limousin by his jongleur Papiols—whose name suggests that he may have been of Catalonian origin—Bertran set out to win the ear of the

Young King by inciting him into war against his brother and, if need be, his father. He taunted him for having a fine title but no wealth or power, and exalted the thrill and excitement of battle. Bertran's most famous poem on this bloodthirsty motif begins with what appears to be the conventional praise of spring, but soon changes key:

> I love the merry Eastertide
> With leaves and flowers in bloom.
> I love to hear the joyous sound
> Of birds whose melodies are sung
> > Through many a wooded grove.
> I love to see in proud array
> Tents and pavilions on the plain
> > And I rejoice to see
> Drawn up in ranks on either side
> Knights and their steeds in arms.

In the fourth stanza Bertran describes the clash of armies in clangorous rhythms reminiscent of the old *chansons de geste*:

> Maces and brands and painted helms,
> Escutcheons hacked and stabbed with holes,
> All this we'll see when battle joins,
> And many a baron trading blows.
> > Horses in panic flee.
> Their masters dead or wounded lie,
> And in the fury of the fray
> > Each valiant-hearted knight
> Takes savage toll of heads and limbs,
> Preferring death to life in chains.

The heraldic vividness of Bertran's imagery has been compared to the battle scenes of Paolo Uccello, except that Uccello's warriors and their horses are as stylized as chessmen and have no real blood flowing! Bertran longed to provoke the lords into fighting one another; the thought of war gave him more delight than "eating, drinking and sleeping," and he believed that the great nobles were especially generous with gifts and favors in wartime. He ended this *sirventès* with an exhortation:

> Barons, I bid you pledge
> Your castles, towns and cities too,
> Stay not at home in craven peace!
>
> Papiols, go with speed
> And tell Sir Yea-and-Nay [Richard]
> That peace has lasted far too long.

The only comparable glorification of war can be found in the bombastic rhetoric of Marinetti and the Italian Futurists in their manifesto of 1909, in which war was praised as "the only health giver of the world," by people who themselves had never experienced it! It was natural that Ezra Pound, whose truculence matched that of Bertran de Born and who later supported Mussolini's fascism, should have chosen this poem as the basis for one of his extremely free adaptations from the Provençal, the "Sestina: Altaforte," which is a brilliant elaboration of the original rather than a translation. "Altaforte" is the Italian form of Hautefort, Bertran's castle. Pound's version begins:

> Damn it all! All this our South stinks peace.
> You whoreson dog, Papiols, come! Let's to music!
> I have no life save when the swords clash.

Bertran's songs appealed to the Young King's pride and made him even more defiant and demanding. It is not known when and where he and Bertran met, but they were both present at a Christmas court held by Henry II at Caen in Normandy, in December 1182, in a final effort to make peace between his feuding sons. While at Caen, Bertran abandoned his martial manner to pay court in verse to Henry's daughter, Princess Matilda, whose husband, Henry the Lion, Duke of Saxony and Bavaria, was then on a pilgrimage to Santiago de Compostela. It would appear that, after the Christmas court had dispersed, Bertran followed Matilda to Argentan, another of Henry II's Norman castles, but the princess gave him little encouragement.

In a pique Bertran wrote a poem attacking what he chose to call the "niggardliness" and dullness of Henry's palace. He declared that a court without merry conversation and laughter and without largesse was "no better than a baron's warren" and that only the presence of Saïssa (the Saxon, meaning Matilda) had saved him from dying of depression amid "the boredom and meanness of Argentan." "We in Limousin," he wrote, "prefer folly before wisdom and are by nature gay and fond of lavish living and laughter."

Even Henry II's most generous offers failed to satisfy the Young King's ambition, and Bertran continued to pour out his inflammatory *sirventès*. Young Henry had sworn allegiance to his father, but after the Lenten truce of 1183 he joined his brother Geoffrey in Brittany and some rebellious vassals in a renewed attack on Richard's domains. They began to lay waste the countryside in Quercy and the Limousin. In grief and anger Henry II had no choice but to support Richard.

Young Henry's most spectacular exploit in his futile campaign was a raid on the rocky heights of Rocamadour in the Dordogne (Fig. 62). Rocamadour was a hallowed place of pilgrimage, famous throughout the Middle Ages for its miraculous Black Virgin and for the great iron sword of Roland, called Durandal. According to legend, Roland had vowed his sword to the Virgin of Rocamadour when he went to Roncevaux (although the statue did not then exist). Today a replica of Roland's sword is set in the rock wall near the "Holy of Holies" of Rocamadour, the chapel of Our Lady housing the miraculous statue. The original sword was taken by the English in the 14th century and was never recovered.

Pilgrimages to Rocamadour had begun early in the 12th century. The body of a small man was discovered there by some monks, who declared it to be the body of Zacchaeus, the "little friend of Christ." According to a local tradition, Zacchaeus had escorted the three Marys to Provence, and afterward had come to these lonely heights to devote himself to a life of prayer to the Blessed Virgin's memory. Zacchaeus was also known as Amadour, the spiritual lover of Mary, and Rocamadour was the rock-bound shrine where his relics were preserved.

Thousands of pilgrims made their way up the tortuous, steep paths of Rocamadour to the shrine at its summit, drawn not only by the venerated remains of Zacchaeus but also by the miracle-working power of the Black Virgin, a primitive statue, possibly carved by a

Above: Fig. 62. Rocamadour (Lot).
(Reportage Photographique YAN)

Left: Fig. 63. Lead medallion given to
pilgrims at Rocamadour.

village artisan. Pilgrims who had climbed the steep and narrow steps to the shrine, often on their knees, were given an oblong lead medallion (Fig. 63) with the image of the hallowed Madonna, which they added to their pilgrim's cloak for the return journey. Many illustrious visitors, including Bernard of Clairvaux, came to Rocamadour as pilgrims.

In 1159 Henry II, accompanied by Thomas à Becket, then his intimate friend, had paid homage to the Virgin and had been reputedly cured of an illness. Twenty-four years later young Henry Curtmantle had come on a very different mission. Rocamadour had become immensely wealthy with the offerings of thousands of pilgrims, and the desperate prince looted the shrines in order to pay his *routiers* —his rowdy, rapacious foot soldiers who were little more than brigands. It was reported that as he was leaving Rocamadour after raiding its treasures the great iron bell of the chapel miraculously began to toll.

This was surely a sign from God. As he rode with his companions-in-arms to Brive in the blazing June sunshine, he was suddenly seized with a violent fever, and he was carried to the peaceful little town of Martel, in the heart of the Limousin. The pious were convinced that his sacrilege had brought retribution on the Young King.

In Martel, the "town of seven towers," the Young King was taken to the house of a citizen, Etienne Fabri, which still exists. Feeling that death was upon him and stricken with remorse, young Henry confessed his crimes to two priests who had hurried to his bedside. Messages were sent to his father to ask his forgiveness.

Henry II was then preparing to besiege Limoges, whose viscount had joined the rebel forces. He was deeply distressed at the news of his son's illness, but was dissuaded from visiting him for fear of conspiracy. Instead he sent a precious sapphire ring as a sign of his forgiveness. The messengers arrived to find Henry Curtmantle lying in agony on a bed of cinders, a heavy wooden cross over his breast. He kissed the ring and put it on his finger. The priests, thinking of the dying prince's salvation, exhorted him to renounce all worldly possessions. At first he refused to part with the ring, saying that he valued it, not for its worth or for any frivolous reason, but as a proof on the Day of Judgment "that my father has restored me to the fullness of his grace." Then he agreed to give it up, but the monk was unable to remove it from his finger, and this was seen as a sign of divine mercy.

Young Henry sent a farewell message to his mother, Eleanor, still a prisoner in far-off England, and bade his followers see to the welfare of his young wife, Marguerite, then living in exile at the French court. Willful, thoughtless and hotheaded though he was, the death of the handsome young prince in June 1183 was bitterly regretted by his father and by all who had known him.

There is no record that Bertran de Born was at the deathbed of young Henry. According to his biographer, the poet withdrew in sorrow to his castle of Hautefort. When Henry II, torn between rage and grief, came with his men-at-arms to attack him, Bertran realized that resistance was useless and surrendered, expecting to be put to death. But first he asked to sing a *planh*, a lament, he had composed for young Henry, and the King was so moved by its beauty and by Bertran's deep attachment to his beloved and wayward son that he forgave him and restored his castle to him.

This funeral elegy for the Young King is considered Bertran's most perfect work. It is impossible to do justice in English to its stately cadences, as solemn as a funeral march, and to the impact of certain repetitions, such as the word *marriment*—grief, distress—at the end of the first line of each stanza. Here at least is the rhythm and meaning of the second stanza:

> Mournful and sad and full of grievous woe,
> They weep for him, the gallant men-at-arms,
> The jongleurs and the comely troubadours.
> They found in death a deadly warrior;
> He bore away the fair young English king
> Whose bounty made the gifts of others small,
> No tears, no fury in this cursèd age
> Can ever with this misery compare.

Bertran laments the passing of "*del mon lo plus valens del pros*"— "the bravest of the world's most valiant knights"—and urges others to model themselves on the Young King, advice hardly conducive to the peace of the realm!

Not long after the prince's untimely death, Bertran made his peace with Richard, who became heir to England and Normandy and had, after all, many of the fighting qualities he admired. From then on Bertran spent most of his time in his castle of Hautefort, lamenting the decline of chivalry and liberality among the great lords of Limousin.

As with many troubadours, the facts of Bertran's public life are scarce. After Henry II's death at Chinon in 1189 and Richard's accession to the English throne, Bertran, in a rousing *sirventès*, tried to stir up war between Richard and the French king, Philip Augustus. But this was largely rhetoric, as Bertran was in middle age and had no intention of leaving Hautefort, where he was comfortably settled with his second wife and several children. He taunted Philip for being an unworthy heir of Charlemagne, a lamb to Richard's lion, and hurled insults at Alfonso II of Aragon, who held territory in Provence.

There have been attempts to present Bertran as the heroic champion of the liberty of the Midi against French, English and Aragonese domination, but he was inspired more by adventurism and opportunism. Warfare for him, when he chose to take part, was a source of excitement, pageantry, personal advantage and stirring poetic imagery, not a matter of principle.

Bertran wrote no poems after 1194, and like a very different troubadour, Bernart de Ventadour, ended his days in the monastery of Dalon—whether from religious conviction or sheer exhaustion is not known. He became a monk in the abbey before 1197 and died there in 1215.

Bertran's pious end did not redeem him in the eyes of Dante, who, in spite of his own debt to troubadour poetry, placed him in the eighth circle of Hell in his *Inferno* for having incited a son against the authority of his father. John Ciardi's translation goes:

> I saw it there: I seem to see it still—
>   a body without a head that moved along
>   like all the others in that spew and spill.
>
> It held the severed head by its own hair,
>   swinging it like a lantern in its hand,
>   and the head looked at us and wept in despair.

Then the "unquiet spirit" reveals its identity:

> When you return to the world, remember me,
>   I am Bertran de Born, and it was I
>   Who set the young king on to mutiny,
>
> Son against father, father against son
>   As Achitophel set Absalom and David,
>   and since I parted those who should be one

in duty and in love, I bear my brain
    divided from its source within this trunk
    and walk here where my evil turns to pain.

an eye for an eye to all eternity:
thus is the law of Hell observed in me.

CHAPTER XVII

The Plantagenet Empire in Decline

T HE DEATH OF THE YOUNG KING did not end the woes of the Plantagenets. Henry II decided to redistribute the lands he had rashly bestowed on his sons at Montmirail. Unwilling to see the new heir apparent, Richard, grow too powerful, Henry invited him to renounce Poitou and Aquitaine in favor of the youngest of the princes, John, on whom Henry now placed his fondest hopes. Richard was strongly attached to the southern provinces where he had spent his youth; the duchy of Normandy, of which he was the heir, had no appeal for him, and England, whose throne would one day be his, was always a foreign country to him and no more than a useful source of revenue.

Richard temporized, and took the fateful step of seeking the help of Philip Augustus, the Plantagenets' archenemy. To counter this move, Henry, whose judgment was increasingly erratic, bestowed Richard's possessions on Eleanor, ending her long captivity. By this double ploy he hoped to humble Richard and appease his wife. Richard yielded, but from that time on became his father's bitter enemy. Eleanor, sixty-two years old and as strong-minded as ever, could hardly feel gratitude toward her jailer. She gave Richard her full support. Henry II was ill and prematurely aged; he had grown corpulent over the years and had difficulty mounting his horse. Richard's forces were powerful, and Henry was chased ignominiously from Le Mans to Angers and forced to buy peace by granting all that was demanded of him. Richard insisted that he be recognized immediately as his father's successor.

The old king's repeated defeats and the prospect of utter disaster aggravated his ailing condition, but his heart was broken by the discovery that John, on whose behalf he had alienated Richard, was in secret league with his enemies. Henry had predicted earlier: "My sons will never give me peace." On June 26, 1189, in his castle at Chinon, the great Henry Plantagenet died attended only by his illegitimate son Geoffrey, who was a priest and who administered the last rites. Richard arrived in time for his burial at Fontevrault, where Henry's effigy now lies (Fig. 64). The new King of England knelt at his father's bier in respectful silence.

Under Richard I's rule, Eleanor again became a political personage of the highest importance. Her influence on Richard caused him to reverse his father's autocratic policies in Poitou and Aquitaine, but the people there never believed that he had their interests at heart. But the popularity that Eleanor still enjoyed in those territories was most valuable to Richard, and she acted as regent in England during his long absences on the Third Crusade. In his entire reign Richard spent little more than six months in England, and it is ironic that he should have become one of England's national heroes.

Fig. 64. Tomb of Henry II of England in Fontevrault Abbey. This figure, carved between 1189 and 1199, is not a true portrait. Henry was clean-shaven, thickset and obese in his later years.

Even during his lifetime Richard was a favorite hero of poetry and romance. While on his journey home from the Holy Land, Richard was seized by Leopold, Duke of Austria, whose hatred he had incurred during the Crusade, and he was held prisoner for two years in the Castle of Dürenstein on the Danube. There may be some foundation for the story, which first occurred in a French romantic chronicle of the 13th century, that during his imprisonment his location was discovered by his favorite minstrel, Blondel de Nesle. According to the tale, Blondel, wandering through Germany and Austria, sang a song known only to himself and his lost master as he passed by the Castle of Dürenstein. Richard answered him with the subsequent stanzas of the song, and because of this Blondel was able to tell the English where their king was held captive. Richard's own compositions were mostly in the *langue d'oïl*, and Blondel was a Northerner.

Eleanor helped to frustrate a conspiracy against Richard which Prince John, the most treacherous of all the brothers, had launched with Philip Augustus during his brother's captivity. After Richard's return from imprisonment in 1194, Eleanor reconciled the King and the prince in order to save the succession for John.

Richard made a token visit to England, then left that country in charge of a trusted deputy, the prelate Hubert Walter, who had raised the ransom that obtained Richard's release from imprisonment and in return had been made Archbishop of Canterbury. To the great satisfaction of Bertran de Born, who could never get enough of war, although he rarely participated in the actual combat, Richard then devoted all of his energies to making war on Philip Augustus. He had increasing difficulty in raising funds for his campaign.

In 1199 a claim to a treasure trove embroiled him with the Viscount of Limoges. Richard invaded the Limousin, to besiege the Castle of Chalus. While directing the assault he was wounded in the shoulder by a bolt from a crossbow shot from the ramparts. Through neglect or unskillful treatment, gangrene developed, and Richard died of his wound on March 26, 1199, aged forty-two. His last act was a magnanimous one, in keeping with his reputation for chivalry. The young Limousin soldier responsible for the fatal bolt was captured and brought before the dying king. The youth, who was of lowly origin, explained that Richard's campaign had been the cause of the deaths of his own father and brother. Richard forgave him, bidding him go in peace and adding, "By my bounty behold the light of day." In his last moments Richard confessed to his chaplain that he had betrayed his father to the French king and asked that as a sign of his remorse he should be buried at Henry's feet in the crypt at Fontevrault.

In spite of his preference for the *langue d'oïl*, Richard did not neglect the Occitan troubadours. Among those he patronized was Gaucelm Faidit, a prolific poet who was also a protégé of Marie de Ventadour. The *planh* composed by Faidit on Richard's death is more conventional in style than Bertran de Born's lament for the Young King—but Faidit paid sincere homage to the ideal of chivalry symbolized by the glamorous Coeur de Lion, whatever his disastrous shortcomings as a king:

> Ah God! the valorous Richard, England's king
> Is dead. What sorrow and what grievous loss . . .

> Of all the bravest knights he was the first . . .
> A thousand years will never see his peer.

> Not Charlemagne, men who love truth will say,
> Nor Arthur e'er outmatched his valiant deeds.

CHAPTER XVIII

Eleanor's Last Years

RICHARD COEUR DE LION captured the imagination of many of his contemporaries, but the people of Poitou had little cause to regret his sudden death. He had been more concerned with his fame and his place in history than with the welfare of his subjects. Even judged by the standards of medieval chivalry, Richard's great adversary, the Moslem ruler Saladin, had a more admirable character.

Richard's death was a terrible blow for Eleanor. Her son Geoffrey, Duke of Brittany, had died in Paris three years before while negotiating with Philip Augustus. During Richard's captivity she had written to Pope Celestine II: "I have lost the staff of my old age, the light of my eyes. . . . My posterity has been snatched from me." She was seventy-seven, an astonishing age for the period, but she was to have no rest. She had arranged the marriage of Richard to Berengaria, the Princess of Navarre, but there had been no heirs.

Her one surviving son, John, became King of England. At an early age he had been given the nickname Lackland because, unlike his elder brothers, he had been left out of Henry II's division of the royal dominions. His father had always shown him great indulgence. He had been given scattered possessions in England and France, and in 1185 had been sent to govern Ireland. This was a calamity, and some of John's worst faults were revealed—his insolence, his treachery, his ingratitude to loyal supporters and his underlying cynicism. He lacked neither energy nor intelligence, but his actions were invariably ill considered and ill timed. Though shrewd in small matters, he had no breadth of vision or real competence. His capacity for cruel vindictiveness was not then apparent—it would later shock even that far from tenderhearted age. John's mismanagement of Ireland was so obvious that he was soon recalled. Before long John deserted his father to aid the rebelling Richard, and after Richard's departure for the Crusades, John changed allegiance again and conspired with King Philip to supplant Richard on the English throne. Richard generously pardoned his brother when he returned from his captivity in Austria, and they lived on fairly amicable terms for the next five years.

Whatever Eleanor's apprehensions were about John's character, she supported his claims to the English throne on Richard's death. It is a tribute to Eleanor's restraining influence that John at first acted with prudence and diplomacy in Poitou and Aquitaine. He flattered the local barons and extended their powers, and he granted franchises to Poitou, Niort, Saintes and other important cities, hoping to win the loyalty of the rising bourgeoisie and the common people. Eleanor made sure that special favor was shown to Poitiers. The city was made into a free commune and in 1200 was given its first mayor. The last remnants of serfdom were abolished as Eleanor decreed that even the lowliest of peasants could marry those of their own choosing, instead of a spouse selected or approved by their overlord. This was revolutionary. Everyone settling in the city could enjoy the same freedoms as its residents—these provisions remained in force even after Poitou passed to the French monarchy.

The old queen's strength was failing, but she began the new century with an act that had great consequences. Over twenty-five years earlier, Eleanor had married her daughter of the same name to King Alfonso VIII of Castile. The young Eleanor, known in Spain as Leonora, was very young when she arrived in Castile, but she must have brought something of the culture and intellect of her mother's court with her. Alfonso, an able ruler who had restored order in his kingdom after the chaos of the preceding reign, founded the first university in Spain at Palencia, and his luxurious court, under his young queen's influence, became a center for poetry, music and courtly ritual. Both the *langue d'oc* and Castilian Spanish were spoken. A visiting troubadour, the Catalonian Raimon Vidal de Besalù, described a gallant assembly of knights, barons and jongleurs at Alfonso's court as "Queen Leonore" entered:

> In rich red mantle modestly arrayed,
> Its silver border wrought with golden lions . . .

After bowing to the King, she took her place at his side.

The Castilian marriage had prospered and eight children were born. Eleanor resolved to arrange the marriage of one of her Castilian granddaughters to the son of the old foe of the Plantagenets, Philip Augustus, and thus settle the long enmity between France and England. In the winter of 1199, despite her advanced age, Eleanor undertook the strenuous journey through Gascony, across the Pyrenees to Castile. She arrived at Burgos, its capital, in January 1200. Leonora was then a gracious woman of middle age, and the reunion was a happy one. It was a joy for Eleanor to find something of the cultivated atmosphere she had not experienced since Henry II dispersed her court in Poitiers over a quarter of a century earlier.

Eleanor did not choose the eldest princess, Urraca, but her equally beautiful younger sister, Blanche, to accompany her back to France. Some claimed that this was because the name Urraca would sound harsh and strange to French ears, but Eleanor, an astute judge of character, seemed to have sensed the greater strength of purpose in the fifteen-year-old Blanche. Shortly after the arrival of the royal party in France, Blanche was married to Philip Augustus' son, Louis Capet, the future Louis VIII.

As Blanche of Castile, the domineering mother of Louis IX—St. Louis—she was destined to make her mark in history, but her authoritarian, narrowly pious character was to help to create a world drastically different from that envisioned by Eleanor in her great days at Poitiers—a world which would eventually bring about the destruction of Provençal civilization.

Another important royal marriage, that of John himself, took place later that year under very different circumstances, which revealed John's devious and unpredictable nature. His twelve-year marriage to Isabella of Gloucester had been childless. The union was dissolved after John's coronation without any protest from Isabella.

While in Bordeaux with his court, John was invited to Lusignan to attend the festivities celebrating the betrothal of another Isabella, the daughter of Adémar, Count of Angoulême, to Hugues IX, the Brown, Count of Lusignan. John had won over his often troublesome vassal, Hugues of Lusignan, by giving him the county of Marche, and their relations at that time were good.

When John saw Isabella he was so violently attracted to her that he secretly resolved to marry her himself. In addition, it was to his advantage to prevent an alliance between two such powerful lords as the Counts of Angoulême and Lusignan. Marriage with Isabella would give him direct control over the Angoumois.

After sending the chief members of the Lusignan family on various missions in different directions, John went to Angoulême, where Isabella was visiting her father the count in preparation for her marriage. John had brought with him the Archbishop of Bordeaux and he ordered the astonished prelate to marry him then and there to Isabella. The archbishop did not dare refuse, and the proud and ambitious Isabella was apparently quite willing to exchange the coronet of a countess for a royal crown. John took his bride first to Normandy and then to London, where she was crowned in Westminster in October 1200.

Eleanor was not overjoyed at this maneuver, conducted without her knowledge. She feared its consequences. Nevertheless, she accepted John's second queen with good grace and gave her the cities of Niort and Saintes as a dowry.

John's trickery caused a general uproar, and the enraged Poitevin nobles appealed to John's titular suzerain in France, Philip Augustus. Philip ordered the confiscation of John's French territories in favor of young Arthur, Duke of Brittany, the English king's nephew. War broke out, and John seemed at first to have the better of his adversaries.

Arthur was defeated and captured. He was murdered in Rouen in 1203 at John's instigation. This ruined John's cause in Normandy and Anjou. All were convinced of his guilt in the death of the young prince, and the future of the Plantagenets had never looked more ominous.

Eleanor, weary of the struggle, retired to Fontevrault. She was over eighty, and her long, arduous pilgrimage was drawing to an end. Bertran de Born, in one of his last *sirventès*, refers to *"la vielha reina d'Englaterra,"* the old queen of England, who owned "Font Ebrau"—an abbey *"on si rendon totas la vielhas richas,"* where all old ladies of high rank retire. Eleanor died in March 1204, in her

eighty-third year. Her tomb, with its noble Gothic effigy (Fig. 65),
lies in the cool choir of the abbey church, between her second husband, Henry Plantagenet, and her beloved son, Richard the Lion-
Hearted.

The splendid *gisant*, or reclining tomb figure, of Eleanor was
carved very shortly after her death and gives the impression of being
a portrait, far more than the effigy of Henry II with its generalized
features. The Queen is shown in her later years, but the face, framed
by the wimple, has an ageless beauty and serenity, and radiates
intelligence and dignity—the *franc vis*, or noble countenance, once
sung of by Bernart de Ventadour—and there is the faint suggestion
of a smile. The drapery on the gracefully elongated figure is arranged
in ornamental folds, but the most unusual detail of the statue is the
little open book that Eleanor holds in her hands. It may have been
intended as a prayer book. Some have imagined it to be a book of
poems, but this is too romantic an interpretation. In the spring of
1973, a symposium on the court of Eleanor of Aquitaine was held in
Austin, Texas, attended by delegates from many countries, and there
the historian Elizabeth Brown suggested that in view of Eleanor's

*Fig. 65. Tomb statues of Eleanor of Aquitaine and Richard Coeur de Lion in
Fontevrault Abbey. (Archives Photographiques)*

lifelong interest in political power, she could well be studying the Book of Kings! We can never know all the secrets and all the facets of this extraordinary woman, whose death marked the end of a great era.

The sensitive features of Richard's effigy—how close a likeness one cannot tell—are more those of a troubadour than of the warrior-king who fought the Saracens.

With the death of Eleanor, John lost his only source of support in lands where he was regarded as a cruel and unscrupulous usurper. After occupying Normandy, Anjou, Maine and Touraine, Philip Augustus made his triumphal entry into Eleanor's old capital of Poitiers on August 10, 1204. He annexed most of Poitou to the French royal domain. Aquitaine, with its capital, Bordeaux, remained in English hands. The results of Eleanor's divorce from Louis and marriage to Henry Plantagenet had been all but wiped out by Louis' wily, patient and determined son, Philip Augustus.

Philip's victory over John and his allies ten years later at Bouvines was a deadly blow to the Anglo-Angevin empire and laid the foundations for a unified France. The Occitan lords who once dreamed of a glorious Southern federation between Richard Coeur de Lion, Raymond VI of Toulouse and Peter II of Aragon—all generous patrons of the troubadours—found their hopes destroyed. They feared a very different future, dominated by the strategy of the French king in Paris and the Pope in Rome. Southern independence, and with it the rich and varied troubadour culture, would soon face its deadliest challenge.

CHAPTER XIX

Conflicts in Provence

COMPARED TO THE TURMOIL in Poitou and Aquitaine, Provence in the second half of the 12th century was relatively peaceful. It was not an unbroken calm; there were sporadic clashes, just as the radiant sunshine of the Midi is interrupted from time to time by the violent gusts of the mistral.

The Provençaux, under the command of Raymond IV, Count of Toulouse and Saint-Gilles, had taken an important part in the first Crusade, and in the following decades the country had prospered. The Crusades led to considerable activity in the ancient metropolis of Arles and the bustling port of Marseilles, and there were constant commercial and cultural exchanges with all the Mediterranean countries. Considering the intricate network of political allegiances, it is surprising that there were not more armed conflicts.

In 1112 the daughter of Geoffrey, Count of Provence, a young woman with the attractive name of Douce, married Raymond Bérenger III, Count of Barcelona. By this marriage Provence passed over to the house of Barcelona. Since both the Catalans and the Provençaux spoke the *langue d'oc*, there was no cultural division. In the palaces of the counts and the castles of lesser nobles the songs of the troubadours and courtly romances had an enthusiastic audience.

Fig. 66. Les Baux-en-Provence (Bouches-du-Rhône), with the ruins of the medieval castle demolished in 1632 by order of Louis XIII and Richelieu.

(Reportage Photographique YAN)

There were, however, dynastic rivalries. Raymond Bérenger III had many struggles with the powerful feudal family of Les Baux, which had extensive property in Provence. The strange city of Les Baux, near Arles, virtually carved out of limestone, is still an amazing sight, even in its ruined state (Fig. 66). Bauxite, named after the town, was discovered in a nearby ravine, aptly named the Val de l'Enfer—the Valley of Hell—which is said to have inspired Dante's *Inferno*.

The proud and turbulent lords of Les Baux entertained troubadours and held Courts of Love in their castle on the great rock. The winners of poetic contests are said to have received a crown of peacock feathers and a kiss from the most beautiful lady present. A legend popular in the 16th century and later tells a lurid tale of fierce Provençal passions and the terrible fate of those who transgressed the code of courtly love.

The lovely Berengère des Baux, eager to secure the undying love of the handsome troubadour Guilhem de Cabestanh, served him a magic philter, with predictable results. Her husband, in a jealous fury, killed the troubadour, tore out his heart and had it cooked and presented to his wife as a rare delicacy. Only after she had drunk the blood and eaten the meat did her husband tell her what she had consumed. She replied, "So sweet is that meat and so pure the wine that none other shall pass my lips." She then ran to the highest cliff of Les Baux and threw herself over the edge. Because of this legend the wine from the grapes that grow at the foot of the highest cliff is called to this day Sanh del Trobador—troubadour's blood.

According to another version of this story, Guilhem de Cabestanh, after receiving the love potion from Berengère des Baux and incurring the jealousy of her husband, fled to his native Roussillon near the eastern Pyrenees and visited the Castle of Roussillon. Once again the poet's talents and winning ways enraptured the chatelaine, Countess Seremonda. The jealous count, meeting the poet out hunting, killed him in the same horrible fashion as in the other version and served the heart to his wife. The countess's response was identical, but Seremonda threw herself to her death out the castle window, not over a cliff. The count's cruelty caused such outrage that the nobles of the county rose against him, headed by King Alfonso of Aragon. They hunted him down and killed him. The bodies of Seremonda and Guilhem were buried with great pomp in the Cathedral of Perpignan and became the objects of pilgrimage. Ever since the story of Tristan and Iseut, the romantic theme of tragic lovers united by death has had its appeal. Needless to say, no such tombs are to be found in Perpignan.

Raymond Bérenger III was killed at the siege of Nice in 1166. His cousin Alfonso II, King of Aragon, claimed his inheritance and took the title of Count of Provence as well as Count of Barcelona.

His succession was disputed by Count Raymond V of Toulouse, whose son had married Raymond Bérenger's daughter. The situation was further complicated by the fact that ever since Carolingian times the county of Orange and the kingdom of Arles had belonged to the Holy Roman Empire, although its imperial deputies had exercised little control. The Holy Roman Emperor, Frederick I, Barbarossa, who had hoped to unite Provence and Burgundy under the aegis of the Empire, was crowned King of Arles in the superb Romanesque Church of Saint-Trophime in 1176.

Reflections of the many conflicts, rivalries and conquests of Provence occur in a *tenson* written by Raimbaut IV, Count of Orange, and the mysterious "Countess of Die." Long thought to be a love poem, it is now believed to contain several political allusions and in this instance love and politics were closely intertwined.

An earlier Count of Orange, Raimbaut III, was the first specifically Provençal troubadour—using the term to refer to the province, not the language. He was related to the Counts of Montpellier, all of whom either practiced or encouraged poetry. Raimbaut was the first in Provence to write the *trobar clus*, or "closed" troubadour poetry, which relied more on formal virtuosity than on originality of theme or depth of emotion, and appealed to aristocratic connoisseurs. Giraut de Borneilh from the Dordogne, called the "prince of troubadours," and Arnaud Daniel, extravagantly praised by Dante and Petrarch, were also masters of the *trobar clus*. For Guiraut de Borneilh, the best song was one which "at a first hearing is not understood."

Raimbaut III's verse was often obscure and lacked direction but had considerable style and charm. Typical of his verbal ingenuity was his poem based entirely on the idea of "the world turned upside down," a belief in the power of love to transform nature and transcend its laws. The poem begins, *"Ai resplan la flors enversa"*—"When upside down the flower appears." The second stanza can be roughly translated:

> I turn the whole world upside down,
> I see the plains as little hills,
> I take the frost and snow for flowers,
> The biting wind grows soft and warm,
> The storm's a piping melody.
> The prickly thorns are green with leaves.
> So fully am I bound to Joy,
> Nothing in nature is my foe.

In a later verse Raimbaut elaborated on the theme:

> My verse, I turn you upside down
> That you may woods and hills withstand!
> Go, serenade in accents clear
> My lady, with her heart of thorns!

Raimbaut III was considered by other troubadours to have too high an opinion of his own poetry. He actually claimed that since Adam ate the apple, no poet born could compete in skill with himself!

One anecdote in the biography of Raimbaut, even if it is probably fictional, illustrates that peculiar mixture of sensuality and chastity in courtly love that seems so strange, even perverse, to the modern mind. After the Countess of Urgel, beloved of Raimbaut, had become a nun—with many great ladies this was more for political or family reasons than out of any deep religious vocation—she said, as quoted in the *Vidas*: "If Raimbaut had come to the convent at that time she would have granted him the pleasure of touching her naked leg with the back of his hand"!

Peire d'Auvergne, in his satirical verses on Bernart de Ventadour and other troubadours quoted earlier, wrote that he found Raimbaut's poems lacking in gaiety and warmth and that for his own part he preferred the music of itinerant bagpipe players!

The often convoluted imagery of the *trobar clus* was also linked to the idea of secrecy and concealment of the identity of the lady. In another poem Raimbaut III seems to mock his own verbal acrobatics:

> I only love—and what is love?—
> My ring which is my great delight
> 'Twas on the finger of—but hush!
> Be still, my tongue; to speak too much
> Can do more harm than mortal sin:
> And therefore is my heart shut tight.

The anonymous author of the *Vidas* gives Raimbaut many relationships with noble ladies, but they are largely fabrications. The poet's elaborate concealments seem to have worked!

CHAPTER XX

The Countess of Die:
A Woman Troubadour in Provence

T HE AUTHOR OF THE *Vidas* WRITES: "The Countess of Die was a beautiful and good woman. She fell in love with Lord Raimbaut of Orange and made many good poems about him" (Fig. 67). This *trobairitz*, or woman troubadour, did exist, but there has been much debate as to her exact identity; it is not even certain that the name Béatrix, given her by early biographers, was her real name.

Of the five poems attributed to her by modern scholars, four are entirely hers. The fifth is a *tenson* in which she and her *ami* wrote alternate stanzas. Careful study of this poem has led to the conclusion that the object of her love was indeed the Count of Orange—not Raimbaut III, but his great-nephew, Raimbaut IV, who was also a troubadour. This is the *tenson* which has come to be regarded as political as well as romantic.

This younger Raimbaut, like his great-uncle, tended to express himself in the oblique *trobar clus*; the countess's verses have greater simplicity and poignancy. She always implied that their love was a one-sided relationship and that it was she who had all the sorrow:

> If but a fourth part you might bear,
> Friend, of the pain that tortures me,
> You then would see my suffering . . .

The mention of the "fourth part" is deliberate, for Raimbaut IV had inherited only a quarter of the seigniory of Orange, on his great-uncle's death.

The Countess of Die and her family were evidently supporters of Raymond V of Toulouse, who also claimed Provence, for several times she mentioned the Knights Hospitalers as enemies and feared that Raimbaut might take their side against her own. Raimbaut's aunt, who had also inherited a quarter of Raimbaut III's estate, had presented her share to the Hospitalers, a religious and military order also known as the Knights of St. John of Jerusalem, which was under the special protection of Alfonso II, King of Aragon and Count of Provence.

In one of her poems the Countess of Die wrote:

> I hold you to be far more true
> Than those men of the Hospital.

And Raimbaut, realizing the delicacy of his position, wrote in *trobar clus* fashion:

> Lady, above all else I fear
> I lose the gold [*l'or*] and you the sand [*l'arena*].

Fig. 67. The Countess of Die. Bibl. MS. Fr. 854. fol 141. (Bibliothèque Nationale, Paris)

This is a play on words. *L'or*, gold, has the same sound as the name Laure. Biographical details relating to the countess are scanty. This use of a pun for the name Laure may identify the mysterious countess as Laure de Castellane, whose husband, Blacatz, a member of the Baux family, inherited the Castle of Die. Raimbaut feared that because of conflicting family allegiances, aggravated by malicious gossip, their love would be destroyed—he would lose *l'or*, or Laure, and she would lose the "sand"—that is, the arena of the famous Roman amphitheater in Orange.

In her fourth *canso* the countess lamented that her lover had left her—she wondered if it was through pride, because she had confessed her love to him but had then declared she would never be his except by marriage (presumably she would seek separation from her husband)—and at the end she asked, "Or was it hatred?"

The nearest equivalents in the Provençal art of this period to the verbal intricacies and limited imagery of the *trobar clus* are some of the ornamental carvings on late Romanesque church façades and capitals in the Midi (Fig. 68). Their extreme elegance became an end in itself; this lush style was succeeded by the more disciplined Southern Gothic.

The Castle of Castellane, belonging to the countess's father, Boniface, an ardent supporter of Raymond of Toulouse, was being threatened by the Aragonese forces. She hoped against hope that Raimbaut's devotion would give her support. The *tenson* may date from around 1187 or 1188, when Alfonso of Aragon ordered an expedition against Castellane, for the countess wrote:

Fig. 68. Detail of capital in former monastery of Saint-Paul-de-Mausole in Saint-Rémy-de-Provence (Bouches-du-Rhône), late 12th century. The monastery was later converted into an insane asylum, where Vincent van Gogh was confined from 1889 to 1890.

> Your soldiers strike our hearts with fear
> And with their loud and angry cries
> Have put us in such dire distress
> We cannot spend one joyful hour.

Castellane was besieged in 1189, and its defenders, who probably included the countess's husband, Blacatz, surrendered to the Aragonese. She felt humiliated by this defeat, and bitter that Raimbaut IV, who had seemed a loving friend, had not supported her cause. His allegiance had clearly been with the house of Aragon.

The following year Raimbaut died, leaving his quarter of the seigniory of Orange to "those of the Hospital." This was the final insult to the beautiful and talented Countess of Die.

The issues are now remote, but it is interesting to find that what were long considered simple love poems are also documents on the political history of Provence at a critical period. At the same time we find a passion and an urgency in the countess's lyrics that move us far more than the clever and studied verses of Raimbaut:

> Why do you claim to be my love
> And then leave me with all the pain?
> For we do not share equally ...

The medieval language of territorial claims is eloquently applied to the emotions. Women troubadours such as Marie de Ventadour and the Countess of Die never hesitated to affirm the principle of absolute equality in love.

While not all the Provençaux welcomed the Aragonese, the period of their rule was an age of peace and enlightenment compared to the terrible scourge that was soon to descend on the Midi. The "Empire of the Sun" was to endure the horrors of the Inquisition, the relentless persecution of the Albigensians and the savage fury of Simon de Montfort's Crusaders.

CHAPTER XXI

Lords and Poets of Toulouse

Toulouse, on the river Garonne, is the warmest and friendliest of the big cities of France. Its early builders used bricks made of local clay, and the result is the beautiful rose-red of its houses and churches. In the 12th century, the period of its greatest glory, the city was surrounded by a wall of the same glowing brick with many fortified gates. In past centuries Toulouse was often called the Ville-Rose; by a play on words this meant not only the rose-red city but the "Rose of Cities." It has been described as a town "rose-colored at dawn, red at noon, and purple at twilight."

The Counts of Toulouse, rulers of an independent Languedoc extending to the Alps and founders of colonies as far away as Tripoli in Syria, were known as the "Kings of the Midi." They were actually descended from a Carolingian official called Fulguald, but they liked to trace their origins to the marriage of the first count, Hursio, to a fairy. It was to commemorate this fabled origin that the name Raymond was handed down from father to son. This was a play on words: in *langue d'oc* the name meant both "pure ray" (in French the word *immonde* still means "impure") and "king of the world" (*rex* or *rey* + *mundi*).

Writers on Toulouse have pointed out that the city's rust-red hue is also a reminder of violent and bloody episodes in its long history. Even the martyrdom in the 3rd century of the apostle of Toulouse, St. Sernin or St. Saturninus, had a particularly gruesome character. St. Sernin was martyred by being tied to a wild bull which dragged him through the streets of Tolosa (the Roman name for the city) to a certain spot and then gored him to death. The place is now marked by the Church of Notre-Dame-du-Taur (Our Lady of the Bull). Its crenelated brick belfry is one of the few surviving remains of the old perimeter wall.

At the north end of Old Toulouse the splendid tower of the Basilica of Saint-Sernin rises up. (See page 115.) This great belfry, with its five octagonal stories, was a landmark for thousands of pilgrims in the Middle Ages and the center of one of the city's most popular *bourgs*, or boroughs. Even today Toulouse has the informal quality of a collection of villages, each with its own character.

In the 12th and early 13th centuries Toulouse enjoyed an independence comparable to that of some of the Italian city-states, and its civic government had a basic conception of law and justice inherited from long years of Roman rule. The municipal cartulary, or register, of 1205, preserved in the city's archives, has an illuminated page (Fig. 69) with three medallions representing three branches of the government. Above, holding a scepter and the city charter, is Count Alphonse-Jourdain, who had been born in the Orient during the crusading expedition of his father, Raymond IV, and had been brought to Toulouse as count in 1112. Below is a young noble with a sword, a tablet and a knight's emblazoned shield—he represents an aristocratic member of the communal chapter. The third medallion shows a bearded consul, or legislator, in a long robe. These consuls, or *capitouls*, governed the city, and the counts consulted them on the maintenance of defense and the conclusion of trade treaties. The *capitouls* were part of a merchant aristocracy which considered itself no less "noble" than the military aristocracy and had greater influence.

In the 12th century the Bishop of Toulouse never tried to exert political power over the township, as happened in some of the other cities of the South, especially Narbonne and Albi. Even though most of the people of Toulouse were Catholics, there was a robust anti-clerical tradition which has never altogether died out.

Above all, Toulouse, like Montpellier, was a city in which many cultures and races existed side by side. In the busy streets one could see Spaniards, Northerners, Byzantines, Orientals, Arabs and Jews and hear many languages. Some were drawn by the city's thriving commerce, but others came to study law. The School of Law in Toulouse was as famous as Montpellier's School of Medicine.

In this multiracial community there were Moorish families who had adopted Christianity but preserved many of their traditional customs. The knights returning from the Crusades brought back from the East a taste for sumptuous, brightly colored fabrics, and the shops, opening on the streets, sometimes had the aspect of an Oriental bazaar. Toulouse also had a small Jewish community, with a synagogue known as the Schola Judeorum. There had always been greater religious and intellectual tolerance in the Midi—some of the ablest teachers of Montpellier's School of Medicine were members of the Jewish colony. In Toulouse the Jews were subject to special taxes, but were protected by the count. Some loaned money at interest, but this was not a monopoly as in other parts of Europe. They were under the administration of a Jewish bailiff and allowed to own property. Some were converted to Christianity and had distinguished careers—the David family helped to develop the central mint, and one of the converted Jews, Eliazar, became a consul in 1180. Those who kept the faith were neither hated nor persecuted, although a curious custom survived in Toulouse which reflected the stigma attached to being a Jew by the medieval Church.

Every Easter one member of the community had to appear in the portal of Saint-Sernin and receive a symbolic blow on the cheek from a priest as punishment for rejecting Christ. This bizarre practice was first recorded in an early 11th century chronicle by Adhémar de Chabannes, who was also an artist and whose sketchbook is the earliest one to be preserved. In the heyday of the counts, this blow, however humiliating in itself, was merely a harmless tap, not taken seriously. After the coming of the Inquisition in the 13th century, the blow was applied so viciously that the victims were sometimes permanently injured. Conditions for the Jewish community were certainly not ideal in the 12th century, but compared to the plight of the Jews in England, Northern France and Germany, their situation in the Midi, and especially in Toulouse, was relatively favorable.

The tolerance shown by the Counts of Toulouse to Moslems, Jews, and especially the Cathar heretics and the generally secular spirit of the Midi were soon to bring terrible retribution by the forces of orthodoxy and repression. Meanwhile the courts of Raymond V and his son, the amiable and open-minded Raymond VI, were the most pleasant, luxurious and cultivated in all Europe after Eleanor of Aquitaine's court at Poitiers had been dispersed. They were centers for poets and troubadours, and the last representative of this gaiety and *douceur de vivre* before the clouds lowered was the reckless, high-spirited troubadour from Toulouse, Peire Vidal.

Fig. 69. Page from the municipal cartulary of the city of Toulouse, 1205. In the top medallion is Count Alfonse-Jourdain (1112–1148) with the town charter. This document is preserved in the Archives Municipales, Toulouse. (Reportage Photographique YAN)

CHAPTER XXII

Peire Vidal: The Adventurous Troubadour

PEIRE VIDAL (Fig. 70) was the son of a furrier of Toulouse—the garments of nobles and well-to-do citizens were often lined with fine fur to ward off the cold of winter—and his varied career was yet another proof that humble origins were no barrier to success as a troubadour. His anonymous biographer calls him "the maddest fellow in the world," one who enjoyed advertising his eccentricities. Since there are many specific references to places and people in his poems, it is possible to follow his career as an itinerant court poet with some degree of accuracy. He was one of the most widely traveled of all the troubadours, and the variety and originality of his verse have greater appeal to the modern reader than the more formalized poetry of his colleagues.

Most of Vidal's poems were written between 1180 and 1205. He left Toulouse quite early and went to the court of Barral de Baux, Viscount of Marseilles and himself a poet; he became a close friend of Barral—he and the viscount called each other Rainier, a nickname which indicated great familiarity.

Vidal paid court, in troubadour fashion, to Barral's wife, Azalaïs, whom he addressed in his poems as "Vierna." Azalaïs was also wooed in verse at this time by that strange figure Foulques of Marseilles, who later became the Bishop of Toulouse and a fanatical persecutor of the Albigensians and their sympathizers.

Promising Barral that he would return to Marseilles, Vidal went on his first trip to Spain and stayed for a brief period at the court of King Alfonso II of Aragon, who was also Count of Barcelona and Provence and who himself wrote Provençal verse. In a humorous poem addressed to Alfonso, Peire asked his patron for a new horse. If he had it, he wrote, he would maintain such order in Provence and Montpellier that even the wickedest bandits would stop their looting. He deserved a new horse, he explained, because he rivaled Roland and Oliver in wisdom, and the epic hero of romance, Bérard de Montdidier, in gallantry! No one knows whether or not he got the horse.

After a short stay in Aragon, Vidal returned to Toulouse, where he was welcomed at the court of Raymond V. He may well have met Bernart de Ventadour there, for Bernart spent his later years at Raymond's court, before retiring to the monastery of Dalon. Vidal would certainly have known the troubadour Bernart de Durfort— as a sign of perfect equality, Raymond V and Bernart de Durfort addressed each other by the same nickname, Albert, just as Peire Vidal and Barral de Baux had called each other Rainier. This may seem quaint or odd, but it illustrates the privileged position enjoyed by the troubadours at the courts that patronized them.

This easy relationship on an intellectual and literary plane, transcending social differences, was an expression of the ideal of *paratge*, or spiritual equality based on personal merit, not rank. It originally

Fig. 70. Peire Vidal, from a manuscript in the Bibliothèque Nationale, Paris.

derived from chivalry, and was closely linked to the troubadour ethic of love.

Alfonso II of Aragon wrote a *tenson* with the troubadour Guiraut de Borneilh (see Frontispiece) debating the problem of love between a great lord and a lady of lesser station. Guiraut claimed that such a love was not possible since "you, the powerful one, on the pretext that you are the greater, first ask to lie with her." Alfonso replied that he had never flaunted his high position in order to "conquer" a lady of quality, although he admitted that certain great lords were "gross and inconstant lovers."

Vidal spent some time in the Toulousain and the Carcassès—the hilly region near Carcassonne—and then returned to Marseilles to revisit Barral and Azalaïs. The anecdotes in Vidal's biography in the *Vidas*, if not always reliable, do convey a probably accurate impression of the whimsical Vidal's dual role of troubadour and licensed jester at the various courts and castles he visited.

According to one of the most colorful stories, the poet one day entered the room where the lady Azalaïs was sleeping, went to her bed, took her in his arms and stole a kiss. She woke up and was furious, not because of any social indignity—a mere poet taking liberties with a great lady—but because the kiss was *stolen*. Vidal had broken the rules of *l'amour courtois*, which required absolute reciprocity. A kiss should be freely given, not stolen! Her husband, Barral, evidently did not take this escapade very seriously, for he succeeded in reconciling Azalaïs and the poet and persuaded her to "grant the kiss as a gift." Any real adultery would have had a very different outcome. This story was based largely on a passage in one of Vidal's poems which includes the lines:

> *E lh baizei a lairo*
> *la boca e. l mento . . .*

> I've laid a tender kiss
> Upon her mouth and chin;
> I've had no more of her than this;
> I'll die unless I reach the rest!

In spite of Barral's good humor, Vidal may have felt that he was becoming too attached to Azalaïs, for he left for a long journey to Italy and the Orient. In Cyprus, it is said—but there is no confirmation by any known fact—that he was introduced to a lovely Greek girl who claimed to be the niece of the Byzantine Emperor. He married her and jokingly assumed the title of Emperor, which he sometimes gave himself in his poems. His biographer said that from that time on he carried a throne with him wherever he went so that he could receive his friends in proper style!

Back in the Midi, Vidal again visited Barral de Baux in Marseilles. Whether or not the relationship became strained, it is known for a fact that Barral and Azalaïs became estranged and separated sometime before the viscount's death.

While in Provence, Vidal sang the praises of Richard Coeur de Lion and spoke scornfully of the machinations of Philip Augustus. He made many references in his poems to a lady called La Loba (the she-wolf), who was also mentioned in the songs of Raimon de Miraval. Biographers called her La Loba, lady of Pennautier, and wrote that she was married to the lord of Cabaret, one of the castles in the Aude region near Carcassonne which later became a Cathar stronghold. Whatever the facts, it is certain that La Loba was given her nickname, not for any ferocity of character, but because she inhabited a mountainous region bounded by the Pyrenees. Vidal asserted that because of her he preferred wild country and mountains to the tranquil plains and rivers below.

On the basis of a few lines of poetry the biographer invented the picturesque tale that Vidal was inspired by La Loba's nickname to dress up as a wolf and be hunted by a pack of hounds through the woods near the lady's castle—a medieval idea of a "happening"! This extraordinary tale was based entirely on these lines:

> And if they call me Wolf
> I'm not thereby disgraced,
> Not even if I'm chased
> By shepherds' hue and cry.
> The woods and bushes please
> Me more than palaces.
> To her I'll gladly go
> Through ice and wind and snow.

The anonymous early 14th century biographer may have been influenced by the Italian prose romances of his day, for he could never resist weaving a colorful anecdote around the few names and events referred to in Vidal's poems. But these stories gave the feeling, if not necessarily the facts, of the period and the society.

Both Peire Vidal and Raimon de Miraval wrote that La Loba was

Fig. 71. Foix (Ariège), with a view of the castle. (Reportage Photographique YAN)

being courted by a great lord, and Vidal complained, none too seriously, that she had left him for *un comte ros*—a blond count. The biographer identified the nobleman as Raymond Roger, Count of Foix, who was like a king in his domain in the Ariège and whose beautiful castle on its high promontory (Fig. 71) still overlooks the town of Foix amid the green foothills of the Pyrenees. Vidal declared that La Loba would "commit a folly" and lose her reputation if she placed her love too high and if she scorned the sincere homage of needy but loyal poets.

Raymond Roger, Count of Foix, later became an important ally of Raymond VI of Toulouse in the Albigensian wars. Several of the castles in the Aude and Albigeois regions, mentioned by Vidal in his poems, including Montréal, Gaillac and Fanjeaux, were owned by nobles sympathetic to the Albigensian heretics and became Cathar fortresses. Vidal was hostile to the French and made veiled allusions to rapacious barons and hypocritical clerics, but during his years as a poet the terrible conflicts that were to overtake the Midi had not yet erupted.

After the death of his patron, Raymond V, in 1194, Vidal traveled widely, visiting courts in the Piedmont and in Hungary. After another trip to Spain, as the guest of Alfonso VIII of Castile, Vidal left on the Fourth Crusade in 1202 in the company of the Marquis of Montferrat.

Facts are scarce after that. In 1204 Vidal was in Malta and received the patronage of the island's Genoese ruler. His last-known poem dates from around 1205. He may have returned to Provence, for in his later years he was in contact with a troubadour called Blacatz, with whom he wrote a *tenson*. Blacatz maintained that love should yield quick results. Vidal defended the delaying endurance required in love's pursuit. Preferring as always a direct, lively approach rather than the elaboration of the *trobar clus*, he used a concrete image:

> *Gran jornada volh far per bon ostal*
> *Ne lonc servir per recebre gen do.*

> I'll walk a whole day to a goodly inn—
> The more delay, the sweeter the reward.

Inveterate traveler though he was, Vidal's most moving *canso*, among the freshest and most lyrical in all troubadour poetry, was written in praise of the land of Provence. Although there is practically no description of "locale," he evokes the sunshine, the soft breeze and the vivid colors of the countryside he always loved:

> *Ah! l'alen tire me l'aire*
> *Qu'en sen venir de Proënsa:*
> *Tot quant es de lai m'agensa . . .*

> I breathe the gladsome air
> That blows from fair Provence:
> I love all things from there.
> Hearing her praises sung
> I listen joyfully,
> And wish that every word
> A hundred words could be.

He declared that the sweetest abode on earth was

> Between the Rhône and Vence,
> The sea and the Durance.

And his homage to Provence in the last stanza carries more conviction than all the tributes to inaccessible ladies:

> For what I say and do
> To her all credit be!
> She gave me art and skill
> And joyous gift of song.
> Her loveliness inspired
> The best of all my verse,
> And tender reverie.

CHAPTER XXIII

The Cathars in Languedoc

EVER SINCE THE BEGINNING of the Church of Rome, heresy had been a problem in many parts of the Christian world. The lands south of the Loire came to be regarded by the Popes as breeding grounds for dangerous ideas and doctrines. The Visigoths, who ruled in Poitou, Aquitaine and Languedoc for three centuries after the collapse of the Roman Empire, and founded the original kingdom of Toulouse, had adopted Christianity, but in the form of Arianism (Fig. 72).

Arians were strict monotheists. They believed that Jesus Christ was neither equal nor eternal with God the Father, but was created as a perfect being, not quite human and not quite divine. Arius, its founder, had taught in Alexandria in the 4th century. In addition to the refusal to identify Christ with God, the Arians rejected the cult of saints, whose numbers the Catholic Church was steadily multiplying. There was no equivalent in the Midi of the mass conversion to Catholicism of the Frankish king Clovis and his warriors in Rheims in 496. This had been largely a political move, and the Franks helped the Church extend its temporal power so that Clovis would be able to claim the sanction of the true religion for his conquests in Gaul.

The Visigoths were defeated by Clovis near Poitiers in 507 and

Fig. 72. Visigothic bas-relief with Christian symbols, including the Cross of Glory and Grace as the source of life. The original is in the Musée Lapidaire, Lamourguier (Aude), near Narbonne.

moved their capital from Toulouse to Toledo in Spain. But Languedoc, especially the Toulouse region, never wholeheartedly adjusted to orthodox Catholicism. There was always a core of resistance.

When the Moslems in the 8th century invaded Languedoc and Provence, many of the inhabitants found that they had more in common with the Arabs than with the Merovingian Franks. The Arabs at that time had a far superior culture; the fierce Saracen horsemen were merely the advance guard. The Moslems brought medicine to Montpellier and science and mathematics to Toulouse. They were pioneers in astronomy, then closely linked to astrology. They planted beautiful gardens in Avignon and Orange with colorful tiles and cool fountains.

Three centuries after the expulsion of the Arab rulers by Charles Martel, the Spanish Moors still influenced architecture, music and the earliest troubadour poetry. Whatever the intentions of the Crusades in Spain and the Orient, these expeditions multiplied the cultural and commercial ties with the East, affecting both the awareness of the senses and the development of the mind.

Fragrant spices and silken fabrics awoke a feeling for luxury and refinement among the southern nobles and burghers, and the presence of Arab and Jewish scholars in Narbonne and Montpellier promoted the study of philosophy and mathematics. The life of Buddha was translated into the *langue d'oc* in the 12th century. This ferment of ideas was a constant threat to orthodox dogma, just as the relative openness of Occitan society and the greater freedom enjoyed by women in the South was a challenge to the entire feudal structure.

In the 11th and 12th centuries, when the growth of the population enabled the cities of the Midi to acquire a certain degree of independence, another Eastern trend caused even greater alarm to the heads of the Church. This was the religion of Catharism, a word derived from the Greek word *katharos*, meaning "pure."

The original group of Cathari, known as Bogomils, had been formed in Bulgaria and the Balkans in the 10th century. Like an earlier group, the Paulicians, who had flourished in Armenia, the Bogomils based their creed on the doctrine of Manichaeism. According to this belief, there was a perpetual dualism between God, represented by light and spiritual enlightenment, and the realm of Satan, symbolized by darkness and all material things. Man was composed of matter, which belonged to Satan, but Christ, the ideal light-clad soul, could redeem from each human the portion of light given him or her by God. The Bogomils' movement in the Balkans had political as well as religious implications, as it reflected intense resentment of Byzantine imperial authority and Slavic serfdom.

Similar groups were known in other countries as Patarenes, and early in the 11th century they began to proselytize in Italy. Their teachings met with great success in Lombardy, whose inhabitants centuries earlier had been Arian Christians, like the Visigoths. From Italy the Cathari crossed over into Southern France, where they made many converts. The center of the new movement was Albi, and the heretics of the Midi were usually known in France as Albigensians. They did not call themselves Cathars, but Christians.

According to the monk Raoul Glaber, who died around 1050, it was a woman from Italy who introduced Catharism into France. Her name is not given, but she is credited with converting some priests as far north as Orléans to the Manichaean or dualist doctrine. Count William VII of Poitiers gave them his protection, regardless of the Church's disapproval. Much of the Cathars' creed and ritual remains obscure because of their need for secrecy. They are known to have rejected baptism by water, for water is matter. They rejected the Christian cross as an object of worship, as this was associated with the material body of Jesus, and they refused to make the sign of the cross.

Like the disciples of Mahatma Gandhi in modern times, the Cathars renounced all violence. Homicide, war and secular justice were rejected, along with any form of lying or evasion of truth. They repudiated not only the outward symbols of Catholicism but the entire hierarchy of the Church with the Pope as its head. To the Cathars the official Catholic Church, in assuming the mantle of imperial Rome, had abandoned the pure simplicity of the Gospels. Rome stood for Babylon, or the beast of the Apocalypse. Their own creed was in many respects a return to primitive Christianity. The Cathar "bishops" and "deacons" were men, but both men and women could be "perfects," the name given by their followers, not by themselves, to those who preached the faith.

The Cathar leaders—the perfects were also known as *bons-hommes,* or good-men—were ascetics who practiced the complete surrender of the flesh to the spirit as a means of perfection. Besides being bound to absolute chastity, they abstained from flesh in all its forms, including milk and cheese. Such an austere religion with its ban on sexual relations would have been doomed to failure had not its founders wisely allowed for two classes of members—the perfects and the "believers." No strict rules were enforced on the believers. The perfects were ordained by receiving the Cathars' one and only sacrament, the "consolamentum," a "laying on of hands" accompanied by the kiss of peace. The believers usually received the consolamentum only when death was thought to be approaching. It could be administered by either a man or a woman. Until that point the believers were able to live as they pleased. The perfects were never authoritarian in forcing their way of life on others, but once the dying person had received the consolamentum, his or her remaining time on earth had to be spent as a perfect. For those who unexpectedly recovered from their illness, there was no turning back— they were perfects as long as they lived!

The Cathars believed that since God was good and loving, and Satan was responsible for all the evil in the world, mankind must eventually be saved. They could not accept the Catholic doctrine of Hell and eternal damnation for sinners. No human soul could be shut out of Paradise; it might, however, take several incarnations to attain the necessary perfection.

Preaching outdoors in the 11th and 12th centuries was virtually unknown in ordinary parish customs, and the eloquence and fervor, as well as the absolute sincerity, of the Cathar perfects, who would stand in squares and near marketplaces to preach their beliefs, contributed to their rapid success among all classes of the population. They were inspired preachers, but not a single Cathar sermon has survived. A manuscript of Cathar ritual preserved in the library of the Palais des Arts in Lyons shows that they based many of their beliefs on the gospel of St. John and the Book of Revelations. The pages of ritual follow a translation of the New Testament into Provençal, in itself a daring achievement. Even if few people were inclined to practice the ideal of asceticism, the contrast between the apostolic simplicity of the *bons-hommes* and the self-indulgence, arrogance and greed of many of the local clergy could not fail to impress those who listened to these sermons.

There were no injunctions and no threats of excommunication, just as there were no churches or temples to confine the spirit. With their gentleness, modest bearing and genuine humility, the perfects shunned all display and exercise of power. The Cathar religion was not a series of formal rituals and decrees, but a way of life, a religion by example.

One of the greatest living authorities on Catharism, René Nelli, has said of the perfects: "They were like that because they were like that." He believes that if they had triumphed they would have practiced far more tolerance toward other faiths than ever was shown to them.

The first official mention of the Cathar heresy in the Midi occurred in 1119, in a Church council in Toulouse, which denounced as heretics all those who denied the sacraments, the priesthood, and Catholic hierarchy and the ties of marriage. Similar pronouncements

Fig. 73. Aryan heretics being driven out of Milan by St. Ambrose, from a 12th century bas-relief on the Porta Romana, Milan. This may have been an allusion to the Cathars of Lombardy.

were made in Italy, and the earliest representation in art of the Church's attack on heretics occurs in a 12th century bas-relief on the Porta Romana in Milan (Fig. 73). It represents the expulsion of the "Arriani," or Aryans, from Milan by St. Ambrose in the 4th century. The saint wears the miter of a 12th century bishop and has a rod, or scourge, in his right hand. He is accompanied by a priest with a cross, and the unfortunate heretics are carrying away bundles, small casks and other belongings. While the word "Arianni" is inscribed on the border, the relief is believed to refer to the many Cathars then living in the vicinity of Milan.

Cathar iconography in Southern France and elsewhere is extremely scarce and has been the subject of much study. A few carvings of flying doves, symbolizing the Holy Spirit and freedom of inspiration (Fig. 74), fish, an early Christian symbol (Fig. 75), and a lamb's head have been discovered which seem to relate to Cathar symbolism. The fish also appears in an initial letter and in the margin of several pages

Fig. 74. The so-called dove of Montsé-gur, a Cathar symbol of the free-ranging spirit. This little sculpture, probably dating from the early 13th century, was discovered in 1906 near the donjon of Montségur. Part of the beak and the end of a wing are missing. It is in the collection of Mme. Fois, of Foix (Ariège).

Fig. 75. Icthys, or fish symbol, from the Lyons MS of Cathar ritual, 13th century. The Greek word icthys (fish) must have reminded the Cathars, as it had the early Christians, of the initials in Greek of Jesus Christ, ιχ.

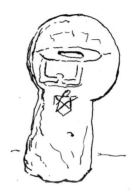

Fig. 76. Discoidal stele from Baraigne in the Limoux Museum (Aude). On the obverse is a Greek cross, with a twelve-branched filiform cross incised into the upper right-hand section. On the reverse is a weaver's shuttle—many weavers in Languedoc were Cathars—and a five-pointed star, an esoteric symbol associated with Catharism.

of the manuscript of Cathar ritual in Lyons mentioned earlier. Although the Cathars rejected the Roman or Latin cross, in which the upright is longer than the transom, they apparently favored the so-called "discoidal" cross, of which several examples have been found in the Lauraguais region of Languedoc. This was the Greek cross—the equality of its four branches was itself significant—enclosed in a circle. This type of cross may have been of pre-Christian origin.

Some of these discoidal crosses in stone planted in lonely places in the countryside must have seemed suspect, as on a few of them crude Latin crosses have been inscribed, probably to "exorcise" the heretical signs (Fig. 76).

Another Cathar image was the star with five rays, which some scholars think may be an abstraction of the human figure with outstretched arms and legs. Other esoteric symbols are thought to derive from either mystical Eastern sources or the Book of Revelations, but what little remains of this mysterious imagery provides more questions than answers.

Catharism was the most important of several heretical sects active in the Midi—and many of the leaders came from the nobility. A reformer from the Dauphiné, Pierre de Bruys, who had attracted a huge following, was burned at the stake at Saint-Gilles. His disciple, the monk Henri, after preaching in Poitiers and Bordeaux, spread the Manichaean doctrines in the Toulousain and was so successful that in 1145 Bernard of Clairvaux himself went to Toulouse and, according to a chronicler, effected another of his miraculous conversions.

Henri renounced his heresy and was taken back into the bosom of the Church. Bernard rebuked Count Alphonse-Jourdain for his "spiritual neglect" of his capital, Toulouse, and, partly as a penance, the count, in 1147, left on the Second Crusade, taking with him the troubadour Jaufré Rudel, who has already been discussed. Alphonse-Jourdain's soul may have been saved by his pilgrimage but not his body—he died of poison in the Holy Land.

In the reign of his successor, Count Raymond V of Toulouse, Catharism made tremendous headway throughout Languedoc. The cities of Béziers, Montpellier and Nîmes were administered by consuls (Fig. 77), mostly from the merchant class, men jealous of their liberties and opposed to any encroachment on their freedoms by either ecclesiastical or feudal powers. Women often took part in elections to the municipal government, or "*commune.*" Many of the burghers were either Cathar sympathizers or secret adherents. The

Above: Fig. 77. Seal of Nîmes (Gard), 1226, showing four consuls. The people of Nîmes supported the Albigensians, but the city surrendered to Simon de Montfort and his Crusaders in 1207. This seal ratifies an agreement to obey the papal legate.

Below: Fig. 78. Seal of Constance of France, wife of Raymond V, Count of Toulouse and sister of Louis VII. The sun and the moon are emblems of the territories of the house of Saint-Gilles in the West and in the Orient.

Cathar preachers would travel through the countryside in pairs, the perfect and the "socius," or assistant. Both men and women wore long black or dark-blue gowns and there would be special signs on walls and trees pointing the way to houses that would receive them.

When the persecutions began, the perfects would dress as ordinary artisans and earn their living as itinerant carpenters or weavers. For this reason the perfects were often called *tesseyres* (weavers) as well as *bons-hommes*. In the Lauraguais region there are still such family names as Cathary, Bonhomme and Tesseyres. Near Béziers there are also Visigothic names, including Got and Reswingle.

In addition to its strong popular appeal, Catharism impressed many of the nobles. Since they were accustomed to open discussion, they were not afraid to receive the perfects in their castles and give them overnight hospitality. These lords might be sincere Catholics who maintained a chaplain, but they were interested in fresh ideas and stimulating conversation. As the independence of the South became increasingly threatened from the outside, many of these lords, even if they were not themselves Cathars, felt an obligation to defend these courageous and sincere people. Many burghers, artisans and peasants also gave the Cathars help and provisions. Later, in order to elude the Inquisition, some of the Cathar perfects became peddlers or traveling retail dealers. Their absolute honesty and integrity impressed the merchants of Toulouse, Marseilles and Avignon, and so did their policy of mutual economic assistance, which was quite new. Even in as Catholic a city as Narbonne, the tradesmen could not regard the Cathar merchants as enemies, for they had removed the moral stigma attached to commerce by the Church.

In 1165 the situation became so serious for the Catholic Church that a colloquy was organized by the Bishop of Albi at Lombez to discuss their policy toward the heretics. It was attended by Raymond V and his wife, Constance (Fig. 78), sister of the devout Louis VII. The easygoing Raymond favored tolerance, but Constance was all for repression and this disagreement led to their separation. Two years later Raymond became apprehensive when a heretic council was held openly in Saint-Félix-de-Caraman, presided over by Nicetas, a Manichaean or "dualist" bishop from Constantinople.

The Catholic clergy in the Occitan lands felt that action was necessary, but they did not have the authority they later acquired, and even the official Church had a more inquiring and less dogmatic attitude than it was to have in the 13th century. Some open-minded churchmen were willing to explore ideas of cabalistic, Celtic or Arab origin and try to absorb them into Christian beliefs. But the growth of Catharism threatened the very foundations of the Church. Raymond V, alarmed at the increasing divisions in the country, wrote in 1177 to Pope Alexander III, "Heresy has penetrated everywhere. It has sown discord in every family . . . even priests yield to the temptations. Churches are abandoned and falling into ruins."

A papal delegation was sent to Toulouse the following year, headed by Cistercian monks. The Cathar bishop Bernard Raimond and his associate, suspected of heresy, concealed their beliefs, but refused to take an oath of loyalty to the Catholic Church and were banished from the city. They went to Carcassonne, where Viscount Raymond-Roger Trancavel and all the nobility were strong Cathar sympathizers. Six years later another papal delegation, this time with an armed escort, captured Bernard Raimond and his assistant and took the two heretics to Le Puy, where they recanted and were rewarded with comfortable ecclesiastic appointments in Toulouse.

Count Raymond VI, who succeeded his father in 1195, was faced with gigantic problems. This genial, tolerant and popular ruler, a handsome, cultivated and sensual *bon vivant* who tended toward stoutness in middle age, was always attractive to women. His flexible policies have been misunderstood by historians, and if he sometimes appeared irresolute, it must be remembered that his position was extremely precarious, and he had to steer a careful and at times devious course to protect his domains and their inhabitants.

Fig. 79. Seal of Raymond VI, Duke of Narbonne, Count of Toulouse and Marquis of Provence. (Reportage Photographique YAN)

The only surviving representation of Raymond VI is on his seal, showing him on horseback in full armor (Fig. 79). He carries a spear with a long pennant, and his shield is adorned with the cross of Languedoc, the "cross with the twelve pearls," which has since become one of the most cherished symbols of the Midi.

Although valiant in warfare and forced to spend years on the battlefield, either defending or regaining his territories, he would have preferred a peaceful existence in his beloved Toulouse, entertaining troubadours and beautiful women in his stately palace and dealing with the business and welfare of the Toulousains. Raymond VI was extravagant in his mode of living but never authoritarian, and he was genuinely loved by his subjects. In many ways he was in advance of his time.

The troubadour Raimon de Miraval, already mentioned as an admirer of La Loba, was a close friend of Raymond VI. Following the usual custom, they called each other by the nickname Audiart, which was a woman's name, but this in no way implied a homosexual relationship. It was a refinement of the masculine name Albert, used by the count's father, Raymond V, and Bernart de Durfort, and it was also a homage to the idea of woman as a free and equal partner; while this seems far-fetched to modern minds, it was in keeping with the involved attitude and code of that era.

This gallantry was not carried over into Raymond's relationship to his wives during his five marriages. Like other great lords of his time, Raymond used marriage primarily as a means of political advancement. His first wife, whom he had married long before coming to power, was Ermessinde de Pelet, who died in 1176. His second wife, Béatrix, sister of the Viscount of Béziers, was repudiated in 1193 on the grounds of consanguinity as soon as Raymond saw the beautiful Bourguigne of Lusignan, whose father, Guy de Lusignan, was King of Cyprus and titular King of Jerusalem. But that marriage too was of brief duration.

Eleanor of Aquitaine was uneasy about the alliance between the future Count of Toulouse and the troublesome house of Lusignan and was instrumental in persuading Raymond to dissolve this alliance and marry her own daughter, Joanna. Later, Raymond, fearing that Toulouse might pass to the Plantagenets if he died leaving no male heirs, repudiated Joanna, who retired to Fontevrault—that asylum for rejected wives of nobles—where she died in 1199.

Raymond married his last wife, Leonor, the sister of Peter II of

Aragon, because he needed a powerful ally against the French troops of Simon de Montfort. However callously he acted toward his wives, Raymond VI believed in the ideals of *l'amour courtois*, contradictory as this might seem. Marriage had nothing to do with love —it was a matter of expediency.

The mercurial, pleasure-loving Raymond VI could hardly be expected to sympathize with the Cathars' ideal of chastity, nor was the luxury of his court in keeping with their austere way of living, but he respected their integrity and felt that they were entitled to the same protection as his other peace-loving subjects. Like most of the Southern nobles he was a Catholic but the idea of a Holy War was abhorrent to him.

The troubadours and the Cathar preachers had the same noble audiences in the counties of Toulouse and Foix and in the viscounty of Carcassonne, but the relationship between troubadours and heretics remains ambiguous. Although the troubadours had created a secular mystique of love, they were essentially worldly court poets and had little interest in metaphysics.

Raymond VI's friend the troubadour Raimon de Miraval was, like most of his colleagues, a Catholic. Even the poet Peire Cardenal (Fig. 80), who later was strongly influenced by Catharism and attacked the papacy, never renounced the Catholic faith, but amid the growing violence he rejected the Church's idea of Hell. He was inclined to believe, like the Cathars, that the true God would not punish or chastise or destroy human souls, but would ultimately redeem them through love.

Both the troubadours and the Cathars took a negative view of marriage, but for very different reasons. The troubadours saw marriage as a venal and "utilitarian" institution involving the subjugation of women—with few exceptions, true and equal love, they believed, could exist only *outside* of marriage. The Cathar perfects renounced marriage for themselves but tolerated it for the "believers," because although the sexual act, either within or outside of marriage, was "Satanic," there was always the possibility that it might lead to the reincarnation of a soul as part of the necessary progress toward perfection. To the extent that the Cathars countenanced marriage, they favored equality of the sexes, not the male dominance implicit in Catholic dogma. In the belief in the spiritual equality of men and women, however different the context, Cathars and troubadours had certain ideas in common. They both attacked the greed and material-

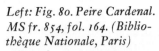

Left: Fig. 80. Peire Cardenal. MS fr. 854, fol. 164. (Bibliothèque Nationale, Paris)

Right: Fig. 81. Foulques de Marseilles. Bibl. Nat. MS fr. 854, fol. 61. (Bibliothèque Nationale, Paris)

ism of many of the clergy. To the troubadours this was an example of *cobeïtat*, covetousness; to the Cathars it was a sign of worldly corruption, the mark of Belial.

At first the troubadours made little distinction between Cathar *bons-hommes* and Catholic monks. The anonymous author of the late 12th century romance in verse "Flamenca" had the squires of young Guilhem tease their master for dressing up as a priest in order to exchange a few words with his lady at Mass. They told him that he looked like a *bon-homme* and that all he lacked was a complete monastic habit to resemble a Carthusian or Cistercian monk.

Only after the Occitan society was threatened by war and persecutions did the troubadours seriously concern themselves with religious matters. When the courts on which their living depended were dispersed and the poets became simple citizens, they made common cause with the Cathars and attacked the French king and his ally, the Pope in Rome. Guilhem Figueira, the son of a Toulouse tailor and the author of the most violent satire on the Roman papacy written in the

Middle Ages, was one of the few troubadours known to have been a
Cathar. He is reported to have died in Lombardy "in a state of
heresy." Another was Pierre-Rogier de Mirepoix, the future defender
of Montségur, but none of his work has survived.

Foulques de Marseilles (Fig. 81) took the opposite course. The son
of a wealthy Genoese merchant established in Marseilles, Foulques
began his career in commerce. He married and was the father of two
sons. Around 1180 he began to write poetry, and composed songs in
praise of Alfonso II of Aragon, Richard Coeur de Lion and Raymond
V of Toulouse. He visited Barral de Baux in Marseilles and, like
Peire Vidal, but with much less originality, paid homage to the
charms of Azalaïs. According to his anonymous biographer,
Foulques found no favor with Azalaïs, and addressed his poems to
Eudoxia, wife of Guillaume VIII of Montpellier.

Foulques composed a *planh* in memory of Barral de Baux on the
latter's death in 1192. He was discouraged by the lack of success of
his love poems, which relied on dry logic rather than feeling, and
took holy orders in 1200, when he was about forty. He became the
abbot of the Cistercian abbey of Le Thoronet in the mountainous
region north of what is now the Riviera; his wife and two sons also
joined the austere Cistercian order. In 1205 Foulques became Bishop
of Toulouse, and for a while continued to write verse, but of a
devotional character, anticipating the strained poems of the troubadours of the post-Albigensian period of decline who felt obliged to
dedicate their songs to the Virgin instead of to a beautiful lady. The
only one of Foulques' religious compositions with any interest is the
poem on the theme: "One Must Think About God." The chorus
faintly recalls the response to nature of earlier and better poets. It
begins:

> The night departs, the daylight comes,
> The skies are calm and clear ...

The mocking Toulousains considered Foulques a self-serving hypo-
crite who had become a bishop in order to satisfy his "will to power"
and to compensate for his unprepossessing personality and lack of
worldly success as a poet—a clear case of sour grapes! It is recorded
that they would deliberately sing the more amorous songs of his
early years under his window, and if he chanced to hear them he
would fast for two days in penitence! Later Foulques was the most
hated man in Toulouse when he became the zealous collaborator of

Simon de Montfort against his suzerain, Count Raymond VI, and the pitiless persecutor of his fellow countrymen.

When Foulques gave the southern lords the order to banish the Cathars, one of them, Aymar de Rodéla, replied with words that summed up the tolerant and humane policy that was incomprehensible to their fanatical adversaries: "We have been raised together, we have relatives among them, all we seek is to live in peace."

CHAPTER XXIV

St. Dominic's Mission

I N THE YEAR 1203 TWO SPANISH CLERICS crossed the Pyrenees into Southern France: Diego, Bishop of Osma in Old Castile, and his canon, the thirty-three-year-old Domingo de Guzmán. They were on a diplomatic mission for King Alfonso VIII of Castile. In his boyhood Domingo, or Dominic, had thrilled to tales of warlike exploits of the Christian knights of Spain against the Saracens, and the love of struggle was part of his character. In Toulouse, their host was a Cathar. Dominic spent the night trying to convince him of his error; his fervor and eloquence prevailed, and at dawn the Cathar gave in. From that time Dominic saw it as his sacred duty to redeem errant souls.

After the mission for the King of Castile was completed, the bishop and Dominic went to Rome, where Pope Innocent III charged them to preach against the Albigensian heretics in Languedoc. The Pope still hoped to overcome heresy by persuasion rather than by force. Dominic went directly to Fanjeaux, near Carcassonne, in the heart of Cathar territory.

Peire Vidal, in one of his poems, compared the castle of Fanjeaux to Paradise, and the site commands one of the loveliest panoramas in the Midi. Dominic saw the town as the arena for an intense spiritual campaign. In 1206 he founded a monastery, and a convent for women at Prouille at the foot of Fanjeaux, which became a center for the cult of the Rosary. Some of the nuns were converted Cathars.

Dominic soon realized that the best way to combat the Cathar perfects, with whom he had many heated debates, was to adopt their poverty and austerity. He even borrowed their costume, sandals on bare feet and a long hooded gown of rough serge, but it was white instead of black—the positive as opposed to the negative. Over it he wore a black cape, and this was the origin of the black-and-white habit of the Dominican order, founded ten years later.

Like the Cathars, Dominic's emphasis was on preaching, and, like the Cathars, the Dominicans traveled in pairs. The population was impressed by their dedication and humility, so different from the behavior of most of the local prelates and priests, but at first Dominic and his companions made little headway. A rough and powerful 13th century woodcarving (Fig. 82) preserved in the convent of Prouille is probably the earliest and most authentic likeness

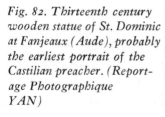

Fig. 82. Thirteenth century wooden statue of St. Dominic at Fanjeaux (Aude), probably the earliest portrait of the Castilian preacher. (Reportage Photographique YAN)

of this zealous, proselytizing saint (canonized in 1234, thirteen years after his death).

The Church organized several colloquies with the heretics in an attempt to win them over by argument. The most famous of these meetings was held at Pamiers in the Ariège, near Foix, in 1207, and the Catholic priests were astonished and indignant at the presence and active participation of some highly articulate women.

Chief among these noble ladies was Esclarmonde de Foix. This brilliant and beautiful woman was the sister of Raymond Roger, Count of Foix, who, like his father, Count Roger Bernard I, received many troubadours and jongleurs at his court. One of them, Ramon de Bexandun, wrote:

> And when to Foix they came
> They found its gracious lord
> Both wise and bountiful,
> As all the world did say.

The name Esclarmonde, popular at that time among noblewomen of the Midi, means "light of the world" (*esclaire-monde*). Esclarmonde de Foix became a zealous protectress of the Cathars and supported their cause. Her husband, Jordan de l'Isle Jordan, was a Catholic, but he loved his wife and was proud of her, and never reproached her championship of the heretics. They were a remarkable family. Esclarmonde's sister Zebelia was the patroness of another and far less numerous heretical group, the Waldensians, or Vaudois, who also preached apostolic poverty as the way to perfection, and her sister-in-law Philippa became a Cathar deaconess and in her castle at Dun directed a community of perfects recruited from the nobility.

Esclarmonde, then over forty, her two daughters and Philippa, along with many other women, attended the colloquy at Pamiers in 1207. She joined in the debates and expressed her point of view with such force and intelligence that Brother Etienne de la Miséricorde, one of Dominic's companions, was profoundly irritated and finally rebuked her, saying, "Madame, go wind your distaff! It is not fitting that you should argue matters of this kind!"

In 1204, three years before the colloquy at Pamiers, Esclarmonde and three of her friends had received the consolamentum in Fanjeaux, in the house of the famous Cathar bishop Guilhabert de Castres. According to tradition, this was the house in which Dominic lived after 1214 and which is now a small museum.

After becoming a perfect, Esclarmonde distributed part of her fortune among the poor, and founded schools, charity workshops and hospitals, where she would soon, to her great distress, receive the first victims of the Albigensian War.

With the support of Raimon de Mirepoix, a Cathar deacon, Esclarmonde contributed part of her wealth to the rebuilding of the mountain fortress of Montségur in the Ariège. This had been chosen by Guilhabert de Castres as a place of refuge for the Cathars, who were being subjected to increasing harassment. Esclarmonde was bitterly attacked for this aid to the heretics by Foulques, Bishop of Toulouse.

Montségur was to become one of the last strongholds in the defense of the South from the French onslaught, and it was the scene of the tragic climax and the end of the Albigensian history.

A modern statue of Esclarmonde in the city of Foix (Fig. 83) shows her standing proudly, a spear in her hand, as the heroic symbol of the struggle of the Midi to preserve its independence against overwhelming odds.

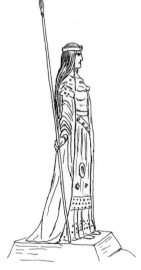

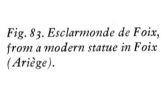

Fig. 83. Esclarmonde de Foix, from a modern statue in Foix (Ariège).

CHAPTER XXV

The "Holy War"

THE COLLOQUY AT PAMIERS in 1207 was one of the last attempts to convert the Cathars to the Catholic Church by argument and persuasion. Dominic's tireless preaching made a number of converts, but the result from the Church's standpoint was disappointing.

Raymond VI was under constant attack for his failure to suppress the heresy. Pope Innocent III (Fig. 84) threatened the count with anathema and hinted that he, the Pope, might appeal to Philip Augustus for help. It was obvious that ecclesiastical censure would have little effect without the assistance of the secular powers. As Dominic said in a sermon some years later, quoting a Spanish proverb: "Where blessing can accomplish nothing, blows may avail."

Raymond VI was unwilling to risk excommunication and a devastating war. Unlike the Dukes of Aquitaine in an earlier and less complex period, Raymond was faced with a strong French monarchy and a determined papacy. He played for time, and declared that he would submit to the will of the Pope in the person of his legate, Pierre de Castelnau. Pierre's own parish of Saint-Gilles was near Arles. The Counts of Toulouse were also Counts of Saint-Gilles, and the splendid Romanesque abbey church was the count's family chapel. On January 14, 1208, Raymond solemnly swore allegiance to the

Pope's deputy, and Pierre, satisfied with his efforts, set out the next day for Rome.

The papal delegate and his retinue were fording a river near Saint-Gilles when fate struck a terrible blow. Pierre de Castelnau was assassinated by a man who stabbed him with a hunting spear and escaped before his identity could be discovered. Some believed that the assassin was a young squire of the Count of Toulouse who bitterly resented papal interference and the humiliation to which his master had been subjected.

It has been established that Raymond had no share in the murder. The last thing that he would have wished was a disastrous event which was certain to bring down the wrath of the Church. It was as fateful in its consequences as the murder of the Austrian archduke at Sarajevo which triggered the First World War.

The Pope was so furious that he was speechless for two days. When he was able to talk, he ordered the Cistercians to preach a Crusade against the Albigensians and appealed to the Christian princes to join in suppressing the heretics by force of arms.

Philip Augustus, then preparing for a confrontation with King John of England, respectfully declined to head the Crusade, but the covetous feudal barons of the North had been waiting for just such an opportunity to invade the prosperous and peaceful lands of the Midi. The Cathar issue provided the perfect pretext for their ambitious designs, and the motives of the Albigensian Crusades were as much political as religious. A council of the Crusaders elected as their leader the able, ruthless and fanatically religious Anglo-French baron

Fig. 84. Innocent III, Pope from 1198 to 1216. From a 13th century fresco in the Lower Church of Sacro Speco, Subiaco.

Simon de Montfort, who was also the Earl of Leicester. He had twice been to Palestine as a Crusader and was eager to answer the Pope's call and march against the enemies of the Church. He is not to be confused with his son of the same name, the famous English statesman and soldier who was also Earl of Leicester, the real founder of the English Parliament.

In his desperation to spare his country the horrors of war, Raymond VI was willing to undergo the ultimate humiliation. In June 1209 he submitted once again to the Pope's authority. Barefoot, stripped to the waist and with a rope around his neck, the proud and handsome Count of Toulouse was publicly flagellated in front of the portals of Saint-Gilles. He then went down into its crypt to make penance in front of the tomb of Pierre de Castelnau.

An inscription added to the tomb centuries later called the murdered legate, beatified after his death, "the honor and the glory of the Cistercian order" and a victim of treason perpetrated by the "odious Raymond VI"—an extremely biased statement, not a fact.

The excommunication was lifted, and as a conciliatory step Raymond made a show of joining the Crusade, since by papal decree the lands of a Crusader could not be invaded or violated. He was determined to do as little as possible and to leave the ranks of the Crusaders at the earliest opportunity. The strategy was too subtle to be understood by Raymond's supporters, especially his young and chivalrous vassal Raymond-Roger Trancavel, Viscount of Béziers, Carcassonne and Albi. (The family name Trancavel means "cut-well" or "pierce-well" and is the exact equivalent of "Parsifal.") The courageous young viscount, a truly romantic figure and a patron of the troubadours and of the arts, whose audience hall in his castle in Carcassonne was adorned with frescoes of charging Frankish knights fighting the Saracens, had the awesome responsibility of being the main defender of the Cathars and of the freedom of the southern cities against the savage onslaught from the North.

The Crusaders came charging down the valley of the Rhone, over five hundred thousand strong, their ranks swollen by soldiers of fortune, mounted German mercenaries and a horde of *ribauds*, or vagabonds, who had their own "king." Dominic, although on friendly terms with Simon de Montfort and praying for the success of the Crusaders, took no direct part in the war, but continued to travel over the country preaching against the heretics.

On July 22, 1209, the crusading army appeared before the walls

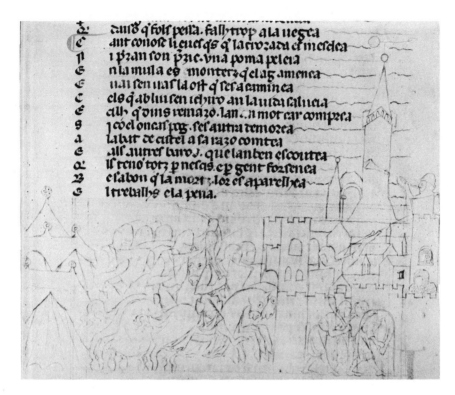

Fig. 85. *The Capture of Béziers. From the* Chanson de la Croisade Albigeoise, *Bibl. Nat. MS Fr. 25425, fol. 11. (Bibliothèque Nationale, Paris)*

of Béziers, a prosperous and flourishing city on a steep hill overlooking the river Orb. The city gates were open and the inhabitants were celebrating the feast day of St. Mary Magdalen, to whom Béziers' most important church (the fortress-like Gothic cathedral had not then been built) was dedicated.

The Bishop of Béziers, realizing the seriousness of the situation, went into the Crusaders' camp and brought back an ultimatum. The citizens were to surrender two hundred and twenty-two Cathars, listed by name. The city's elected consuls, who were not Cathars but respected freedom of thought, proudly refused, and one of them replied: "We had rather be drowned in the salt sea than surrender our fellow citizens."

At a given signal the Crusaders, along with their attendant hordes of mercenaries and brigands, plunged through the open gates into the city (Fig. 85), killing and burning until, it was said, the streets ran with blood. But the most horrible massacre of all took place inside the vast Romanesque Church of Sainte-Madeleine (Fig. 86), where seven thousand citizens, including women and children, had sought sanctuary. Even the monks who tolled the bells during this carnage were put to death, for some of the clergy were known to be in sympathy with the Cathars.

It was impossible to distinguish between Catholics and Cathars, and at the height of the slaughter the papal legate Arnaud Amaury, Bishop of Citeaux, is said to have commanded, "Kill them all! God will know his own!" The authenticity of this atrocious order would be suspect if it had not been reported by a Cistercian monk, and it was in keeping with the fanatical spirit of the Holy War. In his report to Pope Innocent III, Amaury wrote: "Without regard to age and sex, our forces have put to the sword twenty thousand persons. Divine vengeance has wrought wonders."

From Béziers the crusading army moved to the city of Carcassonne, which with its mighty fortifications (Fig. 87) seemed impregnable. The earliest legend concerning Carcassonne appears in various versions in the *chansons de geste* and has to do with a siege. Charle-

*Above: Fig. 87. Aerial view of Carcassonne (Aude). (Reportage Photogra-
phique YAN)*

*Left: Fig. 86. The Church of Sainte-Madeleine, Béziers (Hérault), scene of the
massacre of July 22, 1209.*

magne and his Frankish army had besieged Carcassonne, then occupied by the Saracens, for five years and the inhabitants were starving. A woman, Dame Carcas, thought of a ruse. She had the garrison's remaining supply of wheat collected and fed to the last sow in the city, who gorged herself on it. She then ordered the sow thrown from the ramparts. The hungry townspeople were horrified, but the stratagem worked, for the sow, swollen with her feast, burst open on striking the ground, and the wheat was strewn in all directions. The Franks concluded that the people of Carcassonne had plentiful supplies and informed Charlemagne, who raised the siege. From a tower Carcas waved farewell to the departing army. When Charlemagne learned the truth, he was so filled with admiration for Carcas' cleverness that he decided that the town should bear her name. A bas-relief has been discovered on the ramparts with the figure of a woman and below it the inscription *Carcas sum*, "I am Carcas," which became "Carcassonne." According to another version, favored by the troubadours, Dame Carcas, on learning that the Franks were about to raise the siege, had the trumpets sounded for a parley, and the garrison shouted to Charlemagne, "*Carcas te sonne!*" ("Carcas is calling you"), and the besiegers repeated, "*Carcas sonne!*" The story is told with great charm in Alphonse Daudet's delightful tales of the Midi, *Lettres de Mon Moulin*. It is interesting that it is the Franks, not the occupying Saracens, who are regarded as the enemy. In actuality it was Charlemagne's father, Pepin the Short, who drove the Saracens from Carcassonne, but all the epics made Charlemagne the central figure. A large, much-mutilated 16th century bust of Dame Carcas stands outside the Porte Narbonnaise, one of the gateways into the walled city.

Viscount Roger de Trancavel had entrenched himself in the city, in which thousands of terrified peasants had taken refuge with their cattle. Carcassonne held for many weeks, until the water gave out. It is said that jongleurs stood on the walls, singing and playing their viols and taunting the Crusaders, who were sweltering in the summer heat.

When Simon de Montfort invited Trancavel to a parley, the young viscount agreed to meet with him, hoping against hope for some solution other than a massacre. He was seized as he entered the Crusaders' camp and imprisoned in a dungeon cell. The fifty knights who had accompanied him were hanged, and on August 15, in exchange for their viscount, the inhabitants of Carcassonne were allowed to leave, one by one. The men were allowed to wear only their breechcloths and the women were clad only in shifts. Many took refuge in Spain. But five hundred prisoners were burned alive, to make Simon de Montfort's message clear to everyone.

Six months after his imprisonment, Roger Trancavel died in his narrow cell. Officially, it was reported that he died of dysentery, which was in epidemic proportions, but many believed that he had been murdered by his captors. The troubadour Guillaume de Béziers, who escaped the holocaust, wrote in a *planh* on the death of his patron:

> They slew him, and so great a wrong
> Was never seen by mortal man,
> Nor so iniquitous a deed
> 'Gainst God and our most blessèd Lord
> As this, by Pilate's cursèd seed,
> Those traitorous curs who cut him down.

Raymond VI, still hoping to stave off an invasion of his territories and end the slaughter, hurried back to Toulouse from the Crusade. Simon de Montfort had assumed the title Viscount of Carcassonne and Béziers; the ex-troubadour Bishop Foulques de Marseilles, a close ally of the legate Arnaud Amaury, began a campaign to undermine the morale of the Toulousains from within. He founded the so-called "White Brotherhood" in Toulouse with the aim of stirring up hatred against Jews and Cathars and increasing the power of the clergy in the city.

To counter this organization, the civic leaders of Toulouse who supported the popular Raymond organized a "Black Brotherhood," and the city was on the verge of civil war. A contemporary wrote that Foulques was responsible for the death of thousands of his fellow countrymen, and that he acted "more like Antichrist than like an envoy of Rome." It is ironic that Dante, who with some justification placed Bertran de Born in Hell, chose to put Foulques de Marseilles among the blessed in Paradise!

The Crusaders continued to spread devastation and death in the territories of the Trancavels. In 1210, Simon de Montfort, accompanied by Arnaud Amaury, besieged the Castle of Minerve, an "eagle's nest" surrounded by a little village, perched on a towering promontory between two rivers (Fig. 88). By cutting off the water supply, Simon de Montfort forced the surrender of the stronghold,

Fig. 88. Minerve (Hérault), with the ruins of the castle, a Cathar stronghold, destroyed by Simon de Montfort and his Crusaders in 1210. The little Romanesque church can be seen in the background. (Reportage Photographique YAN)

which had been the refuge of many Cathars. The following day the Crusaders burned one hundred and forty Cathars alive, and Arnaud Amaury's nephew and secretary wrote that the victors watched this mass burning "with intense joy." A street in the little village is called Rue des Martyrs.

Equally horrible was the capture in 1211 of Lavaur, a small town between Toulouse and Albi. The lady of Lavaur, Giralda de Laurac, was a Cathar, famous throughout the region for her kindness and charity and her protection of poets, scholars and heretics. In the absence of her husband, her brother Aimery de Montréal helped her defend the Castle of Lavaur, which held out against Simon de Montfort for two months. Finally Simon took the castle, Aimery de Montréal and eighty of his knights were hanged, and four hundred Cathars were burned alive on the field outside the town. Then Simon ordered his soldiers to throw Giralda down the castle well, and they pelted her with heavy stones until she died. The blocked well-head is still pointed out to show where this kind and gentle woman met her horrible death.

After Lavaur, Simon de Montfort was ready for the bigger prize of Toulouse. Raymond VI was watching and waiting. By constant denunciations and a steady "war of nerves" against the Toulousains, Simon induced the Pope to excommunicate Raymond a second time. The count had no further illusions about altering the course of events by diplomacy, and he appealed for military help to his two most trusted allies, his brother-in-law, Peter II of Aragon, Count of Barcelona, and his neighbor Raymond Roger, Count of Foix. A full-scale war was inevitable. The troubadour Peire Cardenal struck a hopeful note in his *sirventès*:

> We have Lord Raymond in Toulouse,
> Our noble count whom God directs:
> No Frenchman and no caitiff priest
> Shall ever bring him to his knees.

But another troubadour, Bernard de Marjevoir, thinking of all the terrible events of the past two years, lamented:

> Ah! Toulouse and Provence
> And the fair land of Argence,
> Ah! Carcassonne and Béziers,
> I saw you then—I look on you today!

Peter II, King of Aragon, Count of Barcelona and Lord of Montpellier, a curious and contradictory character, had distinguished himself in Spain as a Crusader by scoring a resounding victory over the Almohavide Moors at the Navas de Tolosa in Andalusia in 1212. As sovereign of lands north of the Pyrenees, he had come into close contact with the Cathars. He was a keen patron of the troubadours and had a rakish reputation in the Provençal courts. By his marriage in 1204 to Marie of Montpellier, the daughter of that city's ruler, Guilhem VIII, Peter became Lord of Montpellier. He was a fickle husband and was so enamored of a new mistress that he contemplated repudiating the unfortunate Marie. According to a chronicle written soon after his death, the resourceful burghers and consuls of Montpellier resorted to a stratagem similar to that used in Shakespeare's *Measure For Measure* to entrap the faithless Angelo. They replaced Peter's mistress, with whom he had made a nocturnal rendezvous, with his wife Marie in the royal bed. From this cleverly planned reunion a son was born in 1208, the future James I of Aragon. Subsequently Peter made further attempts to repudiate Marie and she fled to Rome, where she died in April 1213.

In that same year, 1213, Peter took up arms against Simon de Montfort's Crusaders, moved less by sympathy with the Albigensians than by the hostility he shared with other Southern princes to the aggressions by the North under the pretense of religious zeal. He hastened to join forces with Raymond VI and the Count of Foix, but the handsome and amorous young king found time every evening to send messages in Provençal verse to the beautiful chatelaines of Toulouse. One of them was:

> Tremble my fairest turtledoves,
> Peter has come to fight for your kisses!

On September 12, 1213, the Catalonians, the Toulousains and their allies joined battle with Simon de Montfort's Crusaders near the town of Muret. Simon was eager for the death of the chivalrous Peter of Aragon, whom he considered his special rival. Peter was maneuvered into a vulnerable position and killed. A small stone monument by the roadside marks the spot where, in the words of the inscription, Peter of Aragon "died for Occitan freedom." The citizen army of Toulouse was destroyed, and the Crusaders had won. Raymond VI escaped into Spain, with every intention of returning.

Encouraged by the victory of the Crusaders, Philip Augustus sent his son Prince Louis, the future Louis VIII, south to join Simon. The prince was the first member of the French royal family to participate in the Crusade against the Albigensians. Simon and Prince Louis entered Toulouse together, watched by a sullen populace.

At the Lateran Council of 1215, the Pope acknowledged Simon de Montfort as master of the lands he had conquered, and the following year he was officially proclaimed Count of Toulouse by Philip Augustus, and had a seal struck with his new title, substituting the Crusaders Cross for the sun and moon of the House of Toulouse. Simon began dismantling the city's fortifications and demolished the towers of the nobles.

The Church and the armed might of Simon's Crusaders seemed to have triumphed, and the troubadour Peire Cardenal, a native of Le Puy who had been Raymond's secretary from 1204 to 1208, wrote in a bitter *sirventès*:

> Injustice and lies
> Have joined the battle
> With justice and right,
> And lies have won!

Although a pious Catholic, Peire called St. Dominic "mensongier Castella,"—the liar of Castile. After the battle of Muret, Peire Cardenal went into exile and lived at the court of Peter II's young son, James I of Aragon, until the time was ripe for his return to Languedoc.

Events then took a surprising turn. Raymond VI, who was thought to be in Spain, landed in Marseilles with his nineteen-year-old son, Raymond the "Young Count," and was welcomed by the population as a deliverer. Provence rallied to his side and Raymond began his amazing reconquest of his lands.

The Crusaders sent urgent messages to Simon de Montfort, who had gone north to quell an uprising. The people of Toulouse, who had formed themselves into an improvised "citizen's army," imprisoned the French garrison, and on September 13, 1217, Raymond VI crossed the Garonne with his son and his Toulousain *faidits* (exiles deprived of their lands) in triumph. They received a rapturous welcome from the citizens. Bells rang out in defiance of Church regulations and there was dancing in the streets. Banners with the cross of Languedoc were flown from the housetops.

Simon de Montfort returned south and began a nine-month siege of Toulouse. Lords, burghers, Cathars and Jews were all united in the defense of their city, and men and women stood guard on the walls, armed with crossbows.

At dawn, on June 18, 1218, Simon de Montfort, whose brother

Guy had just been killed, was advancing on the Porte Saint-Sernin when he was hit by a stone from a catapult, fired by a woman from the ramparts. In the words of the anonymous troubadour who wrote part of the "Song of the Crusade":

> *E vene tot dreit la peira lai oun ers mestiers—*

> And the stone went straight and landed exactly where it should. [Literally: "there where its duty was."]

Simon de Montfort's skull was split open, and his huge frame fell to the ground in front of the city he had never understood. The cry went up, "*Mounfort ès mort!*" and the whole South rejoiced. The women of Toulouse were acclaimed as heroines, and the cruel tyrant's death was seen as a manifestation of divine justice.

A curious stone bas-relief known as the *pierre du siège* in a chapel in the Cathedral of Saint-Nazaire in Carcassonne (Fig. 89) may possibly represent the siege of Toulouse. It is thought by some to show the death of Simon de Montfort outside the city walls, but this is hard to determine. Simon was buried in the Cathedral in front of the Chapel of Sainte-Croix, but his remains were later dug up and reburied in his family estate at Montfort l'Amaury in Seine-et-Marne.

Many of the dramatic events in the early years of the Albigensian War are described in the remarkable epic chronicle in Provençal verse, the "Canso de la Crozada"—"Song of the Crusade." The manuscript of this poem in the Bibliothèque Nationale is illustrated with line drawings representing the capture of Béziers and the siege of Carcassonne.

This *canso* is the work of two different authors. The first part, covering events up to the spring of 1213, when Peter II of Aragon joined his brother-in-law, is the work of Guilhem de Tudela, a native of Spanish Navarre who, after some years in Montauban, became attached to the court of Raymond VI's brother, Count Baldwin.

In his poem, Guilhem defends the house of Toulouse, but blames the "obstinacy" of the Cathar heretics for the disasters which had overtaken the country. The anonymous author of the second part of the "Song of the Crusade" had a completely different point of view. He was probably a jongleur from the county of Foix and he narrated events from the spring of 1213, through the death of Simon de Montfort, up to the siege of Toulouse by Prince Louis in June 1219. He was a passionate, violent poet, deeply attached to the Counts of Toulouse, sympathetic to the Cathars, and angrily protesting against

Fig. 89. The so-called "pierre du siège", a 13th century bas-relief in the Cathedral of Saint-Nazaire, Carcassonne. It may represent the siege of Toulouse in 1218, when Simon de Montfort was killed. (Reportage Photographique YAN)

the barbarism of Simon and the Crusaders. He used troubadour language when he said that Simon de Montfort's death "brought Pride to the ground and raised up *Paratge*" (that untranslatable word implying gallantry and equality). Raymond VI's own device was "*Prets* [Worth] *et Paratge.*"

Simon de Montfort's body was taken to Carcassonne, and the poet of the chanson made a blistering indictment. He wrote that on Simon's epitaph in the Cathedral of Saint-Nazaire at Carcassonne, he is called "a saint, a martyr, who will rise from the dead and win a heavenly crown in God's kingdom." The poet wrote with savage irony:

> If killing men and shedding blood,
> Destroying souls and murdering,
> Heeding false counsel, lighting fires,
> Debasing barons, shaming Worth,

Seizing lands by violence,
Causing Pride to mount on high,
Kindling evil, quenching good,
Killing women, slaughtering babes,
If for all this one can indeed
Win a reward from Jesus Christ,
If that is so, yes, I agree,
Simon de Montfort wears a crown
And sits in glory in the sky.

CHAPTER XXVI

The Inquisition and the Last Troubadours

RAYMOND VI DID NOT HAVE MANY YEARS to enjoy his triumph. One year after the death of Simon de Montfort, Prince Louis came south again; joined by Simon's feeble but vengeful son Amaury de Montfort, his army took Marmande on the Garonne, and the entire civil population was massacred. Raymond successfully withstood a siege of Toulouse by the French forces, who withdrew northward, and the prestige of the house of Toulouse was largely restored.

In 1222 Raymond VI died, still excommunicated by the Pope, but confident in the belief that his subtle tactics had finally prevailed over brute force. Because of the excommunication he was denied Christian burial, and after the 16th century all traces of his coffin were lost.

His young son Raymond VII—a grandson of Eleanor of Aquitaine (Raymond VI's fourth wife was Joanna Plantagenet)—was fully prepared to carry on the struggle. On his seal (Fig. 90) he sits enthroned with a sword of justice across his knees and holds in his left hand a castle symbolizing the city of Narbonne. The sun and crescent moon on either side of him symbolize the count's territories in the West and in the Orient.

Raymond VII succeeded in reconquering most of the regions occupied by the Crusaders, and in 1223 Philip Augustus, worn out

[*269*]

Left: Fig. 90. Seal of Raymond VII, Count of Toulouse, dated 1242. He holds a three-towered edifice symbolizing the castle of Narbonne.

Below: Fig. 91. Blanche of Castile and Louis IX, from a 13th century Moralized Bible. Below the royal personages, a monk is giving instructions to a scribe-illuminator, who holds an ink-horn in his left hand. Pierpont Morgan Library MS 240, fol. 8. (The Pierpont Morgan Library, New York)

after his reign of forty-three years, died. Prince Louis became King Louis VIII; his cold nature and frail physique made his nickname, the Lion, most inappropriate. Amaury de Montfort, finding his stolen lands in Languedoc too difficult to hold, resigned them to the French king and retired to the Ile-de-France. Louis VIII, determined to conquer the heretical South, led a third crusading expedition in 1226. He forced Avignon to capitulate, but while passing through Auvergne on his return to Paris, he was stricken with dysentery and died. The new king, Louis IX, the future St. Louis, was a boy of twelve, and Raymond hoped for a period of calm. But he had not reckoned with Louis VIII's formidable widow, the Regent, Blanche of Castile (Fig. 91). She offered peace, and Raymond went north only to find that he had been lured into a trap. He was imprisoned, and excommunicated by a Church council. Unable to resist the combined powers of the Church and the French monarchy, now close allies, Raymond yielded to their demands. In order to lift the bar of excommunication, he underwent an even more humiliating ordeal than that of his father at Saint-Gilles.

In the presence of Blanche of Castile, the twelve-year-old Louis IX and the papal legate, Raymond was publicly flagellated, "naked except for his shift," in the open space in front of Notre-Dame in Paris on April 12, 1229, mocked by a jeering crowd. He was then led up the aisle to beg absolution for having sustained the heretics. The few Southerners present could not hold back their tears.

Raymond's submission was confirmed by the treaty of Meaux; his only daughter, Jeanne, aged nine, was to be kept in Paris and married to Louis IX's young brother, Prince Alphonse of Poitiers, on the understanding that on Raymond's death Languedoc and all the southern provinces would fall into the possession of the French crown.

The Archbishop of Auch, a tolerant and gentle prelate who had been removed from his see in 1214 for his refusal to persecute the Cathars, was also a troubadour, and he wrote of the treaty of Meaux:

> Good lasting peace, it likes me well,
> But peace imposed I cannot bear,
> From shameful peace more evils come than good.

Raymond was allowed to keep his county and some of his other possessions, but Carcassonne, Narbonne and Béziers were occupied by the French. Life in Toulouse was never the same again. The papal legate, an Italian, summoned a council of the clergy in Toulouse to lay down rules for the ecclesiastical government of the region and the extirpation of heresy. The council founded the University of Toulouse, but unlike the University of Montpellier with its tradition of freedom, its main obligation was to spread the Catholic faith.

In 1233, twelve years after the death of Dominic, Pope Gregory IX organized the Inquisition, otherwise known as the Holy Office, and charged certain Dominicans with the investigation and suppression of all forms of heresy, the main target being the Albigensians. A court was set up in Toulouse with powers of life and death, and accountable only to the Pope. All the guarantees of justice to which the people of the South had been accustomed for centuries were denied.

When an Inquisitor arrived in a village, the inhabitants were given a "week of grace" to come forward and confess. Those who did not were suspected of heresy, arrested and often tortured. Those who did had to give the names and hiding places of all Cathars they knew or had ever known. The dossiers were filled with denunciations, and the suspect was never allowed to confront his or her accusers or to know who they were.

Since the clergy were forbidden to shed blood—torture was permissible to extract confessions—Canon Law decreed that the condemned should be handed over to the "secular arm" to be punished "without shedding of blood," that is, by burning at the stake (Fig. 92). Over two hundred heretics were burned at Moissac in one day. Those who recanted were imprisoned or subject to heavy penalties; many were financially ruined by being sent on pilgrimages to distant shrines such as Compostela or Canterbury. Saint-Guilhem-le-Désert

Fig. 92. The burning of a heretic, from a pen drawing of around 1250 in the register of Alphonse of Poitiers (reproduced in the Gazette des Beaux-Arts, 1873).

was nearer, but still involved a long, difficult and costly journey. This made a mockery of the original intention of the pilgrimages.

Any means were justified to uncover heresy. Bishop Foulques, who had become very wealthy and who died peacefully in his bed in 1232 after composing some final hymns to the Virgin, was succeeded by Bishop Raimon du Fuga. In 1235 the bishop was informed that a great lady on the point of death had just received the Cathar consolamentum. He immediately went to the designated address accompanied by several Dominicans. When the arrival of "My lord the Bishop" was announced to the dying woman, she thought it was a Cathar prelate. The bishop did nothing to undeceive her and by this subterfuge he was able to obtain a complete confession, even encouraging the old lady to stay firm in her convictions. Then, dropping his "disguise," he threatened her and urged her to be converted. She refused and was immediately condemned. As she was too ill to walk, she was carried in her bed to the stake.

Inevitably there were violent reactions to this reign of terror, even among devout Catholics. In Cordes three Dominicans were thrown into a well. At one point the Catholic *capitouls* of Toulouse, aided by the Augustinian canons of Saint-Sernin, ejected the Inquisitors from their monastery and drove them out of the city with sticks and blows, but they had inspired such fear that they were eventually allowed to return.

Throughout Languedoc, bishops and Dominicans fulminated against the poets and their "vain ditties," which glorified women and celebrated life's pleasures. There were diatribes against feminine luxury and the lavishness of the southern nobles.

Louis IX, who assumed personal power in 1234 but was still strongly influenced by his mother's rigid piety—in her presence he was like a child—encouraged art when it was in the service of the Church—the exquisite Sainte-Chapelle in Paris was his creation—but in the South, he persecuted poets as well as Cathars and Jews. His biographer wrote that the King himself "did not sing worldly songs, nor would he suffer those in his retinue to sing them." Noble knights had to swear to the papal legate that they would never again compose verses.

St. Louis, who is held up in French school textbooks as a model of virtue, benevolence, justice and wisdom, decreed in an edict against blasphemy that sacrilegious language should be punished by "burning the lips of the blasphemer with a glowing hot iron." Informers against

blasphemers or heretics were granted immunity, for St. Louis was
determined to "chase the *bougres*" and other evildoers out of his
kingdom. (The word *bougre*, from which the English word "bugger"
is derived, was a variant of *bolgre* or *Bolgarus*, meaning Bulgarian; it
was in Bulgaria that the Bogomils, the original Cathars, had flourished.)

The troubadours knew that a precious way of life was being
destroyed; not only were many of their patrons dead or in exile, but
they saw that the countryside was devastated and the peasants ruined;
in the cities most of the people could not afford the merchants' wares,
yet those who "collaborated" with the forces of oppression grew
rich and powerful. Songs of protest were called for, not love songs
or celebrations of spring. Peire Cardenal returned from his stay in
Spain and suffered to see his young patron, Raymond VII, reduced
to impotence. He wrote a scathing *sirventès* against the hypocrisy of
the clergy who put on meek and saintly airs but acted like predatory
beasts:

> The priests would shepherds be
> But are assassins all
> Beneath their holy airs.
> When I see how they dress
> I call to mind the tale
> Of Master Ysengrin
> Who entered the sheepfold.
> Fearing attack by dogs
> A sheepskin he put on
> And thus escaped their eyes,
> Then treacherously devoured
> The sheep who pleased him best.

In a later stanza Peire Cardenal, though a sincere Catholic, could not
contain his rage against clerical domination:

> Monarchs and emperors
> And dukes and counts and lords
> Together with the knights
> Are wont to rule the world;
> But now I see that priests
> Have gathered all the power
> By theft and treachery
> And base hypocrisy,
> By preaching and by force.

> They take it much amiss
> If all is not made theirs,
> And thus their will is done.

The most violent satires against Rome were written by Guilhem Figueira of Toulouse, a man of the people, a friend of Count Raymond VII and a Cathar "believer." In his long and passionate *sirventès*, "Rome, Scourge of the World," he lashed out with pounding rhythms:

> *Roma enganairitz*
> *Qu'etz de totz mals quitz*
>   *e sima e razitz!*

> You arch-deceiver Rome,
> The root of all our ills
>   False and perfidious!

He accused the Roman Church of gnawing the flesh and bones of simple people, and listed crimes committed in the name of religion:

> *Roma del cervel*
> *quar de mal capel*
> *etz vos e Cistel . . .*

> Rome, you have decked your head
> With caps of infamy
> You and your own Citeaux
> Who wrought at Béziers
> That monstrous butchery.

The reference was to the papal legate Arnaud Amaury, abbot of Citeaux, who had sanctioned the massacre. Figueira attacked the materialism of the high Roman clergy, whom he called "rapacious wolves and crowned serpents," and although strict Cathars did not believe in hellfire, he declared:

> Rome, vile, corrupt,
> Your heart is all
> On lucre—greed will make you burn
> In flames eternally.

Not surprisingly, Guilhem Figueira's violent denunciations of persecutors and greedy oppressors drew the animosity of the clergy, and to escape the Inquisition he fled to southern Italy, where he joined the brilliant and heretical court of Emperor Frederick II.

Fig. 93. Montanhagol. Bibl. Nat. MS Fr. 854, fol. 124 (Bibliothèque Nationale, Paris)

Frederick, whom the Pope and the orthodox considered the Antichrist, was a Renaissance man before his time. He was a gifted poet, artist and scientist, and he was surrounded by Provençal troubadours who had fled the rigors of their own land and by their gifted German and Austrian imitators, the Minnesingers. In this way the *courtois* tradition was not lost but contributed to the birth of a native Italian literature, as Dante and Petrarch readily admitted.

According to his biographer, Figueira died in Lombardy "in a state of heresy"—many Cathar fugitives settled in this region so long associated with their faith. His "Rome, Scourge of the World" was widely circulated, and a report of the Inquisition in 1274 related that a citizen, interrogated as to whether he or any of his acquaintances owned or had read the book containing the poem, replied that he had heard it sung several times in public, and that he believed it was by a "jongleur called Figueira."

Another troubadour from Toulouse in Raymond VII's circle, Guilhem Montanhagol (Fig. 93), was horrified by the excesses of the Inquisition and by the French suppression of the independence of the South, but was less vehement in tone than Figueira, and at times introduced a conciliatory note. In an early *sirventès* aimed at the Dominicans, he wrote:

> They've made themselves Inquisitors
> And judge according to their whim;
> There should be questions, I agree,
> And error should indeed be fought—

> Those who have strayed must surely be reclaimed
> With gentle speeches, not with savage hate.

He hoped for a return to persuasion, which was out of the question. He deplored the condemnation, by clerics and the Dominican preachers, of Honor and Liberality and other courtly virtues, and their attacks on women's elegant attire—recalling Bernard of Clairvaux's diatribes of long ago. Montanhagol said that a lady was no less deserving of God's love if she decked herself out in beautiful garments embroidered in gold:

> 'Tis not through long black cassocks or white cowls
> That hate-filled souls will ever come to God.

Montanhagol fled to Spain and took refuge in the cultivated court of Alfonso X, the Wise, of Castile, at Toledo. Alfonso, an enthusiastic patron of learning and the arts, commissioned and compiled the *Cantigas de Santa Maria* (Songs of Holy Mary), some of which he probably composed. After Montanhagol returned to Languedoc he settled in Montpellier, where, under the wise and moderate rule of James I of Aragon (Fig. 94), there was still a degree of freedom. Montanhagol tried to adapt troubadour poetry to the new climate by supposedly "raising its moral tone." He constantly tried to reassure both the clergy and those who in their fear of punishment had abandoned poetry and the cult of love, that "Love is no sin but a virtue that makes the bad good, and the good better." He accused earlier troubadours of "heedlessness and frivolity." Love songs should

Fig. 94. Seal of James I, King of Aragon, Count of Barcelona and Lord of Montpellier, 1229.

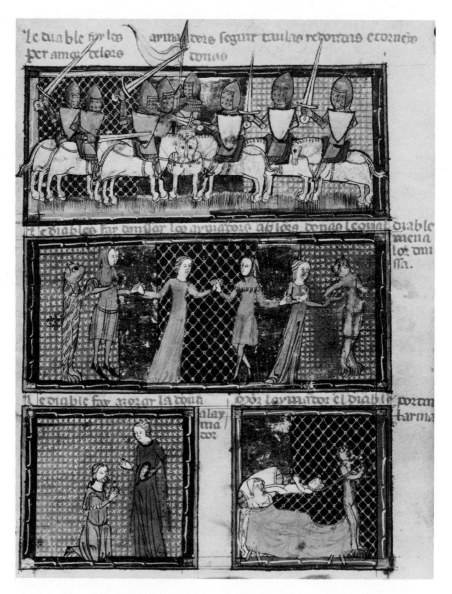

Fig. 95. The Devil leading the dance. From the Bréviaire d'Amour *by Matfre Ermengau of Béziers. Bibl. Nat. MS Fr. 857, fol. 196 v. (Bibliothèque Nationale, Paris)*

conform to Christian morality and be "perfectly virtuous and chaste." It was but one step from this diluted approach to the interminable *Breviary of Love*, a long didactic poem begun in 1288 by a Franciscan monk from Béziers, Matfre Ermengau, and running to 27,445 lines of pedantic verse. Two of the longest chapters are entitled "On the Baseness of Sin" and "On the Vileness of the Flesh," and Ermengau affirmed his impeccable orthodoxy by saying, "Satan, in his desire to make men suffer, inspires them with an idolatrous love of women." Only the pure love of the Virgin was admissible. He also attacked those who for reasons of heresy rejected the institution of marriage. Worldly pastimes were condemned and an illustration to Ermengau's manuscript in the Bibliothèque Nationale shows the Devil leading the dance (Fig. 95).

It should be noted that the Franciscans in Languedoc were often more tolerant and humane than the Dominicans and sometimes gave refuge to condemned heretics, partly from charity and partly in the hope of converting them. St. Francis in his youth in Assisi had known Provençal songs and had even, it is said, thought of becoming a jongleur. As was mentioned earlier, he urged his disciples to practice poetry, saying, "We are the jongleurs of God" whose vocation "is to uplift the hearts of men." By the early 13th century Dominican orthodoxy had prevailed in Southern France, and the Franciscans were never as influential there.

The decline of troubadour poetry and the society that had produced it is exemplified by Guiraut Riquier, sometimes called "the last of the court poets," which is more accurate than "the last of the troubadours." He was born in Narbonne around 1230. His earliest poems, skillful but lacking in feeling, were addressed to Philippa, Viscountess of Narbonne, who did not actually encourage poetry.

Narbonne, strongly Catholic, had been spared the horrors of the Albigensian wars by furnishing supplies to the Crusaders and agreeing to surrender all heretics, many of whom were burned in the city. As French control over the city increased, religious pressures grew and the Jewish community, which included philosophers, doctors, scholars and poets as well as bankers and merchants, was the first to feel the change.

In the 12th century and in the first years of the 13th, the Church had sometimes organized "disputations" with Jews in an attempt to convince them of the truth of Christianity and the absurdity of the Talmud, but usually any counter-argument was shouted down, and

Fig. 96. Jews and heretics debating with Catholic bishops in the presence of the enthroned Church. From a French mid-13th century Moralized Bible in the Bodleian Library, Oxford.

there had been no real debate. A papal bull of 1233 forbade any arguments between Christians and Jews. A miniature in a Moralized Bible of the mid-13th century in the Bodleian Library in Oxford (Fig. 96) shows Jews and heretics disputing with two Catholic bishops, with an enthroned Mother Church presiding.

St. Louis rejected any idea of discussion or association with the Jews and advised that they and other unbelievers should be met not by argument but with "a sword in the belly." The first burnings of the Talmud took place during his reign.

A reflection of this changed climate can be found in a curious *tenson* exchanged by Guiraut Riquier with a Jewish troubadour of Narbonne called Bonfilh. The name Bonfilh in various forms (Boffilus, Bonenfant, Bonfills or Bonus Filius) was not uncommon among Jews in Perpignan and other Southern cities in the 12th and 13th centuries. Riquier asked him maliciously, "I have heard tell, Bonfilh, that you know how to *trobar* and make verses; but I want to know in a few words: What is your reason for singing? Are you afraid of something? Do you have a lady for whom you must sing? Do you sing for love of *jonglerie*, or for the generosity of the first comer? Or do you sing that your reputation may grow?" Bonfilh replied with dignity that his object was not material gain or self-aggrandizement: "Guiraut, I sing to gladden my heart, for love of her who keeps me joyful, for I love renown, joy and youth; but I never sing to earn money: I would rather give money to you, for I give it to several, for the love of my lady who is gracious, generous, gay and full of merit." Then Guiraut brought in religion in an insulting manner. "Bonfilh, I want to ask you one thing more: Since you sing for love, for your pleasure and for your lady, tell me truly what law you obey, and yet I should refrain from questioning you on this point . . . all your words and all your deeds are hateful to Jesus Christ whom you tortured." Bonfilh ironically answered this spiteful question by saying that Riquier was twisting a poetic debate into a theological controversy: "If you abandon talk of love to preach sermons, you may as well speak no more and don a white garment [of the Dominicans]: and great will the dispute be, since my lady absolutely refuses to worship the cross . . ." Riquier replies that it ill becomes Bonfilh to speak of a special garment, an allusion, no doubt, to the distinguishing costume, or at least a special badge, that Jews were compelled to wear after the rise of the new Catholic orthodoxy.

Finally Riquier irritably broke off the *tenson*, saying, "Your reply, your company I will endure no more—my reputation suffers thereby." He decided to break completely with the "perfidious" Bonfilh, about whom one would like to know more. The *convivencia*, or amicable coexistence, of the Midi was rapidly disappearing.

After spending ten years at the court of Alfonso X of Castile, Riquier in 1279 returned to Languedoc and stayed in the castle of Henri, Count of Rodez, one of the last lords of Southern or Central France to gather poets around him. Riquier's one original contribution to troubadour poetry was the *serena*, or "evening song," which he treated with irony and grace, but his last poems, mostly hymns to the Virgin, marked the substitution of religious for courtly lyricism which accompanied the decadence of troubadour poetry.

There is a twilight melancholy in the lines of one of Guiraut Riquier's *sirventès* in which he senses the gathering darkness and the futility of the troubadour's art in a world that has no more use for it:

> Song should express the poet's joy,
> But sorrow weighs upon my heart.
> I came into the world too late.

CHAPTER XXVII

Ordeal by Fire: Montségur

COUNT RAYMOND VII, unable to stop the relentless course of the Inquisition, made one last desperate effort to free his lands from French occupation. He formed a coalition with James I of Aragon, Henry III of England (King John's son) and John's widow, Isabella, who after John's death returned to Lusignan and married her old suitor, Count Hugues the Brown.

Hugues and Isabella persuaded several other nobles of the South-west to join Raymond against the French, but the coalition was made too late to be effective. Louis IX's armies easily overran Lusignan and defeated the Toulousains at Saintes and Taillebourg in 1242 before the English had time to land their troops.

Raymond VII had to capitulate once again, but since he was no longer under excommunication he was spared the ordeal of another flagellation. Blanche of Castile and the Pope had brought pressure upon Raymond and had forced him to execute several leading Cathars.

Young Viscount Raymond-Roger Trancavel II, son of the hero of the siege of Carcassonne, made a gallant attempt to recapture the citadel from the French, but this too ended in failure. He finally submitted to Louis' authority and later accompanied him on the Seventh Crusade.

The reign of terror continued unabated in Languedoc. Even the dead were not allowed to rest in peace, and the bodies of heretics were often dug up and dragged through the streets as threats and grim object lessons.

There were violent reactions even among the non-Cathar population. In May 1242, a bailiff of Avignonet, a little village southwest of Toulouse, learned that the Grand Inquisitor, Guillaume Arnaud, would arrive just before Ascension Day with his tribunal to hold one of the dreaded "weeks of grace." The bailiff sent word to Pierre-Rogier de Mirepoix and his Cathar knights in the Castle of Montségur, and a careful strategy was planned. Sixty armed knights rode down the steep mountain of Montségur to make their way to Avignonet. The people of the countryside knew of their plan, but no one betrayed them. The peasants cheered them as they passed through the villages. The knights were admitted through the gates of Avignonet after dark.

The Inquisitors had arrived and had been lodged in the castle. The castellan, Raimond d'Alfaro, who knew the plan, received the Inquisitors courteously in the name of the Count of Toulouse. The conspirators assembled in a house nearby. The password was "Have you brought the hatchets?" The reply was "We have eleven, freshly honed."

Raimond d'Alfaro went down to admit the knights into the castle. They moved by torchlight through endless corridors, burst open the door where Guillaume Arnaud and his retinue were staying and killed the two Inquisitors and their nine assistants, who had all fallen on their knees on the stone floor, singing the "Salve Regina," which they never finished. The next morning the bells rang out for Ascension Day in villages throughout Aude more joyously than ever before.

The French were struck with amazement at the news of the killing of the Inquisitors. The knights returned to their aerie on top of Montségur. Hugues de Arcis, commander of the garrison at Carcassonne, began the siege of Montségur, determined to avenge the Inquisitors and deal heresy a mortal blow.

For over eleven years Montségur, on its vertiginous height in the Ariège near Lavelanet (Fig. 97), had been far more than a stronghold of the Cathars—it was their shrine, their tabernacle, their holy mountain. A tiny Cathar community settled there in 1202 or 1203 to lead a life of study and prayer. They found the ruined tower of an ancient

Fig. 97. Montségur (Ariège). (Copyright YAN)

castle and a cistern on the western side of the steep mountain to provide water. In 1203 a Cathar perfect, Forneria, the mother of a knight of Mirepoix, had a house there, and since there was no village nearby—the little red-roofed village at the foot of the mountain did not then exist—her son brought her bread, wine and fish.

In those early days most of the community were women, sharing a communal life of evangelical poverty. Their houses were wooden huts and stone cells. They were perfects, and were either widows or women who had lived apart from their husbands after receiving the consolamentum. Not all spent the whole year there; some came to visit friends.

By 1204, the year Esclarmonde de Foix became a perfect at Fanjeaux, the community had increased so rapidly that Raimon de Mirepoix and other members of the Cathar clergy asked Raimon de Péreille, a vassal of the Count of Foix and a friend of Esclarmonde, to rebuild the castle of Montségur for greater protection against brigands and roving bands of soldiers.

Raimon de Péreille, probably aided by Esclarmonde, bore most of the expenses of the rebuilding, which was completed in 1211. The massive square tower became the donjon and the cistern was replaced by a larger and less vulnerable one located where the great hall of the original castle had been. The new fortifications were in the form of an irregular pentagon and had no towers, no openings for the shooting of arrows or the propelling of missiles, and no decorations. It seemed impregnable, but it was intended as a refuge, not as a military fortress. There were two gateways into the castle. The one on the north led to a little village of the perfects, which was perched on the upper slopes of the mountain; the southern gate was the entrance to the castle itself.

The persecution of the Cathars increased after the enforced capitulation of Raymond VII to the French at Meaux in 1229. Pope Innocent III had called the Albigensians "worse than the Saracens," and his successors instigated Crusade after Crusade against them. The heretics were tracked down like wild animals, and they traveled secretly by night and hid themselves in the valleys and clefts of the Pyrenees.

Raimon de Péreille received large numbers of Cathars into the castle at Montségur. It was thought to provide a safe refuge with approaches easy to defend, and was soon to become the religious capital of the Cathars, from which missionaries would go out into

the Languedoc region. The very name Montségur—mountain of
safety—meant that it was protected by God.

At first Raimon de Péreille had been reluctant to receive the many
Cathars within his castle at Montségur, but after consultation with
his knights consent was given. Raimon knew the immense dangers
involved.

The forty knights and squires and hundred-odd men-at-arms in the
Montségur garrison were not all Cathars by any means, but all were
united in their fierce resistance to the French, whom they regarded
as foreign invaders, and in their hatred of the reign of terror established throughout the country by the Inquisition. The perfects themselves were forbidden to bear arms or to shed blood, but were glad to
have these stalwart defenders.

More spacious living quarters were built within the fortifications.
Remains of a great hall with steps carved out of the rock have been
found underneath the donjon: it may have served as a meeting place
or refectory. There was an *"Ostal des Bonshommes,"* where the
perfects lived, and which the Inquisitors called "the house of the
heretics," and next to it, the headquarters of the old and saintly
Cathar bishop Guilhabert de Castres, who had moved from Fanjeaux
to Montségur. Cathar believers could always find perfects at Montségur to advise and comfort them and administer the consolamentum.
Those who were on the point of death were brought up the mountain
on horses and mules to receive the last rites and "die a good death."

Provisions were carried on muleback up the narrow mountain path,
which was then in better condition than it is today. It was protected
by a barbican of stone and wood. Besides being a source of inspiration
and a refuge, Montségur was the hiding place for the Cathar treasures and holy books.

Because of the heavy expenses of rebuilding and sustaining the
castle and fortifications of Montségur and the need to assist fellow
Cathars everywhere, many believers gave the perfects sums of money
according to their means, as well as precious gold and silver objects.
All kinds of legends arose over the years regarding the fabled "treasure of Montségur." Some claimed that it was the repository of the
miraculous "Holy Grail," identified by Christians as the Chalice of
the Last Supper which contained the blood of Christ. It would be
revealed only to a knight whose heart was pure, and in the Arthurian
Legend the purest knight was either Parsifal or Galahad, depending
on the version.

Richard Wagner is said (on doubtful authority) to have visited Montségur around 1877 when he was writing his music drama *Parsifal*; he calls the citadel Monsalvat.

There is still a mystical aura surrounding the ruined fortress, looming four hundred feet above the wooded valleys and green meadows. The place arouses a feeling of awe and wonderment, and somehow suggests, in its remote isolation and rugged majesty, pre-Christian myths and legends and the possibility of miracles. One theory has even been advanced that Montségur was originally built as a solar temple, and that underneath the stones and buildings of the original castle there are the remains of the cult of sun worshippers. In its strange, mysterious beauty Montségur is surpassed only by Delphi.

As many as three hundred perfects, in addition to the one hundred and fifty or sixty knights and men-at-arms, lived at Montségur. Some of the soldiers and knights had their wives or mistresses with them, and a busy community life existed alongside the religious rituals and meditations. Raimon de Péreille, his son-in-law Rogier de Mirepoix and his family and their small retinue lived in the donjon. Pierre-Rogier's natural son, Roquefire, and a surgeon were also part of the household. With the close quarters and the constant coming and going, life at Montségur was crowded, noisy and very uncomfortable, especially in winter, but spirits were high.

The lower hall of the donjon was made cold and damp by the proximity of the new cistern, although there was a large fire burning in the upper hall, where the women gathered.

A battered copper plaque originally plated with gold was discovered at Montségur in 1967, possibly part of a belt or necklace. It represents a woman with delicate features wearing a coif and wimple and is the only portrait to have been found at Montségur.

The Cathar leaders in Montségur were kept fully informed of events in the outside world. They knew of young Trancavel's failure to retake Carcassonne in 1240; they understood when Raymond VII, ordered by the French and the Pope to destroy Montségur in 1241, sent only a small, token army, for they knew that he was preparing his belated coalition against the French. Messengers were constantly journeying to and from Catalonia, and there were frequent exchanges with the Cathar bishop of Cremona in Lombardy, where conditions were more peaceful.

Guilhem Figueira's savage *sirventès* against the Roman Church were sung and applauded in Montségur, and so were the antipapal poems composed by troubadours who had fled to the Emperor Frederick II's court in Capua in southern Italy. The Cathar leaders were seriously hoping for an intervention on their behalf by Frederick II, who was Raymond VII's ally and a bitter enemy of the papacy. But Frederick was fully occupied with the events in Germany, menaced by the Mongols, and he had other problems too complicated to mention here.

There were few young people in Montségur and fewer children. The perfects spent much of their time in their stone cells, but the courtyard was bustling with the activity of the knights and their womenfolk, and the atmosphere was not one of unbroken piety. It was a curiously mixed community. The knights and soldiers acknowledged the spiritual authority of the Cathar perfects, but made no attempt to imitate their austere way of life. The only "legitimate" wives were those of Raimon de Péreille, Pierre-Rogier de Mirepoix and some of the knights related to them, and they had been married according to the rites of the Catholic Church. Catholic marriage had no meaning at Montségur, and no distinction was made between "legitimate" wives and the "concubines" of the knights and soldiers (called *amasiae-uxores*, "mistress-wives," by the Inquisitors). These were for the most part truly loving and passionate relationships, for these women had voluntarily accompanied their men into this dangerous predicament and were sharing the hardship and trials. Many of these mistress-wives were to die by fire with their lovers and make, according to the Cathar belief, "a good end." It was an emotional and physical relationship, "outside of marriage," intensified and sublimated by the element of danger and the ideal of freedom.

René Nelli suggests that "in Montségur, for the first and last time, a society actually practiced and carried to great heights the passionate love of which the troubadours had only worshipped the ideal image under the name of *fin 'amor*."

Blanche of Castile was furious when she heard of the death of the Inquisitors at Avignonet, and declared, "The dragon's head, Montségur, must be cut off." Exactly one year later, on May 13, 1243, Hugues de Arcis, commander of the Carcassonne garrison, and his army of ten thousand pitched their tents at the foot of the mountain and the ten-month siege of Montségur began.

At first the French hoped to starve the defenders into surrender and expected the wells to dry up in the hot summer months. But attack after attack was successfully repelled. Through the summer and the autumn supplies were brought into the fortress secretly by night, carried by men along hidden footpaths unknown to the enemy. Ropes were let down from the castle walls and provisions and men were hoisted up the precipices in the darkness.

A signal code was arranged and, through flares and beacons, Montségur was able to communicate with Raimon de Péreille's castle at Roquefixade, on a mountain to the northwest, and with other distant points. This method of sending and receiving knowledge did not enable the defenders to learn what plans, if any, Raymond VII was able to make. There were rumors that Frederick II would arrive with his army to rescue Montségur.

Life in the fortress went on as before while the siege was endured. The venerable bishop Guilhabert de Castres died and was succeeded by Bertran Marti, who conducted the Cathar rituals and made many new converts.

In November 1143, the situation took a turn for the worse. The French commander, Hugues de Arcis, secured a group of agile Basque mountaineers from Navarre who were able to scale the cliffs with ropes. They succeeded in capturing a shoulder of the mountain, just below the castle, and installed a powerful catapult. Supervised by Durand, Bishop of Albi, a masterful military strategist, the Basque mercenaries began to bombard the ramparts with huge stones.

Raimon de Péreille had dug secret tunnels, hollowed out of the mountain, and through these Bertrand de Baccalaria, one of Europe's leading military engineers, made his way into the castle, sent by Count Raymond VII. Stone-throwing machines were set up to counterattack the French catapult. Late in December a traitor, Jean Bernart, revealed to the Basques the secret way up the sheer cliffs, and one moonless night they scaled the mountainside and captured the east bastion. All of the people in the tower were massacred and fighting raged in the castle and the courtyard. Giant stone-throwers were set up nearer the castle by the Bishop of Albi, and enormous boulders were hurled against the rugged walls, which still held firm.

By February 1244 the narrow courtyard had become an inferno, as fire arrows fell among the defenders and wooden roofs collapsed in flames. The struggle to survive was intense. All of the women, the perfects, the believers, and the soldiers' companions, their garments torn and bloody, worked incessantly side by side, tending the wounded and helping to defend the ramparts.

On March 1 or 2, 1244, Pierre-Rogier de Mirepoix, with the full agreement of the knights and the surviving perfects, decided to seek terms for surrender. The terms given by the French were less harsh than might have been expected. The fortress of Montségur was to become the property of the Pope and the King of France, but the defenders would be allowed to remain in control of the castle for another two weeks. All the knights and men-at-arms, even those who had participated in the episode at Avignonet, were to be free to leave with their weapons and belongings. The lives of the heretics who recanted would be spared—those who persisted in their "error" were to be burned at the stake.

None of the Cathars renounced their faith, and in those last days, marked by a strange unearthly stillness, more and more of the defenders took the consolamentum from their bishop, Bertran Marti. Corba, the beautiful wife of Raimon de Péreille, became a perfect and bade a last farewell to her husband. She was joined by her aged mother, Marquesia de Lantar, and her sick and crippled daughter Esclarmonde (the young girl bore the same name as the great lady of Foix who had died years before in Montségur, the citadel she had helped to create).

Those who awaited death generously distributed all they possessed —clothes, money, wheat and other provisions—among those who were to survive. Bertran Marti gave his supplies of salt, pepper, oil and wax to Pierre-Rogier de Mirepoix.

On the evening of March 15, the day before the "auto-da-fé," Pierre Authier, the treasurer of Montségur, was lowered by rope down the steep mountainside along with three other men, with orders to take the treasure to the Castle of Ussat in the High Pyrenees, where several Cathars had already found refuge. They were to light a beacon on arrival at the summit of Mont Barthélemy as a signal that they had escaped into safe territory.

At dawn the beacon flared from the distant mountaintop at the exact time the Cathars on Montségur were preparing for a different and terrible fire. A huge pile of faggots had been laid on the gently sloping meadow at the foot of the less precipitous side of the mountain to the south. At the appointed hour the heavy gate of the castle swung open, and two hundred and sixteen perfects, men and women, walked solemnly and serenely down the mountainside. Heading the procession was Bertran Marti, his head held high, not because of pride, but because he was willing to accept the responsibility of his conviction. Among those who followed him were three generations of the family of Raimon de Péreille, his mother, Marquesia de Lantar, so feeble that she had to be assisted by the Chevalier de Laurac, her daughter Corba, and her ailing granddaughter Esclarmonde. The Cathars mounted the pyre, and sang hymns as the flames rose, while the Crusaders, who had retreated to a safe distance, sang the "Veni Creator." The Cathars stoically accepted the ordeal of pain and death as a deliverance from a world which seemed to them to be the creation of Satan.

By noon nothing remained but a pile of smoldering ashes in the meadow, which is known to this day as the Camp des Crémats—the Field of the Burned.

No one knows the fate of the mysterious "treasure of Montségur." It may be hidden in any one of the innumerable caves or grottoes of Ussat.

A small altar was erected in 1960 at the foot of the slope of the Field of the Burned, with stones collected from the ruined citadel. It is surmounted by a discoidal cross with four equal arms carved on the front; on the reverse, cut into the stone, is the Cathar star with five rays, beneath a weaver's shuttle. The inscription, in the language of the Cathars and troubadours, reads:

ALS CATHARS
ALS MARTIRS
DEL PUR AMOR
CRESTIAN
16 MARS 1244

TO THE CATHARS
TO THE MARTYRS
OF PURE CHRISTIAN
LOVE
MARCH 16, 1244

In late August 1249, five years after the fall of Montségur, and forty years after the massacre at Béziers, Raymond VII, last of the Counts of Toulouse, was suddenly taken ill while traveling through the Aveyron region, and died in the town of Millau. His last wish was to be buried in the abbey at Fontevrault near his maternal grandmother, Eleanor of Aquitaine, his mother, Joanna, and his admired uncle, Richard Coeur de Lion. This posthumous link with the Plantagenets and the vanished dream of a great realm south of the Loire would compensate, at least symbolically, for his enforced subjection to the French monarchy during his unhappy reign. Raymond's coffin was placed on a barge, which sailed down the Aveyron, the Tarn and the Garonne until it reached the city of Agen, where the nuns of Fontevrault gave it a temporary resting place, before taking it north to their abbey.

During the river journey people lined the banks on either side, kneeling and weeping for the death of their count and the end of Southern freedom. Raymond's only daughter, Joanna (Fig. 98), married as a child by the decree of Blanche of Castile to the new lord of the Midi, Louis IX's brother, Alphonse de Poitiers, was almost a stranger to Languedoc. She and her husband came to the province only twice, to receive the homage of their vassals and to raise money.

The kneeling effigies of the count and his mother, Joanna Plantagenet, in the abbey of Fontevrault were completely destroyed during the Revolution of 1789.

One last Cathar stronghold, the Castle of Quéribus (Fig. 99), on a rocky spur in the Corbières range in Roussillon, held out for six years after the holocaust at Montségur; in the spring of 1255 its commander, Chabert de Barbaira, surrendered the castle to the seneschal of Carcassonne, Pierre d'Auteuil, in exchange for his freedom. By that time Louis IX and his brother, Alphonse de Poitiers, had built new castles and fortress-towns all over the country and had installed French garrisons.

In 1246 another of Louis' brothers, Charles of Anjou, by marrying the daughter of the last Count of Provence and defeating James I of Aragon, took possession of Provence and gradually suppressed the independence of its cities. Louis constructed the fortified harbor of Aigues-Mortes on the Mediterranean east of Marseilles, which gave the French their first southern outlet to the sea, and it was from this protected port that he sailed for the Seventh Crusade to the Orient in 1248 and for the Eighth Crusade in 1270, from which he never returned.

Poitou recovered some of its prosperity under Alphonse's firm rule, but as a "royal city" it was no longer the vital and exhilarating center it had been during the reigns of the Count-Dukes and in the days

*Right: Fig. 98. Seal of Joanna of Tou-
louse, daughter of Raymond VII,
wife of Count Alphonse de Poitiers,
and sister-in-law of Louis IX; 1270.*

*Above: Fig. 99. The ruins of the castle
of Quéribus (Pyrénées-Orientales),
the last Cathar stronghold to surrender
to the French, in the spring of 1255.
(Reportage Photographique YAN)*

when Eleanor had held her court. For better or worse, the destiny of the Occitan lands was from that time on bound up with that of the French kingdom.

The companions of Simon de Montfort, who had seized the territories of many of the Southern lords, were forbidden to marry into the noble families of the Midi. They spoke an alien tongue and despised the *langue d'oc*, which, over the centuries, came to be regarded as a mere patois. It is easy to understand why loyalty to the French crown was never as strong in the impoverished Midi as in the North. The ferocity of the conquest was not so easily forgotten.

Nor did Catharism die out altogether. Although its sanctuary had been destroyed and the Inquisition seemed to have triumphed, the movement survived in various forms for over fifty years. It found sympathizers and at times adherents in certain sections of the Languedoc people in which there had always been an overt or latent anticlericalism. The prestige and influence of the Church had suffered, and as the critical sense grew, there were even members of the Catholic clergy who wondered if Cathars like Corba de Péreille and her family, who had led such blameless and courageous lives, were really damned for all eternity. The Inquisitors were constantly discovering pockets of heresy, but their quarry became more and more elusive. Some Cathars would flee from French territory and return secretly—there were houses in Carcassonne and Albi, for instance, where the consolamentum could be given. Some heretics crossed the Pyrenees into Spain, others went to Germany and England, but a large number, including many of the defenders of Montségur, found refuge in Lombardy and other parts of northern Italy where there was still a climate of freedom. The Genoese Republic, Milan, Pavia, Mantua and Cremona all became Cathar centers. Many of the Cathars were experienced merchants and traders and their presence contributed to the prosperity of Lombardy, much as the banished Huguenots of a later era brought their skills and industry to their adopted countries. In fact, Catharism contained many of the seeds of the Reformation, and in the 16th century the Protestants were to win many adherents in the Midi, especially in Toulouse.

By the end of the 13th century there were very few Cathars left in Languedoc and the South. The atmosphere of alien repression, which, like the Crusades against the Albigensians, was as much political as religious in character, destroyed not only diversity of opinion, but all that had made the rich and beautiful Provençal civilization possible. The troubadours, who were often reduced to the status of *faidits*, or dispossessed persons, and many of whose patrons were either dead or in exile, lamented the end of *paratge*. They dwindled in number, and the quality of their poetry, deprived of its true substance, declined. Even before Montségur, Guiraut de Borneilh sadly recalled the days when

> Minstrels went from court to court
> Richly attired, praising the fair—
> Today we dare not speak a word;
> Honor and courtesy are fled.

Bertran d'Alamanon declared that "the world is so greatly changed that I scarcely recognize it." The gentle Guilhem Montanhagol, who was moved to indignation against French domination and ecclesiastical power and who found one last enlightened patron in King Alfonso the Wise of Castile, realized that the *joi d'amor* sung by the troubadours was more than a romantic concept of love—it had been a way of life, an ideal of kindliness, brotherhood and respect for the individual, the very opposite of tyranny, arrogance, hypocrisy, greed and oppression. He wrote:

> Now Joy and Courtesy offend the great,
> So wicked have they grown . . .

Epilogue

THERE IS NO FINALITY IN HISTORY. A powerful current, dammed in one area, may be diverted into other channels and reappear in unexpected places. If in terms of Provençal civilization—using "Provençal" to cover all the places where the *langue d'oc* was spoken—the "open" 12th century was one of joyous expansion and the 13th century an age of gradual repression, the 14th century, in spite of the Hundred Years' War and the Black Death, produced a mellower climate and a degree of cultural fusion between North and South, the religious and the secular. Curiously enough, one of the main preservers of the Occitan spirit in a modified form was the papacy, for the 14th century was the age of the Avignon Popes.

From 1308 to 1378, during the so-called "Babylonian Captivity," there were seven Popes in Avignon, all born either in the Limousin or in Languedoc. They were dominated politically by the French king, but several of them maintained splendid courts in the immense papal palace, one of the most beautiful Gothic buildings in all France. Both Clement VI (Pierre Roger), the most remarkable of the Popes, and his successor, Innocent VI (Etienne Aubert), were born in the little Castle of Maumont near Ventadour, which is still lived in. Clement VI, affable and tolerant in the best Southern tradition, had written troubadour poetry in his youth. During the ten years of his papacy, from 1342 to 1352, his court was the most brilliant in Europe. Learning and the arts were encouraged. Clement had his study decorated with delightful tapestry-like murals of fishing and hunting scenes by the painter Matteo Giovanetti of Viterbo and his French assistants, one of the few secular decorations from this period to survive. These enchanting scenes, with their charm and delight in nature, contain something of the spirit and grace of troubadour poetry. Nothing comparable existed in painting and decoration during the time when the troubadours flourished. Giovanetti also painted colorful frescoes in the Consistory Chapel of St. John in the papal palace.

Clement's successor, Innocent VI, invited Simone Martini, the greatest Sienese painter of his day, to come to Avignon to paint frescoes in the Cathedral of Notre-Dame-des-Doms. Only a few dim, eroded fragments remain, barely visible. Avignon had become in the 14th century a Franco-Italian enclave.

One last, late troubadour sang in Avignon during Clement's papacy, Bertrand de Pézars, from the town of Pézenas. He was married to a beautiful Provençale who also "sang very well," and as a "husband-and-wife team" they traveled from castle to castle, singing at weddings and other celebrations. All of Bertrand's poetry has disappeared, but it is known that the couple composed and sang nuptial poems and funeral elegies. There is no record in the chronicles of his wife's name, although one anonymous chronicler wrote that Bertrand and his wife were admired for their "talent and good looks." It is recorded, however, that Joanna, Queen of Naples in Avignon, gave the poet a fine silk cloak, and his wife a dress of crimson velvet which the queen had worn herself, as rewards for a performance.

The great Italian poet and humanist Petrarch was for many years a leading member of the Italian colony in Avignon, and a friend of Simone Martini, who painted his portrait. It was in Avignon that, in 1327, Petrarch first saw Laura, in the Church of Sainte-Claire during Mass—a meeting that was to be the main inspiration for his great love poems and sonnets in the Italian vernacular. Little is actually known about the blond Laura, but tradition says that she was Laura de Novès, wife of Hugues de Sade, the mother of eleven children, and an ancestor of the notorious 18th century Marquis de Sade!

After several long journeys Petrarch settled in the lovely little mountain village of Vaucluse, east of Avignon near the celebrated "fountain," the underground source of the Sorgues River, which, during the rainy season, springs out fully formed from a cave in the towering cliffs. The poet's modest house, where, with a few interruptions, he spent sixteen years of solitary study and communion with nature, is now a museum.

Petrarch admired the Provençal poets, and in the third canto of his *Triumphs* he mentioned many troubadours by name, including Peire Vidal, Guiraut de Borneilh, Jaufré Rudel "who took sail to meet death," Arnaud Daniel with his "elegant and polished style" and Bernart de Ventadour. Petrarch owned one of the beautiful manuscripts of troubadour poetry now in the Bibliothèque Nationale, probably compiled in the late 13th century at the Angevin court in Naples. Several miniatures from this manuscript have been reproduced in this book.

Dante, belonging to an older generation, had also praised the troubadours and had at one time considered writing his *Divine Comedy* in the *langue d'oc*. Petrarch, using the Italian vernacular, borrowed many ideas and phrases from the Provençal poets, and Coleridge called him "the final blossom and perfection of the troubadours." Under the influence of Platonic thought, Petrarch sublimated the concept of love far more than even the troubadours had done. His image of Laura was so idealized that some of his contemporaries doubted if she really existed—an assertion Petrarch indignantly denied. His spiritual devotion to Laura, whose death of the plague in 1348 inspired his eloquent *Triumphs*, did not prevent him fathering two children by an unknown woman in Vaucluse, possibly his cook or housekeeper.

In addition to perfecting the sonnet form, which influenced the Elizabethans and the poets of the French Renaissance, Petrarch struck a new note with his keen response to natural beauty. He climbed Mont Ventoux and was overwhelmed by the splendor of the panorama, yet felt guilty at his emotion and hastily read a passage from St. Augustine in a little book he had brought with him.

Two centuries before, Bernard of Clairvaux had journeyed on his mule along the shores of Lake Leman in Switzerland, rapt in thought and blind to the scenic beauties of the region. The troubadours recognized the beauties of nature and responded to the changing seasons with a naïve pleasure without actually describing them. In a pen sketch in the margin of a book Petrarch drew a church, a fishing heron and the cave in Vaucluse that is the source of the river Sorgues, and wrote underneath in Latin, "Solitude beyond the Alps, my greatest joy."

Pope Clement VI made Petrarch a canon and sent him on several diplomatic missions. For all his extravagance and love of luxury, Clement showed generosity and compassion.

When the Black Death came to Avignon in 1348 and carried off tens of thousands of victims, including Laura, the Pope stayed within the city and tended the sick. When the Jews of Avignon were accused by the populace of causing the plague by poisoning the wells, Clement VI took them under his protection and gave them sanctuary. The Jewish communities of Carpentras and Cavaillon were also under papal protection. Carpentras has the remains of one of the oldest synagogues in France—the present buildings in Carpentras and Cavaillon date from the 18th century and are architectural gems.

Clement VI died in 1352; his fine tomb, with its recumbent effigy, is in the Chaise-Dieu in Auvergne.

Avignon always remained suspect to the very orthodox Catholics, and even Petrarch reproached the papal court for its luxury and extravagance. After Pope Gregory XI had returned the papacy from Avignon to Rome in 1378, the papal palace in Avignon housed two energetic Antipopes during the Great Schism which lasted until 1417. The Christian world witnessed the unedifying spectacle of two, and at one time three, rival Popes hurling excommunications at each other! After the ending of the Schism, Avignon was governed by a papal legate from Rome, and from a bustling, overcrowded city, it sank into a drowsy, provincial backwater.

After the death in 1271 of the able but despotic Alphonse de Poitiers and his wife Joanna, the vast inheritance of the Counts of Toulouse passed to the French crown. The city, still governed by its *capitouls*, was allowed much autonomy and regained its former prosperity, but the intellectual and religious freedom favored by the Counts had vanished. The Inquisition was still in force; the few remaining heretics were burned, and the Jews were actively persecuted.

The Gothic style was at its height. Gothic architecture had originated on the Ile-de-France in the reign of Louis VII and had taken a long time to reach the South, where it acquired a very different character. The "nave of Raymond VI" in the Cathedral of Saint-

Etienne in Toulouse, built in 1209, had been the first example of the Gothic in the Midi. The breadth of the nave, as wide as it is high, became characteristic of Southern Gothic. It enabled the worshippers to follow the service and to hear the sermons from any part of the church. The chancel of Saint-Etienne Cathedral was begun much later, in 1272, in the more orthodox Gothic style of the North, and is on a different axis—hence the strange, irregular effect of the church.

In addition to the wide single naves found throughout the South, there were churches with two naves, an entirely new form, as in the brick-built fortress-like Church of the Jacobins in Toulouse, begun by the Dominicans in 1230 and consecrated in 1292. The Dominican monks in Toulouse were called Jacobins because their church was near the Porte Saint-Jacques. The immense brick Cathedral of Sainte-Cécile in Albi was built at the same time, and is an even more forceful expression of the Church Militant. Albi Cathedral was a bastion against the resurgence of heresy in the city which had given the heretics their name, the Albigensians.

Even poetry and letters reflected the new Catholic orthodoxy. On March 7, 1277, the Bishop of Paris formally condemned André Chapelain's *De Amoribus*, the treatise on love adapted from Ovid and composed at Eleanor's court in Poitiers at the request of Marie de Champagne. After this condemnation, poets were forbidden to sing of adulterous love or to cultivate *"l'amour des Dames"*; they were permitted to celebrate only the virtues of the young girls they intended to marry and to sing the praises of the Holy Virgin. The very essence of the *fin 'amor* of the troubadours was denied.

It was in this emasculated spirit that an attempted literary revival took place in Toulouse in the early 14th century, in the brief period of prosperity that preceded the Hundred Years' War and the English invasion. In 1323 seven young burghers of Toulouse—of whom two were merchants, two were moneychangers, one was a notary, one a prominent citizen and one a petty Gascon nobleman of dubious reputation—formed a group which they called the Consistori del Gai Saber—the Assembly, or Company, of Joyful Knowledge. These citizens considered themselves the heirs of the "good and ancient troubadours" and wanted to "preserve" the great literary tradition of the Midi, but in accord with the ideas of their own very different era.

With the notable exception of Gaston III, Count of Foix, surnamed "Phoebus" because of his beautiful blond hair, the Occitan nobility who had fostered the original troubadours had vanished, to be replaced by a bourgeois and mercantile society. Since the *fin 'amor* was forbidden, and satire frowned upon, poetry became didactic, moralizing and mystical, and the verse produced or sponsored by the seven members of the Gai Saber was on the whole trite and insipid. In a proclamation in verse which ended with the line "And may the God of Love assist you," poets were invited to assemble on May 3, 1324, for a competition for which the prize would be a golden violet. The competition took place in the Faubourg des Augustins in the presence of the twelve *capitouls* and a large gathering of nobles, citizens and merchants of Toulouse. The golden violet was awarded to Master Arnaud Vidal of Castelnaudary—no relation to Peire Vidal—for a *canso* dedicated to the Virgin. This poetry competition became a yearly event, which has lasted down to the present day, with golden and silver flowers awarded to the winners.

Around 1490 there was a rumor in Toulouse that a high-born lady, of whom nothing was known except that her name was Clémence Isaure, had left her fortune to the society. But the existence of this benefactor was probably an invention of the *capitouls*, who were at that time seeking means to remove certain funds from the control of the tax authorities. The name Clémence may have been an allusion to one of the attributes of the Virgin, who was addressed in a poem recited in a poetry competition held by the society in 1371 as "Comfort del mon e Clemensa"—consolation of the world and Clemency. A late Gothic tomb-effigy of a woman was given the name Clémence Isaure and converted into a standing statue in the 17th century. She holds a scroll in her left hand and the golden flower in her right, and stands under the arcade of the Renaissance courtyard of the Hôtel d'Assézat. At least Jaufré Rudel's *amor de lonh* had been inspired by a real person; Dame Clémence, the patron of the society, was, as far as we know, entirely mythical.

The Consistori del Gai Saber, whatever its limitations, was the first literary society in Europe, and in the 17th century, by order of Louis XIV, it became the Academy of Floral Games. It kept the *langue d'oc* alive as a literary vehicle in Toulouse and the Pyrenees when it was discredited as a "dialect" and when French had become the generally accepted language. The Academy is now situated in the fine Renaissance Hôtel d'Assézat and contains among its treasures a golden flower awarded to the nineteen-year-old Victor Hugo, which he treasured all his life and kept by his bedside. In exceptional cases,

Fig. 100. Manuscript volume of the Leys d'Amor, *1356, and a silver flower, in the Académie des Jeux Floraux, Hôtel d'Assézat, Toulouse. In the miniature, the poet-laureate offers the golden flower, which he has just been awarded, to the Virgin. (Reportage Photographique YAN)*

as with Victor Hugo, prizes were given for compositions in the *langue d'oïl.*

The Academy archives also contain the manuscript of an important treatise in verse, the *Leys d'Amor* (*Laws of Love*), composed by the seven founders in 1356, with a beautiful Gothic miniature showing a poet laureate presenting his golden flower to the Virgin (Fig. 100). The *Leys d'Amor* stressed the gap between "*los antics trobadours*," who had "grievously sinned" in regard to "God and the Catholic faith," and the "new troubadours," who were instructed how to avoid the fires of the Inquisition and the even greater agonies of "the burning Hell, where the great cauldron is." This fear of death and Hell, accompanying the fear of love—the poet should never ask his lady "to give him a kiss or grant something more secret"—is far removed from Jaufré Rudel's joyous trust in the dynamic force of "God who made all that comes and goes."

Those not adhering to the Catholic faith were barred by the *Leys d'Amor* from the Floral Games; and so were men of "loose morals" and, to all intents and purposes, women, except those of "perfect virtue" who were above suspicion. The authors added, with typical misogyny: "But where can such a woman be found?" In spite of these restrictions several women in the following centuries received awards, and some even presided over the Academy's competitions. But it remains just that—an academy—and the formulae of the contests have never related to the changing life of the times.

Apart from the influence of Provençal verse in Italy and Catalonia, the most vital impact of the great era of troubadour poetry was felt in Germany and Austria with the Minnesingers of the late 12th and the 13th centuries. Their lyrics contain many of the same conventions of courtly love, but they have their own native character, and a warmth, simplicity and directness not always found in their troubadour models. The greatest of the Minnesingers, Walther von der Vogelweide, in a charming verse expresses irritation with the troubadours' constant cult of "the lady" (*frouwe*), and says that, for his own part, he preferred the *wîp*—a flesh-and-blood woman! The Manesse Codex, in the Heidelberg University Library, is the largest collection of Minnesinger poems. It was compiled in Zurich in the early 14th century and contains some delightful illustrations (see jacket) with imaginary portraits and episodes from the poets' lives.

It was inevitable that with the gradual unification of France some of the refinements and values of the earlier Provençal culture, including the greater respect for women, should spread to other parts of the country. Marie de Champagne, Eleanor's daughter, had taken the cultivated spirit of her mother's court at Poitiers to her own county and had encouraged the *langue d'oïl*. In the second half of the 12th century, a poet of genius, Marie de France, wrote in Anglo-Norman, and composed fine narrative poems, some of Celtic and some of Arthurian origin. She spent much of her adult life in London at the court of Henry II. The *trouvères*, less sophisticated and with less individuality than the troubadours of the South, composed lyrics and romances in the *langue d'oïl* in the late 12th and the 13th century. In the early 15th century Christine de Pisan, a French poet of Italian descent, won recognition and royal patronage for her many verse romances, lyric poems and works in prose, and used her great talent and learning to defend the dignity of women. She began to write when she was a widow with three children. Her marriage had been a happy one, and her works tell us a great deal about the society of the time. Christine de Pisan attacked the male premise that "too much harm comes to women through reading and writing." She found it intolerable that men felt that everything was permitted them where women were concerned. But this early feminist was still a long way from complete equality, for in her advice to husbands she wrote:

> Let your wife fear and honor you
> But take good care you beat her not!

The customs of the 14th and 15th centuries sanctioned wife-beating, but if a wife dared to raise her hand against her jealous or irate husband she was subject to the same humiliating punishments as prostitutes.

Christine's last poem was dedicated to Joan of Arc.

In spite of many abuses, courtship, love and marriage in the late Middle Ages were no longer seen as utterly incompatible; one of the most charming miniatures in the exquisite *Book of Hours,* the *Très Riches Heures,* commissioned by Jean, Duc de Berry, uncle of Charles VI of France, and ruler of Poitou, is the betrothal scene for the month of April. The duke had his secretary write down the story of Mélusine in imitation of the Arthurian legends, and this is referred to in the illustration for the month of March (Fig. 43, page 121). During his residence in Poitiers, the Duc de Berry transformed one end of Eleanor of Aquitaine's Great Hall in the palace by building the huge flamboyant Gothic mantel and musicians' gallery (see page 175) and having it adorned with statues. He displayed *largueza* in his patronage of the arts, but *cobeïtats,* or greed (in troubadour parlance), in the exorbitant taxes he levied on his subjects. Manners were more refined, but in that troubled period of the Hundred Years' War and the decaying feudal society, *courtoisie* was to be found more in miniatures, tapestries and delicate Gothic ivories (Figs. 101 and 102) than in everyday life.

At the close of the Middle Ages the last representative of the ideals of medieval chivalry and the traditions of courtly love was the endearing and anachronistic figure Good King René of Anjou. Born in Angers in 1409, René was the second son of Louis II of Anjou, King of Naples. By his first marriage, to Isabella of Lorraine, he was the brother-in-law of Charles VII of France. He was also the

Fig. 101. Leaf of an ivory writing tablet, French, 14th century. The carvings represent four scenes of courtship: the encounter, the gallant conversation, a game of chess, the declaration of love. (The Metropolitan Museum of Art, gift of Ann Payne Blumenthal, 1938)

Fig. 102. The Attack on the Castle of Love. Ivory mirror case with slight traces of gilding, French, Paris School, middle of the 14th century. (Crown Copyright, Victoria and Albert Museum, London)

father of the stormy Margaret of Anjou, who, as the wife of the meek Henry VI of England, became deeply involved in the War of the Roses. In the Museum of the City of Aix, near a 19th century statuette of the young René, by David d'Angers, there is a plaque which lists all of his titles: Count of Provence, Forcalquier, Piedmont, Barcelona, Guise, Chailly and Longjumeau, Marquis of Pont-à-Mousson, Duke of Anjou, Bar and Lorraine, King of Jerusalem, Naples, Sicily, Aragon, Mallorca, Sardinia and Corsica!

Most of these titles were on paper, and had no reality. René had very little power and the only domains where he had authority were Anjou and Provence, where he is still regarded with affection for his benign, kindly and peaceful rule and his concern for even his humblest subjects.

As a young man he had ridden with Joan of Arc, but he preferred the pursuits of peace to those of war. He was never crowned King of Naples and Sicily, and his lifelong struggle with Aragon for control of southern Italy was defeated by his passion for the arts and his love for his second wife, Jeanne de Laval—he hated the long separations! His chief residence was at Angers, but he had castles in Aix and Tarascon and he enjoyed the company of the easygoing, cultivated nobility of the South. René knew Latin, Greek, Italian, Hebrew and Catalonian, played and composed music, dabbled in painting, wrote verses (in French, not *langue d'oc*) and studied mathematics, geology and jurisprudence. He delighted in reviving jousting and the rituals of chivalry, which were outmoded in an age of gunpowder.

His *Book of Tournaments* in the Bibliothèque Nationale is richly and beautifully illustrated, although not by him as was once believed. But for all his romantic medievalism René, who patronized Italian as well as Provençal artists, can be credited with introducing the Renaissance into France a generation before Francis I did so officially. René also served in many ways as a link between the Loire Valley and the Midi.

Since René preferred the wines of Anjou to those of Provence, he had supplies sent to his castle in Aix from Angers, but in order to improve local vintages he imported muscatel grapevines. He also had fruit trees planted in his far-off Duchy of Lorraine.

He was no heretic, and shared the prevalent cult of saints and relics, but neither was he a bigot. He gave hospitality to pilgrims to Compostela and compensated them if they had been robbed by bandits. He encouraged religious festivals for their strong popular appeal, staged mystery plays, organized the elaborate procession of the Fête-Dieu in Aix and revived the colorful pilgrimages of Les-Saintes-Maries-de-la-Mer, a village by the sea in the sandy stretches of the Camargue.

According to an old Provençal legend, Mary Jacobé, sister of the Virgin, Mary Salomé, mother of the apostles James and John, and Mary Magdalen, Lazarus and his sister Martha, St. Maximin and St. Sidonius, all of whom had known Jesus, were cast adrift in a small boat off the coast of Palestine. Sara, their black Egyptian servant, was distressed at having been left behind on the shore. Mary Salomé spread her cape out on the water and Sara was able to use it, miraculously, as a raft to join the others in the boat. Under divine protection the boat finally arrived on the coast of the Camargue and the passengers dispersed to spread the teachings of Jesus. Mary Magdalen went to Marseilles. Martha set out to convert Tarascon, Maximin and Sidonius left for Aix, and Mary Salomé and Mary Jacobé stayed in the little seaside village.

After their death the faithful placed the relics of the two Marys in a primitive oratory dedicated to the Virgin, which was replaced in the 12th century by the fortress-like church (which was painted by Van Gogh). The relics were buried beneath the choir of the new structure to protect them from Saracen pirates.

Because of the association with wanderers and travel, the shrine at Les-Saintes-Maries, from the very beginning, attracted many nomads who came as pilgrims. Gypsies, whose appearance in France was first recorded in 1419, have always had a special veneration for Sara the Egyptian.

The gypsies have their own version of the Sara legend. According to their oral tradition, Sara was already living in the Camargue before the Saints' arrival in their boat. She was a Rom, a gypsy of noble birth, who headed a tribe on the banks of the Rhône and was called Sara-la-Kali. The word Kali in gypsy dialect means "black" and also "gypsy." At that time the Roms were polytheists, and once a year they would carry a statue of Ishtar (or Astarte) down to the water on their shoulders and wade into the sea to be blessed by the goddess.

One day Sara had visions that the Saints who had been present at the death of Jesus would soon arrive on the shores of the Camargue. She saw them approaching in their small boat. The sea was rough and the travelers were in great danger. Sara rushed to the shore she had seen in her vision, waded into the sea and threw her robe on the waters; using it as a raft, she reached the boat and rescued the Saints and brought them to dry land. The Saints baptized Sara and she joined with them in their mission to preach the Gospel.

In 1448 King René had the remains of the two Marys dug up and placed in a splendid reliquary. He instituted two annual pilgrimages, one on the feast day of Mary Jacobé, May 24–25, and another on the feast day of Mary Salomé, the Saturday or Sunday nearest to October 22. This twice-yearly festival is one of the most picturesque ceremonies in all of France. The reliquary, topped by doll-like figures, three feet high, of the two Marys in a boat, is carried through the streets in a procession which includes *gardians* (cowboys of the Camargue) and pretty Arlésiennes on horseback, with each couple sharing a horse. The effigies of the saints, standing stiffly erect in their little boat, are then carried to the seashore on the shoulders of several sturdy men and either dipped into the sea or held above the surface of the water and solemnly sprinkled. This parallels the gypsy tradition which relates to the ancient cult of Ishtar. Gypsies gather there from all over Europe in their colorful costumes, and the real object of their pilgrimage is the statue of the Egyptian, Sara, in the crypt. This dark-skinned Madonna-like effigy is the recipient of gifts of clothing, lace and jewels, and the figure is dressed, redressed and sometimes overdressed in layer upon layer of silk, satin and lace.

Before germs were discovered to be the carriers of disease pilgrims brought bits of clothing from sick relatives and placed them upon Sara's shrine in the hope that she would effect a cure. This pile of soiled cloth has been replaced by a box for gifts of money to accompany the prayers.

Sara's official relics were "discovered" in 1496 at the very time when the first gypsy tribes were settling in the Camargue. There had been no mention of a third skeleton when the remains of the two Marys were dug up by the order of King René in 1448. But the gypsies immediately attached themselves to this black divinity to whom they felt much closer than to the "white Marys" of Christian tradition. There were "Saras" even before Biblical times; Abraham's wife in the Bible was called Sara, but this had also been the name of several mother-goddesses of the ancient Orient. The Church has always been dubious about both the authenticity of Sara's relics and her "sainthood" but has never tried to discourage or discontinue her cult.

Another festival originated by King René was the procession of the "Tarasque" in the town of Tarascon. According to Provençal tradition, an amphibious monster used to emerge at intervals from a cave in the river Rhône, beneath the spot where René's beautifully preserved castle still stands. This monster would devour the inhabitants of the town and devastate the countryside. One year, sixteen young men determined to give battle to the monster, who was able to devour eight of them. St. Martha, who had come to Tarascon from Les-Saintes-Maries, approached the "Tarasque," as the monster was called, and sprinkled holy water upon it. She held up a cross before its glaring eyes. The ferocious beast became as meek as a lamb. St. Martha tied her sash around its neck and led it to the people of Tarascon, who stoned it to death.

To commemorate this miracle, King René organized two annual processions in the streets of Tarascon, which were continued until the end of the last century. The first was held on the last Sunday of June. A huge effigy of the monster was paraded through the town. Its fearsome cardboard head was almost human, and its body was made up of eight youths, representing those devoured by the beast. It was escorted by eight other young men in memory of the eight survivors. The jointed dragon figure was made to careen through the narrow streets, lashing its tail and knocking over all within reach. In the second procession, on St. Martha's Day, July 29, a tamed monster was led through the town on a leash by a young girl. The "Tarasque" is now housed in a shed near the Church of Sainte-Marthe, and admission is charged to see it (Fig. 103).

Fig. 103. The Tarasque, Tarascon (Bouches-du-Rhône). There has been a movement in recent years to revive the famous festival and procession of the Tarasque, which was discontinued in the late 19th century. Festivals are now organized on the last Sunday in June in Tarascon to commemorate the Tarasque and to celebrate the arrival in town of Daudet's immortal Tartarin.

Fig. 104. Love takes the heart of the dreaming King René and hands it to Desire. Miniature by the "René Master" in King René of Anjou's Livre de Coeur d'Amour Epris, 1457. The dramatic nocturnal illumination suggests that the artist may have known Piero della Francesca's fresco of Constantine's Dream, painted in Arezzo soon after 1452. (Bildarchiv der Osterreichischen National-bibliothek, Vienna)

It is no wonder that René himself has become part of Provençal folklore.

King René has been credited, on doubtful authority, with composing the music for the joyous Arlesian *farandole*, and its cheerful rhythms were certainly in accord with his love of festivals. His allegorical poem "The Mortification of Vain Delight," a mystical treatise in verse, dedicated to the Duke and Duchess of Burgundy, makes tedious reading today. His most important work, the verse romance *Livre de Coeur d'Amour Espris*—the *Book of the Heart Smitten with Love*—is much less exciting to the modern reader than the magnificent miniatures that illustrate the manuscript in the Vienna Library (Fig. 104).

In one of these miniatures, among the earliest night scenes in Western art, Love, wearing 15th century hunting boots and with a quiver full of arrows by his side, removes the heart of the dreaming King René and hands it to Desire, dressed like a fashionable courtier.

The most personal of René's poems is the pastoral "Regnault et Jehanneton." It has an ingenuous gaiety and freshness and is of particular interest because, unlike the *pastourelles* of the early trouba-dours, it celebrates in the most romantic terms René's love for his second wife, Jeanne de Laval. Several paintings by the Provençal artist Nicolas Froment (Fig. 105) show René at this time. He had grown stout and far from handsome, and Jeanne, with her pointed, angular features and spare frame, was no beauty, but they were both likable and devoted to each other—a new kind of relationship.

The shepherd Regnault is René himself in the *pastourelle* in which he expressed his love for his wife. He and the shepherdess sit on a bank near a fountain and share a meal of ham, cheese, nuts and wild apples. While eating they engage in an affectionate debate as to

Fig. 105. *King René of Anjou and his second wife Jeanne de Laval, from por-traits in the Louvre by Nicholas Froment. (Archives Photographiques)*

whether men are more fickle than women. Regnault said that he had
abandoned all his possessions "beyond the mountains" and has left
his friends, his sheep and his lambs to be near his love—a transparent
reference to René's abandoning of an Italian campaign in 1453 to be
near his beloved wife Jeanne. The shepherdess accused Regnault of
having had many other loves, and the argument grew more heated.
A pious pilgrim, hidden behind the fountain, heard them and offered
to arbitrate the quarrel. Since it was getting dark and the pilgrim had
to spend the night in prayer, the young couple retired, after agreeing
to meet him again in the morning. René described nightfall far more
vividly than any troubadour had done:

> Out of his hollow came the owl
> And perched on his accustomed branch,
> Singing his rough and mournful chant.
>
> My very fingertips could feel
> The mounting chill as night drew near.

At sunrise the pilgrim returned to the fountain to complete the
arbitration, but the lovers had become reconciled and had gone about
their affairs without waiting for his decision.

The somewhat contrived charm of this pastoral would probably
not have appealed to François Villon, the down-to-earth antihero,
who was at that time introducing a new, sardonic and far more
modern note into poetry, but it is not likely that he knew of its

*Fig. 106. Left: King René of Anjou and Jeanne de Laval, from a medal by
Francesco Laurana, 1462. Right: Reverse of a medal of Jeanne de Laval by
Francesco Laurana, 1461. The original medals are in the Bibliothèque Nation-
ale, Paris.*

existence. King René's poem has tenderness and warmth, and reflects his love for his wife.

In the Bibliothèque Nationale there is a medal by Francesco Laurana with portraits of René and Jeanne (Fig. 106a); there has been no attempt on the part of the artist to idealize the royal couple. On the reverse of another Laurana medal two turtledoves are shown, tied together with a ribbon (Fig. 106b). The troubadours had assumed that married love was all but impossible, and in feudal society this was true. At the eve of the Renaissance it was rare enough, but Christine de Pisan and King René had shown, in their own lives, that even in matrimony the "equality in love" sung by the troubadours could be achieved, given affection and good will on both sides.

One emotion King René did share with Villon and many others in the waning years of the Middle Ages was a preoccupation with death, never found in the earlier poets. In a *Book of Hours* made for René in 1475, a miniature designed but not executed by the King shows not a skeleton, but a wasted corpse with a royal crown on his head, rising against a verdant landscape from behind a tripartite banner with the King's coat-of-arms. In a powerful anonymous 15th century fresco at La-Chaise-Dieu in Auvergne, one of the figures being invited by a skeleton to join in the Dance of Death is a young troubadour whose *vielle* lies useless at his feet.

By the time of his death in Aix in July 1480, René had resigned himself to the seizure of Anjou and Bar by the crafty advocate of *Realpolitik* Louis XI. In his will he left Provence to his nephew Charles, Count of Maine, but when Charles died two years later, the annexation of Provence by the French king was inevitable. This region, however, has always kept its individuality. The statue of Good King René (a far more convincing title than "René the Good") stands benevolently surveying the Cours Mirabeau in Aix in the shade of stately plane trees. In his right hand he holds a scepter, and in his left he holds out a bunch of grapes. King René's legacy to his people was not in conquered territories or a powerful army— he bequeathed a humane and civilized attitude toward life, a love of the arts and poetry, and a feeling for the *douceur de vivre* that all the trials of the Midi have not been able to eradicate.

Envoi

THE FREEDOM-LOVING MIDI gave the French Revolution the rousing "Marseillaise," which even the least radical French people accept as their national anthem. The city of Montauban, once an Albigensian stronghold and later a Huguenot center, produced the painter Ingres, supreme master of line, whose rigorous classical discipline concealed a fiery Southern temperament and a sensuous worship of the female form. Ingres maintained that by spending his youth in Toulouse, with its Roman heritage, he had absorbed more of antiquity than was possible for even the most assiduous students in the North. Marseilles was the birthplace of Honoré Daumier, fearless graphic commentator and a forceful painter whose oils were not appreciated until this century. Montauban now has an Ingres Museum and the bust of Daumier looks out over Marseilles harbor, but only in Paris could these artists have made their reputations, and this was true of most Southern writers and painters of the 19th century. Emile Zola and his boyhood friend Paul Cézanne both came from Aix, but only Cézanne returned to his native city to pursue his solitary art. The birthplace in Albi of another genius, Henri de Toulouse-Lautrec, descended from a branch of the ancient dynasty of the Counts of Toulouse, is still lived in by members of the artist's family, and the former archbishop's palace has an unparalleled collection of his works, but it was Paris that enabled him to find himself as a painter.

The Midi, largely untouched by the Industrial Revolution, and with its natural beauty still unspoiled, had become "provincial" in the 19th century. There was a cultivated bourgeoisie in the cities, but much poverty and illiteracy among the peasantry and the new urban proletariat. The *langue d'oc* of the troubadours, greatly adulterated, had become a despised dialect, with many regional variations.

But other forces were stirring. The 19th century Romantic interest in the Middle Ages and in national literature inspired a Provençal revival. An association of seven young Provençal poets, the Félibrige, was formed in 1854 near Avignon to establish a common spelling for the *langue d'oc* and to purify and enrich its vocabulary. The movement produced an interesting body of literature; its greatest poet was Frédéric Mistral, whose verse romance *Mirèio*, or *Mireille*, appeared in 1859 and won international acclaim—even in translation, its moving and picturesque characters and episodes and the ease and beauty of the language captured the imagination. Mistral won the Nobel prize for literature in 1907.

Another fine poet of the Félibrige, less known abroad, was Théodore Aubanel, who combined devout Catholicism with an ardent sensuality, which was strongly condemned by the orthodox bourgeoisie. In the most passionate troubadour tradition, but with more concrete imagery, he composed a poem to the Venus of Arles, the lovely antique statue, in that city's Musée Lapidaire, praising her as the spirit of eternal youth (*jovença*) and warm-blooded passion, whose bewitching beauty "*clareja en tota la Provença*"—"radiates through all Provence." He ends: "And that is why I, a Christian, sing of you, great pagan!"

While the Félibrige promoted a purely Provençal literature, Alphonse Daudet was popularizing the Midi in Parisian circles with his warm, lively and engaging novels and stories in French, including the delightful *Lettres de Mon Moulin*, *Tartarin de Tarascon*, *Tartarin dans les Alpes* and *Numa Roumestan*. The fat, bearded, boastful and loquacious Tartarin, who comes to believe his own tall tales of lion hunting and mountaineering, is as popular in France as Mr. Pickwick in England, but many people in Provence, then and now, have felt that the gifted Daudet made Tartarin, with his heavy Midi "acceng," a caricature of the Southerner to amuse the sophisticated Parisians—much as the Irish resent the comic "stage Irishman."

The Félibrige, though it performed an immense service in giving new life to Provençal literature and reviving an awareness of the past, had serious limitations which became more apparent as the 19th century drew to its close. The regionalist stress on folklore and tradition could easily degenerate into a narrow parochialism, an escape from wider issues. The essentially middle-class Félibrige movement had a conservative and paternalistic attitude toward the peasants and working people—it had no real popular roots. It was out of touch and out of sympathy with the need for change and growth, and many of its devotees, including Mistral himself, became increasingly reactionary. Among his followers, regional pride and religious conformism found an ally in right-wing French chauvinism, especially during the Dreyfus case, which divided all France. Charles Maurras, a disciple of Mistral, and a guiding spirit of the ultra-right-wing, monarchist and anti-Semitic Action Française, was a firm Pétain supporter during World War II, as were most "Mistraliens." On the other hand, the town of Castres gave France and the world the great Socialist leader Jean Jaurès, one of the few truly admirable political figures in any period or country, who was murdered in Paris in 1914 by a fanatical nationalist on the eve of the war he had tried so desperately to prevent. Nearly every town and village in the Midi has its Jean Jaurès square, school, street and monument.

Because of this background, and the bitter experiences of the German occupation in World War II, the tradition of Mistral and the Félibrige has been somewhat discredited in the Midi. Today, the new "Occitan" movement has a very different emphasis, and bases itself on the strong libertarian and egalitarian heritage of the South, already implicit in the society that produced the troubadours and protected heretic dissidents. For the people of the Midi the horrors of the Crusades against the Albigensians and the Inquisition were made all the more real by the agony of the Nazi occupation and the atrocities of the Gestapo. The French Resistance originated in Auvergne and was active throughout the Midi, and daring acts of sabotage brought on savage reprisals. Béziers, where the terrible massacre took place in 1207, now has a Mur des Fusillés, a memorial wall where eighteen members of the Resistance were shot by the Germans on June 7, 1944.

Soon after the war a group of Southern intellectuals, scholars and writers, of whom several were themselves poets, among them René Nelli, Robert Lafont and Charles Camproux, began to study the

Provençal literature of the past, especially the poetry of the troubadours, in a new spirit, free from Romantic idealization and the academic, backward-looking approach of the Floral Games in Toulouse. They saw the troubadours as an integral part of the society of their time and an example to the *"artistes engagés,"* or "committed artists," of the present day. There was all the more reason to give new dignity to the *langue d'oc*, as children in many schools were penalized for speaking it and were made ashamed of their heritage (the same was true in Brittany). Courses in Provençal language and literature were established in Montpellier and other universities. At the time of this writing, over 6,000 high school students are learning the Occitan language. By the late 1960's the movement had attracted many students of both sexes. By the early 1970's, "Occitanie" had clearly become a "cause" with many social and political implications. It was a reaction against the excessive centralization of power inherited from the French monarchy, which had increased under Napoleon and had persisted in various degrees in Republican France. The Riviera had long been commercialized by the tourist industry and was overcrowded and overbuilt—superhighways and ribbon development threatened to ruin the beauty of the countryside of Languedoc and Provence. The establishment of large military bases was deeply resented as another form of "colonization." Such industries as the Midi possessed were owned by Northern entrepreneurs, and the South was experiencing great economic hardships and unemployment. Scarcity of opportunity has caused many young people to leave the South in this century, and they often have found that their chance of employment in the North depended on their losing their Midi accent. Entire villages have been deserted. Many wealthy people from Paris and other cities have acquired second homes in the South, only to leave them vacant for ten months of the year. Mistral's "Empire of the Sun" was no earthly paradise in the postwar world.

The aim of the Occitan movement is not really political separatism —the "Balkanization" of France or any country is anything but desirable—and its spirit is by no means chauvinistic or xenophobic— quite the contrary. But it advocates a greater degree of economic and cultural autonomy and a sense of identity in a world of increasing uniformity and standardization. There is strong sympathy with minority groups in the United States and with Basques and Catalonians in Spain. One of the Occitan newspapers, published in Avignon, is called *Esclarmonda*; another carries the cross of

Languedoc. In this as in any strongly oriented movement, there is always the danger of too narrow a focus—the troubadour ideal of *mesura*, avoidance of extremes, is still valid—but no one can quarrel with the aims of decentralization and a rich cultural diversity.

A new school of troubadours has arisen in the Midi very similar to the wave of folk singers and protest singers in the United States, such as Pete Seeger, Joan Baez and Bob Dylan. The Midi has always had the gift of song, and well before the Occitan movement certain singers from the South, performing in French, won great popular acclaim in Paris and throughout France—Charles Trénet from Narbonne, in a light, romantic vein, and Georges Brassens from Sète, whose ribald and sardonic ditties combine the witty irreverence of Guilhem VII with the disenchanted irony of a modern François Villon. This shaggy nonconformist, a true "original," has been made a member of the Académie Française.

The Occitan singers, on the other hand, perform mainly in the South. They sing in the *langue d'oc* on themes which directly concern their hearers, and even their love songs are edged with social comment. They write their own material and are their own jongleurs—the guitar has replaced the lute and the *vielle*, and the rhythms are more urgent. The bearded Marti, a schoolteacher at Couffoulens near Carcassonne, has the same name as the troubadour Bernard Marti of the school of Ventadour and Bertran Marti, the Cathar perfect of Montségur. His songs are angry and militant and full of allusions to the grim past—the siege of Carcassonne, city of Trancavel; the fall of Montségur, the hour of defeat when *"l'idea brutla sul lenhier"*—"the idea burns at the stake"—and more recent events such as the 1907 rising of the Béziers winegrowers for better wages and living conditions, and the refusal of the Languedoc troops called in by the government to fire on them, because *"poble e soldats eran fraires"*—"people and soldiers were brothers." The songs of Mans de Breish, a nickname meaning "sorcerer's hands," are more lyrical and melodious but at the same time ironic and provocative.

Patric, young and talented, is a student of linguistics. He sings at festivals and gives recitals in villages. He always prefaces his Occitan songs with a summary in French, and he has an enthusiastic following. These singers have deliberately chosen amateur status, and the company that puts out their records, sold mostly by correspondence, is called Ventadorn, after Bernart de Ventadour; it was founded by the poet and writer Yves Rouquette. Two women singers are

Nicola and Rosine de Peyre. Some songs have greater literary quality than others, but there is also a more serious movement in Occitan poetry represented by Pierre Bec, Bernard Lesfargues, who is strongly influenced by Castilian and Catalan verse, Robert Lafont and others.

The original troubadour songs have enjoyed an impressive revival in recent years. Recitals and recordings by Les Menestriers and other groups in France have increased the audience for this form of medieval music. An American group, the Waverly Consort, founded in 1965, have re-created many medieval works, notably the *Cantigas de Santa Maria*, as sung at the court of Alfonso X, the Wise, of Castile. Wearing 13th century costumes and playing recorders, *vielles*, psalteries, lutes, "nun's fiddles" and other instruments of the period, they have performed in the Cloisters in New York—a most appropriate setting—and on college campuses with great success (Fig. 107).

Since the original rhythms of these songs and the exact nature of

Fig. 107. *Michael Jaffee, founder and director of the Waverly Consort, New York, with a psaltery, and Kay Jaffee, with a recorder. The costumes are based on miniatures in the* Cantigas de Santa Maria *and the instruments are modern reconstructions of those played at the court of King Alfonso X, the Wise, of Castile in the 13th century. (Photograph by William Watson, New York, reproduced by permission of Mr. and Mrs. Michael Jaffee)*

their accompaniment are not known, modern interpretations can only be an approximation, but they do seek to convey the spirit of the troubadour lyrics. Michael Jaffee, the group's director, has said that it is not surprising that young people feel an affinity with this old monodic music, because it is far closer to modern folk and pop music than are the works of Beethoven and Brahms. He pointed out that it had "the same casual, impromptu approach, the same small groups and simple themes."

On a bright Sunday on June 24, 1973, the feast day of St. John the Baptist, Montségur of tragic memory was the scene of an extraordinary gathering of over five thousand people, mostly under thirty, who had come from all over the Midi and from far beyond, bringing not death but joy and life. They came from Lyons, Bordeaux, Nice and Narbonne; here and there one saw banners with the cross of Languedoc on its scarlet ground (Fig. 108), but Bretons were also present with their white banners, dotted with heraldic black

Fig. 108. Occitan Festival at Montségur, June 24, 1973. The flag of Languedoc is being displayed, and a young man plays the vielle. *(Photograph by S. Pons, Lavelanet)*

Fig. 109. Speaker at the Occitan Festival at Montségur, June 24, 1973. Behind him is the flag of Languedoc, to his right the Breton flag. (Photograph by S. Pons, Lavelanet)

ermine (Fig. 109). There were Basques wearing berets and Catalans with harsh accents and a number of visitors from foreign countries. Some of the young people had spent the night in sleeping bags and many of the girls wore long flowered or print dresses. An old woman was knitting and children were playing in the grass; the atmosphere was happy and relaxed and the vast crowd was excited but contained as it listened attentively to lectures by Yves Rouquette, Robert Lafont and other eminent poets and writers. The purpose of the gathering, said Roland Péquou, was not to commemorate the terrible event of over seven hundred years ago that had taken place on this same green meadow at the foot of the mountain, but to celebrate a

Fig. 110. La bonne table. Albi.
(Sketch by the Author)

"people's will to live." Other speakers pointed out how little the official French textbooks glorifying St. Louis, Louis XIV and Napoleon take into account the vital forces of history, including the peoples who only now were discovering who they were. Lafont hailed Montségur, rising silently above this festive meeting, as a symbol of tolerance and love. Poetry was recited and exhibited, and the university theater of Montpellier performed one-act plays and satirical skits in French and Occitan. The crowds heard songs by Marti, Rosine de Peyre, Mans de Breish and others, all on the theme of *"lo pais que vol viure"*—"the land that wants to live."

Cathar freedom but not Cathar austerity prevailed as jovial wine-growers from the Corbières sold their delectable red wine that has enlivened so many excellent meals (Fig. 110). When night fell on the celebration that had begun at nine in the morning, a huge *"feu de joie"* or bonfire was lit—a revival of the dying custom of the *"feu de Saint-Jean,"* the bonfire lit annually on St. John's Day. But at this fire there were no victims, only people enjoying music, singing and dancing. It was as if the evil spirits of the past haunting the Camp des Crémats had been driven away by the forces of life. The dove of

Montségur could now soar as freely as the lark in Bernart de Ventadour's poem, who will

> Drift in sweet oblivion,
> So filled with rapture is her heart . . .

Looking at these warm, friendly, alert and attractive young people, who had come here from miles around as pilgrims, but without superstition, as heretics, for they challenged many accepted values, and as lovers of life and of their friends, one had a renewed faith in the future. Here were some of the cherished ideals of the troubadours, which, for this one day, had become a reality—*joven* or youth, *joi*, *amor*, *largueza* or generosity of spirit, more important than material wealth, and *convivéncia*, the ability of people of all kinds to live together in equality and peace.

Bibliography

P. Aimes. La Comtesse de Die, ou Laure de Castellane; article in the bulletin of the Société d'études historiques, scientifiques et littéraires des Hautes-Alpes, sér. 7, no. 45, 1953.

Joseph Anglade. Les Troubadours. Librairie Armand Colin, Paris 1908.

Joseph Anglade. Le Troubadour Guiraut Riquier: étude sur la décadence de l'ancienne poésie provençale. Féret et fils, Bordeaux, 1905.

The songs of Bernart de Ventadour, edited by Stephen G. Nichols and John A. Galm. University of North Carolina Press, Chapel Hill, 1962.

Bernart de Ventadour: chansons d'amour, edited by Moshé Lazar, C. Klincksieck, Paris, 1966.

Pierre Bec. Nouvelle Anthologie de la Littérature Occitane du Moyen Age, Editions Aubanel, 1966.

Gaston Bonheur. Si le Midi avait voulu. . . Editions Robert Laffont—Editions Pierre Charron, Paris, 1972.

Georges Bordonove. Histoire du Poitou. Hachette Littéraire, 1973.

Robert S. Briffault. The Troubadours. Indiana University Press, Bloomington, Indiana, 1965.

Donald Bullough. The Age of Charlemagne. G. P. Putnam's Sons, New York, 1965.

Cahiers de Fanjeaux 3, Cathares en Languedoc. Edouard Privat, Toulouse, 1968.

Cahiers de Fanjeaux 4, Paix de Dieu et Guerre Sainte en Languedoc. Edouard Privat, Toulouse, 1969.

Charles Camproux. Le Joy d'Amor des Troubadours: jeu et joie d'amour. Causse et Castelnau, Montpellier, 1965.

Paul Carbonel. Histoire de Narbonne. Narbonne, 1956.

Les Poésies de Cercamon, edited by Alfred Jeanroy, E. Champion, Paris, 1922.

Alain Decaux. Histoire des Françaises. Vol. I. La Soumission. Librairie Académique, Paris, 1972.

Denis De Rougemont. Love in the Western World. Harper and Row, 1974. Paper.

Gaston Dez. Histoire de Poitiers. Société des Antiquaires de l'Ouest, Poitiers, 1969.

André Dupuy. Petite Encyclopédie Occitane, Editions "Saber," Montpellier, 1972.

Joan Evans. Life in Medieval France. Phaidon, 1969.

François Eygun. Sigillographie de Poitiers jusqu'en 1515. Société des Antiquaires de l'Ouest, Poitiers, 1938.

François Eygun. Saintonge Romane. Editions Zodiaque, 1972.

François Eygun. Art des Pays d'Ouest. Arthaud, 1965.

The Flowering of the Middle Ages, edited by Joan Evans. McGraw-Hill, 1966.

Henri Focillon. The Art of the West. 2 vols. Phaidon, 1963.

Guide de la France Mystérieuse. Les Guides Noirs, Tchou, 1964.

Guide de la Provence Mystérieuse. Les Guides Noirs, Tchou, 1965.

Guide de la France Religieuse et Mystique. Les Guides Noirs, Tchou, 1969.

Les Chansons de Guillaume IX, duc d'Aquitaine, edited by A. Jeanroy. Les classiques français du moyen age. Paris, 1913.

Charles Homer Haskins. The Renaissance of the 12th century. Meridian Books, the World Publishing Company, Cleveland and New York, 1968.

Arnold Hauser. The Social History of Art. Vol. I. Vintage Books, New York, 1957.

Friedrich Heer. The Medieval World: translated from the German by Janet Sondheimer. A Mentor Book, 1962.

Vera and Helmut Hell. The Great Pilgrimage of the Middle Ages: The Road to St. James of Compostela. Barrie and Rockliff, London, 1964.

John Hugh Hill and Laurita Littleton Hill. Raymond IV, Count of Saint-Gilles and Count of Toulouse. Syracuse University Press, 1962.

J. Huizinga. The Waning of the Middle Ages. Doubleday Anchor Books, New York, 1956.

H. W. Janson and Joseph Kerman. A History of Art and Music. Harry N. Abrams, New York, 1968.

Jean de Notredame. Vies des plus célèbres et anciens poètes provençaux, edited by C. Chabaneau and J. Anglade. Paris, 1913.

Alfred Jeanroy. Les Chansons de Jaufré Rudel. Paris, 1915.

Robert Joudoux. Articles on "Deux Campagnes de Fouilles au Château de Ventadour" in magazine "L'Archéologie en Bas-Limousin," Editions Lemouzi, Tulle, 1968.

Amy Kelly. Eleanor of Aquitaine and the Four Kings. Harvard University Press, Cambridge, Massachusetts, 1963.

Amy Kelly. "Eleanor of Aquitaine and the Courts of Love." Article in Speculum, XII, 3, January, 1937.

Y. Labande-Mailfert. Poitou Roman, Editions Zodiaque, 1957.

Robert Lafont. Clefs pour l'Occitanie. Editions Seghers, Paris, 1971.

Jacques Levron. Le Bon Roi René. Arthaud, 1972.

Robert Sherman Loomis. Arthurian Legends in Medieval Art. Modern Languages Association, New York, 1938.

Poésies Complètes du troubadour Marcabru, translated and edited by J. M. L. Dejeaune, preface by Alfred Jeanroy. Edouard Privat, Toulouse, 1909.

Robert Mesuret. "L'art occitan," article in Annales de l'Institut d'Etudes Occitanes, 4me série, Tome II, no. 6, 1972.

La Musique des Origines à nos Jours, edited by Norbert Dufourcq, Librairie Larousse, Paris, 1946.

René Nelli. L'Erotique des Troubadours. Edouard Privat, Toulouse, 1963.

René Nelli. La Poésie Occitane des Origines à nos Jours. Editions Seghers, Paris, 1972.

René Nelli. La Vie Quotidienne des Cathares du Languedoc au XIIIe Siècle. Librairie Hachette, Paris, 1969.

René Nelli. Le Musée du Catharisme. Edouard Privat, Toulouse, 1966.

René Nelli. Dictionnaire des Hérésies Médievales. Edouard Privat, Toulouse, 1968.

Zoë Oldenbourg. Le Bûcher de Montségur. Gallimard, Paris, 1959.

Raymond Oursel. Les Pèlerins du Moyen Age. Résurrection du Passé, Fayard, Paris, 1963.

Robert Payne. The Splendor of France. Harper and Row, 1963.

Les poésies de Peire Vidal: edited by Joseph Anglade. H. Champion, Paris, 1913.

The Popes: A Concise Biographical History, edited by Eric John. Hawthorn Books, Inc., New York, 1964.

Henri Ramet. Histoire de Toulouse. Librairie Tarride, Toulouse, 1935.

Lilian M. C. Randall. Images in the Margins of Gothic Manuscripts. University of California Press, 1966.

Alfred Richard. Histoire des Ducs et des Comtes de Poitou 778-1204. 2 vols., Paris, 1903.

Cecil Roth. A History of the Jews. Schocken Books, New York, 1961.

John Frederick Rowbotham. A History of Music to the Time of the Troubadours. Richard Bentley and Son, London, 1893.

Steven Runciman. A History of the Crusades. Cambridge (Ely), 3 vols. Cambridge University Press, 1951.

Steven Runciman. The Medieval Manichees. Cambridge University Press, 1947.

The Scallop. Edited by Ian Cox. The Shell Company Ltd., London, 1957.

Justin H. Smith. The Troubadours at Home. 2 vols. G. B. Putnam's, New York and London, 1899.

Stendhal. Voyage dans le Midi. Jean-Jacques Pauvert, Sceaux, 1956.

Francis Henry Taylor. The Taste of Angels. Little, Brown and Co., Boston, 1948.

Les Troubadours. 2 vols. Text and translation by René Nelli and René Lavaud. Desclé de Brouwer, Bruges, 1965.

Sir Algernon Tudor-Craig. The Romance of Mélusine and de Lusignan. The Century House, London, 1932.

André Villard. Art de Provence. Arthaud, 1969.

Freda White. West of the Rhône: Languedoc, Roussillon, the Massif Central. Faber and Faber Ltd., London, 1964.

Freda White. Ways of Aquitaine. Faber and Faber Ltd., London, 1968.

Freda White. Three Rivers of France: Dordogne, Lot, Tarn. Faber and Faber Ltd., London, 1972.

Index